THE MATERIAL CULTURE OF TABLEWARE

Staffordshire Pottery and American Values

Jeanne Morgan Zarucchi

BLOOMSBURY VISUAL ARTS
LONDON • NEW YORK • OXFORD • NEW DELHI • SYDNEY

BLOOMSBURY VISUAL ARTS
Bloomsbury Publishing Plc
50 Bedford Square, London, WC1B 3DP, UK
1385 Broadway, New York, NY 10018, USA
29 Earlsfort Terrace, Dublin 2, Ireland

BLOOMSBURY, BLOOMSBURY VISUAL ARTS and the Diana logo are
trademarks of Bloomsbury Publishing Plc

First published in Great Britain 2018
Paperback edition published 2023

Copyright © Jeanne Morgan Zarucchi, 2023

Jeanne Morgan Zarucchi has asserted her right under the Copyright,
Designs and Patents Act, 1988, to be identified as Author of this work.

For legal purposes the Acknowledgements on p. ix constitute an extension
of this copyright page.

Cover design: Liron Gilenberg.
Cover photograph © Jeanne Morgan Zarucchi.

All rights reserved. No part of this publication may be reproduced
or transmitted in any form or by any means, electronic or mechanical,
including photocopying, recording, or any information storage or
retrieval system, without prior permission in writing from the publishers.

Bloomsbury Publishing Plc does not have any control over, or
responsibility for, any third-party websites referred to or in this book.
All internet addresses given in this book were correct at the time of going to
press. The author and publisher regret any inconvenience caused if addresses
have changed or sites have ceased to exist, but can accept no responsibility for
any such changes.

A catalogue record for this book is available from the British Library.

A catalogue record for this book is available from the Library of Congress

ISBN:	HB:	978-1-3500-4127-1
	PB:	978-1-3503-5992-5
	ePDF:	978-1-3500-4128-8
	ePub:	978-1-3500-4126-4

Typeset by Integra Software Services Pvt. Ltd.
Printed and bound in Great Britain

To find out more about our authors and books visit www.bloomsbury.com and
sign up for our newsletters.

CONTENTS

List of Illustrations	vi
Trademark Acknowledgments	ix
Introduction: THE "PICTURE" IN THE SHOP WINDOW	1
Chapter 1 OLD WORLD STYLE FOR THE NEW WORLD	7
Chapter 2 ALLIES IN WAR AND TRADE	29
Chapter 3 AMERICAN HISTORY (THE BRITISH VERSION)	53
Chapter 4 COMMEMORATIVES AND SOUVENIRS	77
Chapter 5 PROSPERITY AND NOSTALGIA	101
Chapter 6 MODERN STYLE, NEW TRADITIONS	125
Conclusion: ENDINGS AND BEGINNINGS	155
Notes	160
Bibliography	176
Index of Tableware Patterns	180
Index	184

LIST OF ILLUSTRATIONS

Plates

1A Sugar bowl, Johnson Brothers late Pankhurst, *c.* 1883.
1B Pattern 131486 sauceboat, Johnson Brothers, *c.* 1889.
1C Wisconsin plate, William Brownfield & Sons, *c.* 1871–91.
1D Aesthetic-style butter pat, Minton (?), *c.* 1860.
2A Rolland covered vegetable bowl, Johnson Brothers, *c.* 1890.
2B Vienna pitcher, Johnson Brothers, *c.* 1898.
2C Savannah sugar bowl, Johnson Brothers, *c.* 1890.
2D Florida plate, Johnson Brothers, *c.* 1890.
3A Oxford covered vegetable bowl, Johnson Brothers, *c.* 1890.
3B Watteau plate, unknown Staffordshire maker, *c.* 1910.
3C Franklin milk jug, Johnson Brothers, *c.* 1909.
3D Davenport sauceboat, Johnson Brothers; Grosvenor spoon, Oneida Ltd., *c.* 1921.
4A Madison plate, Johnson Brothers, *c.* 1920.
4B Petroushka plate, Johnson Brothers, *c.* 1925.
4C Untitled art deco-style plate, Johnson Brothers, *c.* 1925.
4D Greydawn bowl, Johnson Brothers, *c.* 1929.
5A Old Britain Castles "Canterbury Castle," Johnson Brothers, *c.* 1930.
5B Old Britain Castles "Cambridge," Johnson Brothers, *c.* 1930.
5C Old Britain Castles, "Haddon Hall," Johnson Brothers, *c.* 1930.
5D Old Britain Castles, "Blarney Castle," Johnson Brothers, *c.* 1930.
6A English Chippendale, Johnson Brothers, *c.* 1937.
6B Margaret Rose, Johnson Brothers, *c.* 1939.
6C Devonshire, Johnson Brothers, *c.* 1940.
6D Old Blue Historical, "The White House," Wedgwood, *c.* 1900.
7A Historic America, "The Capitol," Johnson Brothers, *c.* 1938.
7B Historic America, "St. Louis Missouri," Johnson Brothers, *c.* 1939.
7C Historic America, "Barnum's Museum New York," Johnson Brothers, *c.* 1938.
7D Historic America, "Covered Wagons and the Rocky Mountains," Johnson Brothers, *c.* 1938.

List of Illustrations

8A Historic America, "Frozen Up," Johnson Brothers, c. 1938.
8B Souvenir plate of St. Louis, c. 1904.
8C A Century of Progress, "First Fort Dearborn," Johnson Brothers, c. 1933.
8D Chicago, Johnson Brothers, c. 1951.
9A Empire State Building, Johnson Brothers, c. 1959.
9B Williamsburg Restoration, "The Governor's Palace," Wedgwood, c. 1950.
9C Piranesi Series, "Basilica of St. Mary Major," Wedgwood, c. 1950.
9D Pennsylvania German Folklore Society, Johnson Brothers, c. 1960.
10A The Oregon Plate, Johnson Brothers, c. 1957.
10B Mount Rushmore, Johnson Brothers, c. 1965.
10C Mount Vernon, Johnson Brothers, c. 1954.
10D Floating Leaves, Johnson Brothers, c. 1955.
11A Day in June, Johnson Brothers, c. 1954.
11B Old Flower Prints, "Rose," Johnson Brothers, c. 1949.
11C Game Birds, "Partridge," Johnson Brothers, c. 1951.
11D Fish, Johnson Brothers, c. 1955.
12A Olde English Countryside, Johnson Brothers, c. 1957.
12B Barnyard King, Johnson Brothers, c. 1950.
12C His Majesty, Johnson Brothers, c. 1959, detail.
12D Merry Christmas, Johnson Brothers, c. 1959.
13A The Old Mill, Johnson Brothers, c. 1951.
13B The Friendly Village, "Village Street," Johnson Brothers, c. 1953.
13C Apple Harvest, Johnson Brothers, c. 1954.
13D Dream Town, Johnson Brothers, c. 1956.
14A The Road Home, Johnson Brothers, c. 1954.
14B Coaching Scenes, "The Coach Office," Johnson Brothers, c. 1963.
14C Jamestown, Johnson Brothers, c. 1965.
14D Fruit Sampler, Johnson Brothers, c. 1965.
15A Alice in Wonderland, Johnson Brothers, c. 1974.
15B Neighbors, "Band Concert," Johnson Brothers, c. 1974.
15C Petite Fleur, Johnson Brothers for Laura Ashley, c. 1976.
15D Heritage Hall, "Georgian Town House," Johnson Brothers for Sears Roebuck & Co., c. 1977.
16A Heritage Hall, "Spanish Hacienda," Johnson Brothers for Sears Roebuck & Co., c. 1977.
16B Eternal Beau, Johnson Brothers, c. 1981.
16C Summerfields, Johnson Brothers, c. 1985.
16D Historic America II, "The Capitol," Johnson Brothers, c. 2002.

Figures

1.1	Johnson Brothers Late Pankhurst backstamp, *c.* 1883.	10
1.2	Johnson Brothers Semi-Porcelain backstamp, *c.* 1890.	12
1.3	Aesthetic-style plate, maker F.W.G., *c.* 1884.	14
1.4	Columbia, Johnson Brothers, *c.* 1889–93.	15
1.5	Johnson Brothers Royal Semi-Porcelain backstamp, *c.* 1890.	16
1.6	Nancy, Grimwades, *c.* 1902, detail.	17
1.7	Queen Victoria Diamond Jubilee backstamp, Johnson Brothers, *c.* 1897. Image courtesy of David Arrowsmith.	23
1.8	Johnson Brothers Crown backstamp, *c.* 1899.	24
2.1	Johnson Brothers Angular Crown backstamp.	31
2.2	William Norbury, 1950s. Image courtesy of William Norbury.	37
2.3	Johnson Brothers WindsorWare backstamp, 1940s through 1970s.	51
2.4	Sheraton backstamp, Johnson Brothers, *c.* 1944.	52
3.1	Historic America backstamp, Johnson Brothers, *c.* 1939–74.	62
4.1	Chicago backstamp, Johnson Brothers, *c.* 1951.	85
4.2	Empire State Building demitasse cup and saucer, Johnson Brothers, *c.* 1959.	86
4.3	Williamsburg Restoration backstamp, Wedgwood, *c.* 1950.	90
5.1	Game Birds backstamp, Johnson Brothers, *c.* 1951	111
5.2	Fish backstamp, Johnson Brothers, *c.* 1955.	112
5.3	The Friendly Village backstamp, Johnson Brothers, *c.* 1953.	120
5.4	The Road Home backstamp, Johnson Brothers, *c.* 1954.	122
6.1	"Old Granite" series backstamp, Johnson Brothers, *c.* 1965.	129
6.2	Paisley backstamp, Johnson Brothers, *c.* 1970.	134
6.3	Petite Fleur backstamp, by Johnson Brothers for Laura Ashley, *c.* 1976.	135
6.4	Heritage Hall backstamp, Johnson Brothers for Sears Roebuck & Co., *c.* 1977.	136
6.5	Summerfields backstamp, Johnson Brothers, *c.* 1985.	139
6.6	Summer Chintz backstamp, Johnson Brothers, *c.* 1985.	140
6.7	Bull backstamp, Johnson Brothers, 1970s–1990s.	142
6.8	Advertisement from *The Sentinel*, October 16, 1991.	143
6.9	Plymouth backstamp, Williams-Sonoma, *c.* 2000.	145
6.10	Johnson Brothers England 1883 backstamp, *c.* 2007.	150

TRADEMARK ACKNOWLEDGMENTS

Johnson Brothers operated as a part of the Wedgwood Group from 1968 to 2014. The following information is accurate as of the date of this publication. The Wedgwood brand and trademark are part of the Fiskars portfolio of brands and trademarks, www.fiskarsgroup.com. Registered office: Wedgwood Drive, Barlaston, Stoke-on-Trent, Staffordshire, ST12 9ER. Registered in England. Company registration number: 6805116. VAT number: GB946915581.

Mintons Ltd merged with Royal Doulton Tableware Ltd in 1968. The Royal Doulton Brand and Trademark are part of the Fiskars portfolio of brands and trademarks, www.fiskarsgroup.com. Registered office: Wedgwood Drive, Barlaston, Stoke-on-Trent, Staffordshire, ST12 9ER. Registered in England. Company registration number: 6805116. VAT number: GB946915581.

Williams Sonoma© is a registered trademark of Williams-Sonoma, Inc. Williams-Sonoma, 3250 Van Ness Avenue, San Francisco, CA 94109.

Introduction:
THE "PICTURE" IN THE SHOP WINDOW

Some years ago, I was wandering through an antique shop in my hometown of St. Louis, Missouri. Amid the randomly assorted items of furniture, glass vases, and silverplate pitchers, something caught my eye: a full set of china on a dining table. It was a pink pattern on an off-white background, and each place setting was stacked with a dinner plate, salad plate, and a round soup bowl with tabbed handles on the side. As I approached, I saw that the bowl had a scene in the middle, surrounded by a decorative border featuring intertwined oak leaves and acorns. The center of the bowl featured a nineteenth-century-style image of a tree-lined knoll with a little covered wagon and a man and a woman standing nearby, looking out on a river with two steamboats. On the far bank, there were buildings and a few church steeples. I turned the bowl over and saw an image of an eagle, the words "Historic America," and two banners with the words "St Louis Missouri."[1] I was immediately taken, both by the pleasure of recognition of my own city and by the charm of the picture, which was extremely detailed and as well-drawn as any "real" historical engraving.

Looking further at the other items in the set, I noticed there were new discoveries. There was an unusual square-shaped salad plate depicting "The Capitol at Washington."[2] The scene was not entirely familiar, because the building seemed incomplete, as if still under construction. It was in the background of the image, and the foreground showed a horse-drawn carriage, a man on horseback, and several people in old-fashioned dress, on a wide dirt road rutted by wagon wheels. The dinner plate showed a "View of Boston Massachusetts" and the butter plate showed "Covered Wagons and the Rocky Mountains." The teacup was too small for a printed backstamp, other than the embossed words "Made in England," but the saucer identified both pieces as "San Francisco during the Gold Rush." Even though I did not need any dishes, I did not recognize the maker's name of Johnson Brothers, and pink would never be my choice of color for a dinner set, I bought it, paying about a dollar per piece. I did not realize it at the time, but my experience was similar to that of millions of Americans throughout the twentieth century, who were the targeted consumers of decorated dinnerware made in Staffordshire, England.

From the second half of the nineteenth century through the end of the twentieth century, a vast amount of decorated tableware was produced in Britain for export to America. This tableware, called "pottery" in Britain, was durable and inexpensive, as distinguished from the finer-quality porcelain known as "china." The majority of production was never considered by its manufacturers or users to have a high intrinsic value, and even in the mid-twentieth century, families living in the townships around Stoke-on-Trent, known as "the potteries," would frequently discard entire sets when some pieces became chipped or cracked. Buying a new set was seen as a way of protecting the jobs of the workers in the community, and there was little or no sentimentality attached to the pattern itself.[3]

The aesthetic qualities of this tableware, however, render it an ideal subject for the study of material culture in the American home. These plates were intended to appeal to consumers on the basis of their visual interest, not merely their utilitarian function, and they provide valuable insights into what Americans of different eras considered to be decorative and stylish. The concept of displaying tableware as home décor is not new, typically occurring in a dining room on the open shelves of a hutch or behind the glass doors of a display cabinet. What was markedly different in this case was that many of the plates were conceived of as works of art, similar to engravings that might be hung in a frame. This perception was enhanced by the fact that there was not just one pattern reproduced on all of the plates, but there was often significant variation of the scenes, so that the display of several plates would be similar to having a row of pictures on the wall. Above all, the subjects being depicted spoke to American cultural identity, in terms of showing scenes of historical relevance to US history or topics that reflected trends of popular taste.

This book will present an in-depth analysis of representative examples of this tableware, focusing on one of the most important British companies that targeted the American market, Johnson Brothers. The pottery produced by Johnson Brothers reflects the broader history of American export tableware produced by a large number of British firms. Rival companies frequently produced similar patterns, and it is therefore possible to study the production of one company and gain an understanding of the trends influencing all of the companies in the industry.[4] Such firms included Wedgwood, Spode, Adams, and what a ceramic historian in 1906 called "the great 'American' firms, that is those which supply the American market, such as Meakin's, Johnson Bros., Maddock's, and Grindley's."[5] The firm of Johnson Brothers, however, was notable for its sheer volume of production. By 1908, the company would be described by the Staffordshire trade publication *The Pottery Gazette* as "the largest pottery manufacturers in the world."[6] As the article noted further:

> The company make chiefly, but not exclusively, for the American, Colonial, and foreign markets. Of course, it is their enormous export trade that finds work for their huge factories. I was shown samples of their best popular staple lines, and also of some of their most recent productions. Johnson Brothers are constantly bringing out novelties in form and ornamentation, in face of the fact that they have some patterns which maintain their popularity for a long time.[7]

In contrast to the high volume of sales and wide distribution of Johnson Brothers pottery in the United States, documentation of the company's history is quite limited, as are records of its patterns. *The Pottery Gazette* made occasional mention of activities at the company, naming a few patterns, but this only allows us to associate those patterns with a specific date, that is, the date of the publication issue, which was not necessarily the date when the pattern was introduced. The *Gazette* was also a trade publication intended to promote the potteries, and relied upon information provided by the companies themselves, a fact that renders its "reporting" somewhat less than objective. For example, an article from April 1, 1909, describes a visit to the Johnson Brothers Hanley Pottery "BY A 'POTTERY GAZETTE' SPECIAL COMMISSIONER," where he had "a short interview with one of their managers, Mr. A. Weston, who was able to give a favourable report upon the company's business in the last year [...] All the forms and decorations of their wares are right up to date. Indeed, for novelty in shape and ornamentation they are well in front."[8]

The principal publications to date about Johnson Brothers patterns are found in books aimed at the market of "collectors," which exist for the purpose of pattern identification. The first such guide was *Johnson Brothers Dinnerware, Pattern Directory & Price Guide*, privately published in 1993 and 2003 by an antiques dealer named Mary Finegan.[9] In preparing her book, Finegan had visited the company headquarters in Stoke-on-Trent, had seen the factory, and had interviewed a company manager, John Healings. He provided her with dates of production for many patterns, information that is extremely useful for this study. According to Finegan, however, "in the early years at Johnson Brothers, records were not kept past the period during which a specific pattern was active. As a result, names and other information on older patterns are literally impossible to find unless they extend within the memories of current or recent employees" (p. iii).

Another source of information concerning Johnson Brothers patterns is a fifty-eight-page booklet compiled for the Flow Blue International Collectors Club, Inc. by William H. VanBuskirk. This work, entitled *The Johnson Bros., A Dynasty in Clay*, was privately published in 1998.[10] VanBuskirk was specifically interested in "flow blue" patterns, which he dated between 1883 and 1913,[11] which will be described in Chapter 1, and he gleaned detailed descriptive information about many patterns from other collectors, as well as obtaining some information from correspondence with the Johnson Brothers company.

A collector's guide, *Johnson Brothers Classic English Dinnerware*, was published in 2003 by Bob Page and Dale Frederiksen, the owners of the pattern-matching company Replacements, Ltd.[12] That work contains over 1,600 pattern images, classified by plate shape and pattern name (if known), but there are no dates given for patterns, and there are only two pages of company history, cited from Finegan. Some references to Johnson Brothers patterns may be found in other publications for collectors, such as *English Transferware, Popular 20th Century Patterns* (2005),[13] but this typically consists of photographs of patterns, with no information provided except for the pattern name and estimated sales prices.

What does exist in abundance, however, is the physical record of the patterns themselves. As mentioned above, the Page and Frederiksen guide contains over 1,600 photographs of Johnson Brothers patterns, photographed in color. In addition, because of the large number of pottery pieces that have survived through several generations, it has been possible for this author to view many examples at firsthand. Only two patterns, *Old Britain Castles* and *Historic America*, have become widely recognized by antique collectors, perhaps based in part on the mistaken belief by some purchasers that the patterns were actually made in the nineteenth century, because of the historical scenes and old-style clothing that they depict. For the most part, other Johnson Brothers patterns are considered simply old-fashioned, and usually what remains of grandmother's prized plates ends up in a charity resale shop.

The research for the present study included a visit to Stoke-on-Trent in 1998. At that time, none of the company personnel interviewed by Mary Finegan were still employed, and although Johnson Brothers company records were stored in the Wedgwood Museum in Barlaston, this consisted only of a handful of news clippings and advertising brochures. During the visit, however, it was possible to conduct interviews with two fourth-generation members of the family, Christopher John Staley Johnson and David Edward Dunn Johnson. Information provided by them will be discussed in the chapters of this book. Most important, there was an opportunity to interview William (Bill) Norbury, a long-retired master engraver who worked for the company for fifty years, from 1927 to 1977, who offered insight into the company's unique success.[14]

As a student at the Stoke College of Art, Norbury caught the eye of the college's director, Gordon Forsyth. Forsyth had served as superintendent for art instruction in Stoke-on-Trent since 1920, and one of his principal duties was to recruit artists for the pottery companies. He offered Norbury a position as apprentice engraver for Johnson Brothers, and in order to help his family financially, Norbury left school and went to work on February 15, 1927, just three months after his fifteenth birthday. He became a chief engraver in 1936 and remained the head of the engraving department until his retirement in 1977. Many of the designs produced from 1936 to 1977 were by his hand or produced under his close supervision.

Norbury recounted his experience at Johnson Brothers in an unpublished personal memoir that he wrote in the years between his retirement in 1977 and his death in 1999.[15] The Norbury memoir is a remarkable document, not only for what he viewed as the most important events of his life, but also for the picture it presents of an industry and the community it supported over the span of several generations.

In producing designs for the American market, Norbury believed that an essential element was charm, but not of a kind that imitated Victorian preciosity. He was quite dismissive of some of the earlier company patterns, and although he admired (and contributed to) images for *Old Britain Castles*, he described its border as resembling the decoration on a "chocolate box." Most important, however, he believed that pottery designs were works of art. To Norbury, a shop window was like a window into an art gallery, and the works displayed should invite the passerby to stop, admire, and be moved by the desire to have the work in her own home.

This concept of tableware design is essential to our understanding of the medium, not merely for its function but rather for its artistic significance. When asked if he ever considered how food would look when served on the plate, Norbury was bemused by the very idea, which was completely irrelevant to him as an artist. He wanted his designs to have integrity as compositions, with elements of balance, depth, and narrative meaning. Even Norbury's floral motifs have a "right side up," because he created them to be viewed from a specific vantage point, and he took particular pride in his abilities in portraiture and landscape. In Norbury's own words:

> The basic reason for the industry's success was [...] because of our efforts to produce better and better and the most artistic engraving in the Potteries since print began at the end of the 17th Century. I remember being told as a boy, that engraving and printing is dying out, that was in 1927. But now I knew, that if it could be done, we were the ones that could do it "Better". (p. 8)

To the designers of this pottery and to its users, it was a form of art that brought visual and cultural meaning to the domestic environment. It offered an aesthetic choice to people ranging from the upper ranks of society to those of the most modest means, in deciding what decorative patterns, images, colors, and shapes would be part of their everyday experience. And in the specific case of British tableware for the American market, the "art of the table," in a very literal sense, both reflected and helped to shape the social values of its time. These patterns constitute a material history of cultural values and identity, in a humble and often-overlooked medium, which nevertheless reached into the life of virtually every American of the twentieth century.

Chapter 1

OLD WORLD STYLE FOR THE NEW WORLD

The history of British pottery made for the American market dates back more than 250 years. The earliest tableware in the American colonies was of wood or inexpensive metal such as pewter, and when ceramic pieces were used, they were of necessity very plain and durable, since all of the goods were shipped from Britain and broken pieces could not be easily replaced. The vast majority of tableware exported to the colonies in the eighteenth century and into the mid-nineteenth century was of this type.[1]

The Staffordshire area was not well populated until around 1700, because the soil was poor for farming; it was ideal, however, for the making of pottery. Coal and clay were available resources, and the town of Hanley was about sixty miles from the western port of Liverpool. A series of canals was built in the early eighteenth century to facilitate the transport of goods to the coast, since barges pulled by horses produced less breakage than transport over a common road. Hanley was the largest of six townships that later incorporated in the twentieth century as Stoke-on-Trent, and this area became the base for most of the export trade to America.

In 1752, the Liverpool firm of Sadler and Green is believed to have invented the technique of transfer printing,[2] and decorated wares became an important part of pottery production.[3] Instead of labor-intensive hand painting, a copper plate was engraved with a design, and a roller of ink was applied, allowing ink to settle in the carved areas. The plate surface would be wiped clean, and a sheet of tissue would be pressed upon the inked copper plate, absorbing the ink. The tissue was then applied to a prefired ceramic object. When the ink dried, the piece was immersed in water to remove the tissue, and the piece was fired again at a lower temperature, to fix the image before a final glazing and firing.

The process of transfer printing involved multiple firings that were still highly demanding in terms of energy; for a single firing, bottle-shaped kilns filled to the ceiling with stacks of dried clay objects had to be heated over a two-day period to a temperature of 1000–2000 degrees Celsius (1832–2102 degrees Fahrenheit), consuming 10 to 12 tons of coal. Transfer printing, however, allowed for greater uniformity of pattern application and eliminated the need for multiple artists to apply a design by hand. The process became more mechanical, allowing more relatively unskilled workers to produce goods more quickly. And above all, the decorated plates could be produced in a limitless variety of patterns, offering choices to accommodate the individual tastes of potential purchasers.

It was typical for the entire community to be involved in the manufacturing process. In addition to the artists who created designs, the potters who shaped the clay forms, and the manual laborers involved in the firing process, artist-engravers were trained to reproduce the design on a copper plate, each plate specially proportioned to fit a piece of a certain size and shape. Many other workers were involved in the preparation and application of the transfer patterns.

The American Revolution brought about a major shift in the economic relationship between Britain and its colonies. The Americans' military alliance with the French, and hostility toward all things British (not just tea), threatened Britain with a potentially devastating loss of its very lucrative colonial market. After the end of the conflict in 1783, British potteries had to face for the first time the necessity of competing for American trade, and imagining what Americans wanted to buy.

One solution was to make tableware decorated with scenes of American cities. These scenes were copied from contemporary engravings of landscapes and city streets, depicting major population centers of the northeast such as Albany, New York. Some potteries even commissioned artists to travel to America, to record scenes that would then be reproduced on pottery back in Britain. An early scholar of historical pottery, Edwin Atlee Barber, wrote:

> The production of Liverpool creamware, with black, brown, green and red printed designs relating to America, extended over a period of some twenty-five years—from about 1790 to 1815. The black printed and lustered creamware and the dark-blue china of the Staffordshire potteries began to take the place of the Liverpool products soon after the War of 1812, and blue printed china continued to be manufactured until about 1830. ... This ware, in turn, was gradually superseded by the Staffordshire crockery, with prints in various colors—red, green, light blue, black, brown and purple—which was made in great abundance for at least fifteen years longer, or down to about 1840.[4]

Among the many known examples of "Staffordshire blue" or "historical blue" are scenes of the "Capitol, Washington," made by Ralph Stevenson around 1820[5] and "Harvard College," made by Ralph Stevenson & Williams of Cobridge after an engraving dating from 1823.[6] As will be noted later on in Chapter 3, the oak leaf and acorn border used by Stevenson & Williams would form an integral part of the Johnson Brothers' design for *Historic America*, when it was launched around 1938.[7]

A dinner service ornamented with American scenery was manufactured around 1840 by William Ridgway & Company. Called "American Views," it was based on engravings by William Henry Bartlett, and was printed on the reverse with a spread eagle and shield, with the phrase "Opaque Granite China, W. R. & Company."[8] The series was produced chiefly in light blue, but some examples are known in black and mulberry. Ridgway owned the Charles Street Works in

Hanley, and in addition to the "American Views," his firm was a producer of white granite ware for the American market.[9] At one point, Ridgway purchased some land in Kentucky, to establish a pottery manufacturing operation there, but due to financial reversals he sold the land in 1848.[10] Ridgway's Charles Street Works was later taken over by J. W. Pankhurst, who continued to manufacture goods for export to the United States.

The original patriarch of the Johnson family was Robert Johnson, born in 1822.[11] According to local legend, as recounted by a hotel proprietor in 1998, Robert was the humble gardener of the prosperous Meakin family, owners of one of the largest potteries in Hanley. On September 9, 1851, he married Sarah Meakin, the youngest of Meakin's eight children; the same local legend claimed that this marriage of two social unequals was prompted by the imminent arrival of a child.[12] The couple eventually had four sons, Henry James ("Harry," b. 1852), Robert Lewis (b. 1856), Frederick George (b. 1858), and Alfred (b. 1862), as well as four daughters. All four sons eventually entered the pottery trade as apprentices with Meakin.

After J. W. Pankhurst declared bankruptcy in 1882, two of Robert Johnson's sons, Alfred and Frederick, purchased Pankhurst's Charles Street Works in 1883.[13] The year of 1883 was subsequently adopted by the company as its official founding date.[14] The firm of Johnson Brothers initially produced earthenware called "White Granite," and according to the company's own unpublished account:

> The end of the Civil War in America had created a great demand for consumer goods in that country and the Johnson Brothers were not slow to take advantage of the opportunities in the market. In addition to supplying well-potted white ware of reasonable weight and price, they were now producing under-glaze printed ware.[15]

The name of "granite ware" reflects an early marketing strategy to suggest that the plates were as hard as stone, which of course they were not. Among the earliest known examples of decorated granite ware made by Johnson Brothers for the American market, dating from 1883 onward, is a square-shaped covered sugar bowl with motifs of a spray of flowers, and touches of hand-applied color (Plate 1A). The floral spray pattern was well suited for this use, because its naturalistic, random quality allowed for less precision in its application than a pattern of symmetrical, repeating images. If the transfer were applied crookedly, no one would know the difference. Even when the transfer pattern or the color was misapplied, however, the piece was still fired and sold. There was no culling of "seconds" when it came to decorating mistakes, which is understandable in light of how difficult and costly it was to produce a finished piece after multiple firings.

The sugar bowl was not particularly well made, as indicated by the fact that the base is uneven, causing it to rock. Its decoration, however, strives hard to be pleasing. The floral engraving is enhanced by four applied colors, gray and beige on the leaves and pink on the flowers. White paint was also applied in heavy dots, which are raised to the touch. As a final embellishment, gilt paint was applied to the rims and handles of the lid and base, and to the feet of the base. The gilt, and possibly the white paint, would have required an additional firing at a lower temperature, so it is somewhat paradoxical that such visual attention was given to a piece of imperfect quality.

The other significant role of the transfer engraving was to make a company mark, or backstamp, on the reverse side or base of the piece of pottery. The earliest known mark used by Johnson Brothers was "Royal Ironstone China, Johnson Bros., Late Pankhurst & Co., England" (Figure 1.1).

The mark also featured the British coat of arms, with a lion and a unicorn flanking an oval shield with the royal motto *Honi soit qui mal y pense* (shame on him who thinks evil of it) topped by a crown. The British coat of arms was used frequently as a pottery mark by many firms,[16] and the term "Royal" further emphasized the British origin of the wares; a very similar "Royal Ironstone China" mark was used by W. H. Grindley & Co. of Tunstall, but that may not have been introduced until after 1891.[17] "Ironstone" is defined as "a hard, heavy earthenware

Figure 1.1 Johnson Brothers Late Pankhurst backstamp, *c.* 1883.

body introduced by C. J. Mason in 1813."[18] The term "china," however, was misleading; this was the thick, durable stoneware known as "pottery" in England. It is possible that the company believed that Americans would prefer to buy goods marked as "china," even if "ironstone china" was an oxymoron. In keeping with the uneven production quality, the backstamp is unintentionally printed off-center.

The company's success led to expansion, and in 1888, Alfred and Frederick were joined by their brother Henry in a deed of partnership. In the same year, they began construction of the Hanley Pottery, which began operation in 1889, and in 1891 they built the Imperial Pottery; both were in Eastwood Road, Hanley, a ten-minute walk from the original Charles Street Works.[19] In 1895, they opened another factory in the north end of the city, naming it the "Alexandra Pottery" in honor of the Princess of Wales.

The Royal Arms backstamp was used by the company from 1883 to about 1913,[20] but in the meantime, other logo designs were adopted, including a globe etched with lines of latitude and longitude, with a crown resting on top (Figure 1.2). The pattern name, if any, was written horizontally, and the word "Semi-Porcelain" formed a half circle above the globe. The words "Johnson Bro^s" and "England" formed a half circle below the globe.

Like "ironstone china," the new term "semi-porcelain" was another contradiction in terms, since "porcelain" correctly applies to the very finest quality of ceramic goods, and while this was lighter in weight and of somewhat better quality than the coarse, heavy granite ware, the term "semi-porcelain" clearly represented a marketing strategy. The term was also used by other companies, including William Adams & Sons, Upper Hanley Pottery Co., and Globe Pottery Co.; "Semi-China" was used by Clementson Bros. Ltd.[21]

The globe logo also indicates that Johnson Brothers considered itself to be an international company. The fact that the crown rests on top of the globe could be seen as an imperialistic statement that "Britannia rules the world," but it certainly creates a visual link between the company, represented by the British crown, and its American customers, represented by the globe. Its use on pottery sold in the United States reflects the importance of that market to the company's fortunes, and in one example of the globe logo, on an unnamed pattern, small splotches of red paint suggest the North and South American continents.

The Johnson Brothers globe mark is not mentioned in Godden's *Encyclopaedia*, but there are other similar examples by companies such as Adams and Grindley, with attributed dates varying widely. A globe mark used by E. Hughes & Company was used between 1912 and 1941.[22] Ralph M. Kovel's *Dictionary of Marks* lists sixteen globe marks, not including Johnson Brothers but appropriately including the Globe Pottery Co. Ltd. of Cobridge.[23] A globe mark dating from around 1891–97 was used by Alfred Meakin,[24] to whom the Johnson brothers were related.

According to a British design registration number of 131486, embossed on the reverse of pieces from several patterns, Johnson Brothers registered a new, asymmetrical body shape in 1889. Although the dinner plates were round as usual, pieces such as tureens, gravy boats, and pitchers were molded with an S-curve (Plate 1B). The decorations were either "random" floral sprays or floral motifs

Figure 1.2 Johnson Brothers Semi-Porcelain backstamp, *c.* 1890.

repeated around the edge, as in *Hop*, which depicted the flowers and leaves of the hop plant.

The asymmetrical shape of these patterns reflects a confidence in the American consumer's appreciation of design that was nontraditional and innovative. The shape was likely influenced by the popularity of asymmetrical motifs popularized by the aesthetic movement of the 1870s and 1880s. In 1854, the American fleet under the command of Commodore Matthew Perry had ended a 220-year period during which Japan was closed to trading with Western countries. An historic agreement was signed, allowing future trade between America and Japan. By the 1870s, a now-thriving trade meant that artists and designers were exposed to Japanese motifs found in such items as woodblock prints, fans, and kimono fabrics. This style of design became known as the aesthetic movement.

Several British pottery manufacturers followed the aesthetic trend. One example is a Japanese-inspired pattern of fishing boats framed by stylized medallions and multiple bands of abstract line patterns (Plate 1C). The edge is formed by a clever fan pattern, made up of wedge-shaped segments of daisies, of which the petals resemble the "ribs" of the fan. The maker's mark, by William Brownfield & Sons of Cobridge, is dated by Godden between 1871 and 1891,[25] and the pattern has the American name of *Wisconsin*. This pattern name clearly indicates that it was intended for sale to the American market, as was the pattern by T.G. & F. Booth of Tunstall, *America*, dating from 1886 (Rd. No. 41252).

Numerous other patterns by other companies were made in the style of the aesthetic movement, although they appear to be somewhat hit-or-miss in their understanding of Asian style. Some designers had enough visual reference material to form accurate impressions, such as in a butter pat (Plate 1D) impressed on the back with the letters "BB," suggesting that it may have been made by Minton, as early as 1855–60.[26] This butter pat features a round paper fan with cranes, a spray of cherry blossoms, a framed rectangular vignette of a lake, trees, and tall mountains, and a repeated pattern of fans, similar to a kimono fabric.

In some cases, an Asian motif was accompanied by a definitively non-Asian pattern name. This may have been due to artists being told to use the "popular" motifs, whereas the people assigned to give the pattern a name were only aware that it was an exotic locale. This may explain a plate dating from around 1886 (Rd. No. 69160) made by W. H. Grindley & Co., Tunstall. It is a Japanese-inspired pattern with geometric motifs and cherry blossom sprays, but it is inexplicably named *Malta*. Another example is a pattern by G. W. Turner & Sons, Tunstall, featuring an Asian-style ginger jar, but named *Brazil*.

Very often, however, the British designers had an imperfect understanding of true Asian style in terms of visual characteristics as well as pattern names. It is unclear whether this was due to inadequate sources of inspiration, or due to the belief that British or American consumers would prefer to see images that were "closer to home," resulting in an odd mixture of styles. A plate made by W. A. Adderley & Co., Longton, with a registration number from 1884, features Asian-inspired flowers and vignettes, but the vignettes are of English scenes, and the pattern name is *Alton*. A butter dish with no maker's mark has a registration number dating from 1881. It features bamboo-like handles, but the center scene shows a European-style castle with crenellation. Another unnamed plate made by "F. W. G.," an unknown manufacturer, dates from 1884 and features pomegranates and a Japanese fan decorated with fish. It also has a "fan" made up of cards on which writing in English can be seen, suggesting a diary, and a cover card featuring a little British or American girl. There is also a vignette showing the same little girl sitting on a wooden fence with a watering bucket nearby (Figure 1.3).

Johnson Brothers patterns in the 1890s were predominantly floral, in the Victorian taste. Not every pattern was named, but many were, and a large number of these were generic names echoing the floral design, such as *Petunia*. In some instances, however, names were chosen to appeal directly to American tastes, and one of those patterns was called *Columbia*.

The figure of Columbia was popular in the nineteenth century as an allegorical representation of the United States as a female goddess. Her name was derived from the name of Christopher Columbus, the fabled "discoverer" of America, and the term "Columbia" had been used to describe British territories in the New World since the 1730s.[27] The word also suggested the Latin word *columba*, meaning "dove," and therefore was associated with peace. In 1790, the goddess Columbia became part of the name of the nation's capital city, Washington, within the federal district called the District of Columbia.

The ceramic historian Robert Copeland observed that in "patterns specifically aimed at the American market […] designs were named appropriately in the

Figure 1.3 Aesthetic-style plate, maker F.W.G., *c*. 1884.

belief that the name would help to attract custom [...] 'Columbia' was a popular name for romantic scenes."[28] The Johnson Brothers pattern was produced after 1889, since it was one of the asymmetrically shaped series registered in that year (Figure 1.4). Its decoration was of floral sprays, with five-petaled flowers resembling the columbine. The leaves are less botanically accurate, and the sprays also include a form of grass.

It is also possible that the pattern was created to coincide with the World's Columbian Exposition, a world's fair held in Chicago in 1893. (This event was planned to commemorate the 400th anniversary of Columbus's voyage in 1492, but due to delays, the opening did not occur until 1893.) The purchasers of this pattern would feel patriotic pride, not only in the symbolic association of America with New World exploration, but also in the fact that a world's fair was being hosted by the second largest city in the United States. The association of Columbia with peace would also be inspirational, presenting America as a powerful agent of world harmony.

At some point around 1890, Johnson Brothers introduced a new style of pottery that was thinner than the semi-porcelain. The other, more solid wares continued to be produced, but there was now a two-tiered production aimed at different markets. The finer goods were called "Royal Semi-Porcelain," and the backstamp logo did not feature the globe, but rather a large angular crown, with a ribbon-style banner beneath it that read "Johnson" on the left and "Bros" on the right, with "England" below (Figure 1.5). It should be noted, however, that the "Royal Semi-Porcelain" backstamp occasionally found its way onto pieces that were identical in

Figure 1.4 Columbia, Johnson Brothers, *c*. 1889–93.

weight and pattern style with the earlier "Semi-Porcelain." A similar "Royal Semi-Porcelain" backstamp was also used by other companies, such as Meakin.

The patterns in the "Royal Semi-Porcelain" style were characterized by detailed molding, including scalloped edges, freeform-shaped handles, and leaf-like motifs in the body of the piece. The transfer patterns were often very delicate, suggestive of lace and embroidery, and there was often gilding applied to the edges and in the body. The transfer engravings were applied with greater care than was evident in the semi-porcelain pottery, and the gilding was also carefully applied to highlight fine details such as the ribs of a leaf. The highly refined quality of this ware is illustrated by covered vegetable dishes in the patterns *Dartmouth, Regis,* and *Rolland* (Plate 2A).

Many of the "Royal Semi-Porcelain" patterns had names that suggested sophistication and wealth, at least in the minds of the purchaser. Two examples of this are *Vienna* and *Paris*. *Vienna*, which has a registration number issued in 1898,[29] features embellishment not only in the form of transfer pattern but also raised motifs throughout the body. In the small pitcher illustrated in Plate 2B, the handle has two circular perforations. Finely stippled lines are used to create "solid"

Figure 1.5 Johnson Brothers Royal Semi-Porcelain backstamp, *c.* 1890.

color areas around the rim of the spout and around the base, and to create shading on the flower petals and leaves.

Paris has a relatively streamlined design in comparison to *Vienna*, but it features a delicate floral pattern of one large spray and two smaller ones, applied asymmetrically to both the rim and the flat center of the plate. The flowers are represented so precisely that they can be identified botanically as poppies, lilacs, and grass.[30] Both poppies and lilacs grow wild in France, and both have been associated with events in French history; the poppy was a symbol of the French republican revolt of 1871, known as the "Commune," and would later become a symbol of the casualties of the First World War.

The name "Paris" was perhaps inspired by the 1900 Paris World's Fair, which introduced the world to the design style of "Art Nouveau," although the pattern does not embody characteristics of that style such as the stylization of organic forms. A much better example of Art Nouveau style may be seen in a plate by Grimwades Ltd., with a pattern name of *Nancy* (Figure 1.6). The registration number of 399029 dates it to 1902, and the name refers to the eastern French city

Figure 1.6 Nancy, Grimwades, *c.* 1902, detail.

of Nancy, renowned as a site where Art Nouveau furniture and glass were being produced by makers such as Émile Gallé, Louis Majorelle, and the Daum Brothers. The plate features highly stylized intertwined vines and water lilies; water lilies were a favorite motif used by Gallé and Majorelle, and the symmetrically intertwined vines suggest designs by Hector Guimard.

In other cases, it seems clear that a name was selected for its significance to the American consumer. *Oregon, Florida, Manhattan,* and *Savannah* are examples of place names derived from native American words, which have no counterpart in Europe. The pattern *Savannah*, seemingly named for the city in the southeastern American state of Georgia, can be seen in a covered sugar bowl (Plate 2C). This piece is much more refined in its appearance than the earlier Royal Ironstone piece; it features rococo-inspired molded shapes for the handles of the bowl and lid, and the lid handle is asymmetrical. The body features very thin vertical ribs around the base, with delicately molded ribbons and olive branches that are only visible upon close inspection. The green engraving pattern features very small flowers and scrolls, with a stippled background, and there is gilt paint surrounding the rim of the lid as well as in various touches on the body and lid. The backstamp is also very delicate, although in typical fashion, it is applied off-center.

In other instances, the pattern name found the ideal blend of referencing both uniquely American sites and sophisticated wealth. *Waldorf* alludes to the legendary hotel founded in New York City in 1893. According to the hotel's official history:

> Millionaire William Waldorf Astor opened the 13-story Waldorf Hotel on the site of his mansion at the corner of Fifth Avenue and 33rd Street, designed by renowned architect Henry Hardenbergh. Four years later, The Waldorf was joined by the 17-story Astoria Hotel, erected on an adjacent site by Waldorf's cousin, John Jacob Astor IV.[31]

In many ways, these patterns marked as "Royal Semi-Porcelain" illustrate the aesthetic values of the American "gilded age." Their rococo-style shapes reference the ceramics of eighteenth-century France and Germany, made by manufacturers such as Sèvres and Meissen, which were recognized as the finest examples of decorative tableware used by royalty and nobility. Even though this semi-porcelain pottery was thicker than the true porcelain it imitated, in many cases it was relatively lightweight, and its delicately molded and painted embellishments declared its user to be a person of refinement and upper-class tastes. It is likely that this type of piece would have been acquired principally for display, and only used very rarely, which helps account for some examples having survived more than one hundred years.

The Johnson Brothers firm had always pursued the American market, but in the late 1890s, a member of the family was dispatched to cultivate those contacts more directly. That was Robert Lewis Johnson (1853–1909), the fourth Johnson brother. As described by the family's history:

The partnership had become a Limited Liability Company in 1896, and a fourth brother, Robert, had by then joined the Company. By living in New York, he set up the Company's office in that city and travelling across the country with his samples, greatly stimulated the demand for Johnson Brothers' products in North America.[32]

This direct American connection may account for the fact that many Johnson Brothers patterns around the turn of the twentieth century were made in the "flow blue" style. This was a type of transfer pottery that originated in Staffordshire around 1820, in which a cobalt oxide ink was applied and allowed to seep into the glaze, creating an intense color. Flow blue was similar to traditional blue-and-white pottery, except that the blue color was deliberately blurred, an effect achieved by adding a cup of lime or ammonia to the kiln during glazing.[33] The flow blue style was very popular in the United States between 1885 and 1915, but it was not considered desirable in England, since the blurred effect was regarded as a production flaw. It is therefore possible to study how patterns of this style appealed directly to the American consumer. According to Christopher Johnson:

> Tastes differ between England and America, then as now, and the best example of this is the popularity of the various "Flow Blue" patterns produced especially for the American market. This type of decoration, where the blue (Cobalt Oxide) has bled into the glaze, has proved enduringly popular in America. Sadly this style of decoration has never been popular in England and can rarely be found here today.[34]

In 1998, William VanBuskirk published a study of Johnson Brothers flow blue pottery.[35] Using his personal collection and research, as well as letters and photographs from the members of the Flow Blue International Collectors Club, VanBuskirk identified sixty-seven patterns produced by the Johnson Brothers company in flow blue,[36] including some pieces created with "mulberry" (deep purple) color ink. He also noted that the Grindley company made a "flow green."[37] There were a number of patterns, including *Paris*, which were made both in flow blue and in the standard transfer process with blue ink, thus increasing the purchaser's options. *Vienna*, also described earlier, is known to have been produced in a wash set in flow blue style.[38]

Many Johnson Brothers flow blue patterns featured American place names, including *Manhattan, St. Louis, Georgia*, and *Oregon*. These patterns reflected the growth of a prosperous American middle class, and purchasers who wanted to acquire material goods in the European tradition, but asserting a distinctively "American" character. Flow blue pieces are in general very rich in appearance, with gilding applied to complement the intense blue color. When combined with the "Royal Semi-Porcelain" characteristics of decorative molding in the body and elaborately shaped handles, a flow blue piece was the epitome of "gilded age" sophistication.

The *Florida* pattern (Plate 2D) is one of only three flow blue patterns identified by VanBuskirk as having its particular body shape, which is roughly hexagonal, with flat edges alternating with rounded scallops.[39] It was produced both with and without gilding, sometimes referred to as "tracings," and a "gilder's trade mark" of dots or small lines would be applied to the back of the plate.[40] This would enable the gilder to receive payment, since these workers were paid by the piece after the final firing.

An advertisement from the 1895 Montgomery Ward catalogue offered the flow blue pattern called *Peach Blossom*, with the following text:

> Peach Blossom Pattern. Manufactured by Johnson Bros., Hanley, England. Best quality of genuine English semi-porcelain, very durable. The decoration is a rich flown blue of beach [sic] blossoms and leaves put on under the glaze; the blossoms are illuminated with gold traced outlines burnt on which conduce to make it the handsomest dark blue ever brought out. All the pieces have full gold trimmings.[41]

The prices advertised seem remarkably low in comparison to the rich appearance of this pottery, even factoring in a century of inflation. A dozen teacups and saucers were $2.10; a dozen 8-inch plates were $1.97; a 16-inch platter was $1.44; and a 3-quart pitcher was 78 cents. The most expensive item on the price list was a soup tureen with ladle and stand, at $3.93.

An inventory of flow blue patterns made by Johnson Brothers allows us to compare and analyze the pattern names. The list was compiled by VanBuskirk,[42] but as is true of every "collector's guide" pertaining to Johnson Brothers, it is not comprehensive. Additional patterns are known to the author that are not included in the inventories of VanBuskirk, Finegan, or Page and Frederiksen, and more will undoubtedly be discovered in the future. Some of the patterns listed subsequently have been dated by their design registration numbers, with dates ranging primarily between 1893 and 1908, and the names can be grouped according to categories of "British Names," "Foreign Names," "Nature," "Hotels," "Women's Names," and "American Names."

Under "British Names," one finds *Argyle, Aubrey, Clayton, Cornwall, English Garden, Exeter, Fulton, Kenworth, Oxford, Regent, Richmond, Royston, Salisbury, Stanley, Sterling, Warwick,* and *Waverly.*

Under "Foreign Names," one finds *Andorra, The Blue Danube, Brittany, Dresden, Hague, Holland, Japan, Mentone, Mongolia, Neapolitan, Normandy, Oriental, Paris, Pekin, Persian, Tokio, Trieste, Turin, Venice,* and *Vienna. Mentone* is noteworthy, in that it is the Italian name for the French town more commonly known as Menton, situated on the French Riviera close to the border between France and Italy.

Under "Nature," one finds *Begonia, Clematis, Lily* (also perhaps a woman's name), *Peach Blossom, Poppy,* and *Tulip.*

Under "Hotels," one finds *Astoria, Regent,* and *Savoy.*

Under "Women's Names," one finds *Clarissa, Constance, Coral, Dorothy, Fortuna* (the Roman goddess of fortune), *Jewel* (also referring to a gemstone), and *Lily.*

Some of these examples are open to a variety of interpretations, such as *Lily*, which is both a flower and a woman's name, or *Raleigh*, which is both a city in North Carolina and the name of the heroic Sir Walter, a romantic figure of British history. *Sterling* is both a British place name and a mark indicating silver of high quality (92.5 percent pure). The important point, however, is that the designers believed that all of the pattern names were appropriate for flow blue pottery, because of all that they might imply about urban sophistication, exotic locales, or feminine delicacy.

The listing of "American Names," however, is the most intriguing: *Albany, Brooklyn, Claremont, Columbia, Florida, Georgia, Manhattan, Montana, Princeton, Raleigh, Richmond, Savannah,* and *St. Louis*. It is interesting to note that *Montana* and *Oregon* were chosen as flow blue pattern names, given that both states in 1900 were still semi-wilderness, and their names would in fact evoke a rough-and-ready pioneer history in the minds of Americans. Claremont was a California town founded in 1887 and officially incorporated in 1907, at which time there were only 131 eligible voters.[43] This would appear to suggest that the British pottery workers responsible for choosing the pattern name did not have a sense of what those places were like; instead, they may have been given lists of names and assigned them somewhat arbitrarily.

In other instances, however, the British designers hit their mark. There are several English towns called Newport, but the namesake of the pattern is likely Newport, Rhode Island, the turn-of-the-century summer playground of New York City's wealthiest families. *Princeton* commemorates the Ivy League university in New Jersey, which was originally called the "College of New Jersey" and only received the name of "Princeton University" in 1896; the pattern is dated 1899, making this a pattern of timely interest. *St. Louis* was also a timely choice, in that it was the site of the 1904 Louisiana Purchase Exposition, commemorating the centennial of the explorations of Lewis and Clark, and better known as the St. Louis World's Fair. While it is not known whether or not the pattern was actually issued in 1904, it is very probable that a large quantity of it was sold to Americans during the year of the fair.

Few of these flow blue patterns attempted to make any connection between the visual characteristics of the pattern and its name or associated location. The motifs are usually very stylized, some more overtly floral, but others resembling the repeated pattern of a fabric or carpet. The designers appear to have given primary consideration to the creation of an appealing pattern that would retain its integrity after undergoing the flow blue process, and the name may have been assigned by someone else, after the fact. One flow blue motif that appears to have been influenced by the aesthetic movement was *Mongolia*, the name given somewhat incongruously to a Japanese-inspired design. This pattern features plates and bowls with a plain round shape, kimono-patterned banded border, and a center image featuring Asiatic pheasants.

It is also evident that transfer patterns were applied to molded shapes that did not bear any relationship to the pattern design or name. A covered vegetable dish in the *Oxford* pattern has a body molded with olive branches (leaves and fruits) in relief, covered with white glaze. The blue transfer pattern does not highlight the molded branches, and its design has no hint of olive or laurel shapes (Plate 3A). This example indicates that body shapes and patterns did not have to match. Rather than creating individualized molded shapes for each design, it would be more economical to use one molded shape and create new styles by applying different transfer patterns.

At this time, another important category of flow blue was the pictorial pattern, a direct revival of the "Staffordshire Blue" wares produced in the early nineteenth century. Johnson Brothers does not appear to have produced any of these pictorial patterns, but several other British companies did. An example of this is a plate made for the L. Straus & Sons store in New York, a company specializing in the importation of "china, porcelain, glassware and crockery."[44] The Straus family acquired part ownership in the R. H. Macy & Co. department store in 1884 and became sole owners in 1896. Perhaps not coincidentally, Macy's and Johnson Brothers would later enter into a close partnership, as will be discussed in Chapter 3.

The flow blue plate made for L. Straus & Sons depicts an imaginary landscape in the center, and a border with repetitions of a small vignette, framed by scrolls (Plate 3B). The center image has a man and woman in the foreground, a castle in the middle ground, and a winding river with a bridge and another castle in the background. The repeated vignette shows another couple, with the man playing a lute-like instrument and the woman seated at his feet, in a pose inspired by paintings of the eighteenth-century French artist Jean-Antoine Watteau. This would be less apparent if it were not for the information in the backstamp, which gives the pattern name of *Watteau* and "Staffordshire England" in gothic lettering, and a registration number dating the pattern to 1910. No name of a specific manufacturer is given, but the backstamp has an elaborate motif of a crowned lion rampant holding what may be a globe (a circle with crisscross marks). The lion is framed by a circle with another crown on top of it, which provides a double reference to British royalty even though this is not the royal coat of arms. The plate has faint traces of gilding around its edge.

This plate is not an "American" scene, as was typical of the original Staffordshire blue wares, but rather it shows an imaginary European landscape, and the pattern name requires some recognition of the French artist in order to be understood. It appeals to a purchaser who seeks to acquire "continental" sophistication, even though such an item, in flow blue, would probably not have been sold on the European continent. Nevertheless, this plate would have been proudly displayed in an American home, as if it were a family heirloom from the "old country."

By 1895, Johnson Brothers was well on its way to becoming what the *Pottery Gazette* would call one of the great "American" firms. It was operating four tableware potteries (Charles Street Works, Hanley Pottery, Imperial Pottery, and Alexandra Pottery), and in 1896 it opened the Trent Sanitary Works, across the road from the Imperial Pottery, manufacturing "sanitaryware" (ceramic plumbing fixtures). All four sons of Robert and Sarah Johnson were involved as managing partners: Henry James, Robert Lewis, Frederick George, and Alfred. Company policy also allowed for every brother to bring two sons each into the business,[45] and these sons joined the firm between 1900 and 1910.[46] Figure 1.7 shows the reverse side of a commemorative plate issued in honor of Queen Victoria's Diamond Jubilee in 1897, featuring an unusually detailed transfer engraving of all of the Johnson Brothers factories.

There were many elaborate Johnson Brothers patterns dating from around the turn of the twentieth century that have an entirely different backstamp: this was a crown, the top of which is formed by small circles suggesting pearls, and topped by a small square cross. The cross has angular arms, reminiscent of the Canterbury Cross, a symbol of the Anglican church. This "rounded crown" image is much smaller and simpler than the "royal semi-porcelain" motif, and it typically features only the pattern name above and the words "Johnson Bros England" below. The

Figure 1.7 Queen Victoria Diamond Jubilee backstamp, Johnson Brothers, *c.* 1897. Image courtesy of David Arrowsmith.

pattern *Edgvale* has both a registration number, 341993, and the printed words "PAT^D NOV 7 99" (Figure 1.8).

The rounded crown motif was used on many pieces that were identical in weight and style to patterns marked "Royal Semi-Porcelain." The popularity of flow blue patterns may have influenced the shift from using the highly detailed "Royal Semi-Porcelain" mark to using the rounded crown, since the former would have the tendency to become unattractively blurred in the manufacturing process. This may have been true especially of the company name, which appeared only in small letters on the banners of the "Royal Semi-Porcelain" mark. The crown, however, could remain recognizable even if some of the details were obscured. The company name printed below in capital letters was also more likely to remain legible.

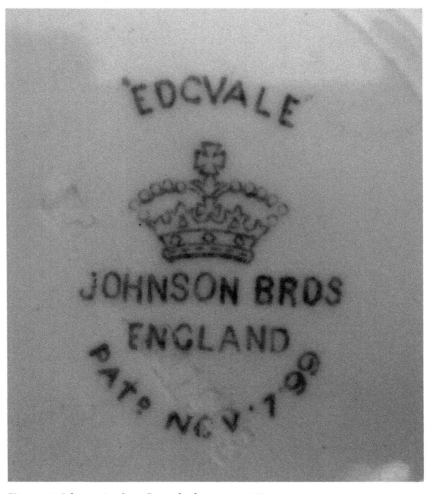

Figure 1.8 Johnson Brothers Crown backstamp, *c.* 1899.

The introduction of the rounded crown stamp also appears to have occurred at around the same time that the company began to produce a much simpler style of pattern, of similar weight as the "Royal Semi-Porcelain" but with less ornamentation. These designs had fewer embossed motifs and a simpler transfer pattern, and in order to offset the relative plainness of the pattern, touches of color were applied by hand, although this was not always done with care. These patterns featured the rounded crown backstamp and usually did not have any pattern name.

While it may be surprising to observe such a significant lowering of the company's quality standards, these simpler patterns could be mass-produced on a much greater scale. The fact that the decorating process became more streamlined and objects could be produced more quickly also meant that there could be an increased number of patterns made available for sale, and the company could experiment with different styles and color combinations. Many of these patterns were apparently in production for only a short period of time, being replaced by newer versions in the hope of reaching new potential purchasers.

Several examples illustrate the way in which the company had created a second-tier quality of production. One unnamed pattern features tiny garlands of roses around the rim and a small bouquet in the center, with embossed ridges around the edge and touches of pink and green color. The crown backstamp states "Pat. 1900." The second plate has a pretty but virtually invisible embossed pattern of curved lines and dots around the end, with no transfer printing, but touches of gilding. The backstamp has no pattern name but states "Pat. Oct. 21st 1902." The inclusion of patent dates suggests that the company wanted to establish a proprietary claim over these designs, even though they were not especially remarkable, and the backstamp quality is very poor. In the case of the pattern of "Oct. 21st 1902," a covered vegetable dish and sauceboat exist which have molded shapes from the higher-quality "Royal Semi-Porcelain," but lacking any decoration other than the gilding. This is evidence that at least for some patterns, the same molds were used for the first- and second-quality production lines, and the difference was in the presence or absence of transfer decoration and/or gilding.

A similar type of pattern made by Meakin has a registration number of 391493, which allows identification of the date of 1902. This pattern is on a plain round shape and has a border motif of beige bands accented with small sprays of roses; a thin rim of gold paint is made to appear wider by an adjacent line of yellowish brown.

The relative simplicity of these patterns, however, did not prevent them from being visually appealing. One example is Johnson Brothers' *The Madras*, which has a pretty motif of an Asiatic pheasant perched on a branch of pink and orange flowers. Another example is an unnamed pattern with only a border design, but that design has curvilinear scrolls reminiscent of Art Nouveau style.

Another important component of the "second-tier" production was tableware produced for the hotel trade. *The Pottery Gazette* of April 1, 1909, describes this as follows:

The company make a very special line in semi-porcelain for hotel and restaurant use. The flat pieces in this "Hotel" ware have roll edges, which effectually prevent chipping. Two especially good printed patterns are applied to this shape—the "Franklin" and the "Valencia Lace," both of which are freely ordered by wholesale houses.[47]

While the name of *Valencia Lace* references a luxury textile, *Franklin* most likely honors Benjamin Franklin, the celebrated Founding Father of the American republic. The monochrome transfer pattern is quite delicate, but the shape is relatively plain. A milk jug in that pattern has molded shapes of elongated leaves in the body and handle, and a scallop-shaped rim (Plate 3C).

Johnson Brothers' diversified production would prove to be strategic when America experienced a major recession in the years 1907–08. The event is described as follows by Jon R. Moen and Ellis W. Tallman: "The Panic of 1907 was the first worldwide financial crisis of the twentieth century. It transformed a recession into a contraction surpassed in severity only by the Great Depression. The panic's impact is still felt today because it spurred the monetary reform movement that led to the establishment of the Federal Reserve System."[48] American industrial output dropped 17 percent in 1908, but the economy recovered within a year.

According to *The Pottery Gazette* of April 1, 1909:

> Johnson Brothers were in the happy position of having maintained their usual volume of trade right through 1908, despite the influence and after-effects of the financial panic in the United States and the general slump felt all over the world. They attribute this to the fact that throughout their various departments they make it a rule to maintain the high quality of their production […] A cursory look at their latest samples suggests that another characteristic of the firm contributes largely to the steady business they are doing. All the forms and decorations of their wares are right up to date. Indeed, for novelty in shape and ornamentation they are well in front.[49]

The success of British potteries in the American market was also due in part to the widespread acknowledgment that British pottery was of lower cost and superior quality in comparison to equivalent wares made in the United States. A report of the US Department of Commerce published in 1915 blamed the higher cost of US goods on American potteries' relative lower efficiency and higher labor costs, which in England were reduced by having more female workers paid at lower wages.[50] A table of wages paid to British pottery workers in 1911 reflected that the highest salary range for "skilled men" was 18.34 to 39.82 cents per hour (converted to US currency); at the highest rate, working 9.5 hours per day, 57 hours per week, a man could earn $15.14 per week. The range for "skilled women," however, was 12.39 to 20.32 cents per hour, and at the highest rate, working 9 hours per day, 54 hours per week, a woman could only earn $5.68 per week. The number of male and female workers was virtually the same, 23,048 males and 23,441 females;

this would clearly keep costs far lower than for American potteries, where female workers were not as involved in the production process.

Historically, there had also been a large number of children employed in the potteries to do menial tasks, and although in 1911 children between the ages of 10 and 12 could no longer be hired, 11.56 percent of all pottery employees in Stoke-on-Trent were under 16, that is, 7.21 percent of all workers were females under 16 and 4.35 percent of all workers were males under 16. The lowest wage for "unskilled men and boys," for a "straw boy," was 3.16 cents per hour, and the lowest wage for "unskilled women and girls," "handle makers," was 4.38 cents per hour. In a 54-hour week, they would only earn $1.51 and $1.64, respectively, and using an inflation calculator, $1.50 in 1911 would only be worth $36.19 in 2015.

At the same time, the Commerce Department report admitted that "in addition to their greater efficiency in the placing and drawing of kilns, English and German potteries obtain a very much greater percentage of firsts, or best ware, from their kilns than do American potteries, indicating greater care and less destruction in the handling of ware." It was reported that in 1913, over two million dollars' worth of earthenware and china was exported from Stoke-on-Trent to the United States, and although no companies were identified, it was stated that "their names and their ware have been known for generations in every State in the Union." The report continues:

> It is frequently stated in the United States that imported pottery has the advantage of prejudice in its favor from the mere fact that it is imported. In fairness it must be said that the best English ware is judged in the United States by its merits and by the test of experience. The investigation of the English potteries [in preparing the report] developed that 90 percent of the best ware is manufactured for the trade of the United States. The pottery made and sold to the local English trade is not up to the standard of that made for and sold to the United States, nor is it up to the standard of the ware made in the United States for our domestic uses.[51]

It is therefore apparent that there were not just two tiers of production, but three: the highest quality for export to the United States, a more moderate quality also for export to the United States, and a lower quality for sale within Britain itself. In the case of Johnson Brothers, the firm continued this multitiered quality of production into the second decade of the twentieth century. By this time, however, the world was on the verge of the Great War. That cataclysmic event would bring the gilded age to a definitive close, and with it ended the manufacture of Johnson Brothers' finest quality wares, including the use of elaborate mold shapes and the production of flow blue. With reduced manpower and resources, the future would lie in the mass production of lesser-quality pottery, and the company's success would depend upon the skill and creativity of its transfer imagery.

Chapter 2

ALLIES IN WAR AND TRADE

In the second decade of the twentieth century, the Johnson Brothers directors became interested in expanding into the German market. This proved to be the wrong decision at the worst possible time. The story should be told in the words of the anonymous author of "The Story of Johnson Brothers":

> It was therefore decided to build a Sanitaryware plant near Frankfurt, and Victor [son of Frederick] and Reg [Reginald, son of Henry] were particularly involved in this development and the plant opened for production in 1913. Disastrously, the Great War broke out in August 1914, which meant the end of the venture and it was never re-started afterwards. Members of the nucleus Johnson Brothers' Staff managed to get home without too many problems but Victor was caught and interned by the Germans in Ruhleben, a civilian prison camp in Berlin, where he remained throughout the war. During the 1914–18 period, business was obviously extremely limited with so many people in the Forces and severe difficulties of shipping goods abroad due to the intensity of submarine warfare. Along with many local men serving in the 5th Battalion, the North Staffordshire Regiment, the local Territorial battalion, Reg Johnson was killed in action in Flanders in February 1915, a black day for North Staffordshire.[1]

The war had a similarly crippling effect on all of the potteries in Staffordshire. According to the Stoke *Sentinel*, "Records obtained from the War Graves Commission shows a total of 13,000 men who were killed during the Great War. These servicemen either fought in the North Staffordshire or South Staffordshire regiments, or had links to Stoke-on-Trent and Staffordshire."[2]

Because of the war's disruption of production, as well as anti-German sentiment, ceramic imports from Germany and France dropped precipitously between 1910 and 1920. This benefited American companies such as Homer Laughlin, primarily in the area of department store and mail-order sales; between 1918 and 1920, 90 percent of the pottery distributed in the United

States was made in American factories.[3] When the British potteries resumed production, they had to do so with reduced resources, including manpower, and the most obvious way to reduce cost was to simplify the type of decoration. Transfer patterns could be reduced to a single band around a plate's edge, or the application of a floral spray in its center. Hand painting of color and gilding could be reduced to a minimum or eliminated altogether, since any measure that reduced the number of required firings in the bottle kilns would result in a significant saving of energy, time, and ultimately money. The consequence of making such simplified designs, however, was that they risked becoming relatively anonymous and undifferentiated.

British pottery manufacturers also had to address the fact that American public taste had undergone a profound change. Flow blue patterns, asymmetric molds, and delicate hand painting were not only more costly both to manufacture and to purchase, they were also associated with old-fashioned divisions of class. It would therefore be a challenge for Johnson Brothers and other British companies to understand what Americans now wanted to buy, and to find cost-effective ways of meeting that demand.

One response that was adopted across the British pottery industry was to produce patterns based on Asian motifs that had been known as far back as the eighteenth century. The *Willow* pattern, also called *Blue Willow*, was created in Staffordshire around 1790, based on images found on Chinese porcelain. Nearly every pottery manufacturer had some form of "willow" pattern, and a search of Replacements Ltd. identified a partial list as including not only Johnson Brothers but also Wedgwood, Adams, Churchill, Meakin, Booths, Wood, Spode, Ridgway, Royal Doulton, Coalport, Allerton's, and Burgess & Leigh. Additional versions were introduced in the mid-twentieth century by American manufacturers such as Royal, Homer Laughlin, and Shenango as well as many Japanese companies. Another industry-wide pattern was *Indian Tree*, which the Coalport company claimed to have created in 1801. A variation of this was reintroduced by Johnson Brothers in the 1920s, and other companies that produced versions of *Indian Tree* throughout the twentieth century included Myott, Spode, Churchill, Aynsley, Maddock, and Royal Doulton. American companies such as Syracuse followed suit.

It should be noted that the backstamp is not a reliable basis for assigning a precise date to Johnson Brothers pottery patterns that were made before and after the First World War. Similar backstamps were in use from around 1900 through the 1940s, based on the crown that had been in use since at least 1899. The crown had variable shapes, both rounded and angular, with the company name in a slightly rounded serif upper and lower case or sans serif capital letters, with the word "England" below the company name (Figure 2.1). It is not known why there were differences in crown shapes and lettering styles, although this may have been a way to distinguish pottery produced by a particular factory among the several that were operated by the company.

Figure 2.1 Johnson Brothers angular crown backstamp.

Colonial Revival

In some instances, there are patterns that clearly relate to a particular American-style trend. Such trends can be identified in other consumer goods, including textiles and flatware. It is not surprising that the Johnson Brothers firm would have responded quickly to American fashions; Robert Lewis Johnson's relocation to New York lasted only a few years, but his sons (Robert) Lewis Johnson, Jr. (1879–1946) and Ernest James Johnson (1881–1962) both travelled frequently to the United States, and Ernest eventually assumed primary responsibility for that market. Ernest also married an American, Anna Shepard Boote from East Orange, New Jersey, which undoubtedly contributed to the company's already-strong interest in that market.

One notable style trend was "Colonial Revival," which Mary Miley Theobald has called "a social and stylistic mindset that peaked during the 1920s."[4] This was a nostalgic reimagining of America in the eighteenth century, which began with the Philadelphia Centennial Exposition of 1876. This movement is also referred to as Neoclassical Revival or Georgian Revival, the latter term being used more frequently in architecture. According to Theobald:

> Preservation fever swept America in the 1920s. Virginia, with more colonial buildings than most states, was hard hit. Private individuals and preservation societies snapped up derelict plantation homes and restored and furnished them for personal use or to open to the public. In Virginia, Monticello, Stratford Hall, Montpelier, Oak Hill, Brandon, Kenmore, Ampthill, Carter's Grove, and dozens more were saved from ruin. Creating museums from historic buildings became a preferred philanthropy for the wealthy: in Michigan, Henry Ford started Greenfield Village; in Delaware, the DuPonts began transforming Winterthur inside and out. And John D. Rockefeller Jr. launched the largest single preservation project the country had seen: Colonial Williamsburg.[5]

In terms of tableware design, Colonial Revival included references to the late eighteenth-century designs by the British decorator and architect Robert Adam. This style was characterized by classically inspired urns and medallions, joined by restrained, stylized swags. Similar patterns of pottery and silverplate include Johnson Brothers' named pattern of *Davenport* and the silverplate pattern *Grosvenor*, introduced in 1921 by the American silver company Oneida Ltd. in their "Community" line (Plate 3D).[6]

The name *Grosvenor* alludes to Grosvenor Square in London, named for the English peer who owned and developed the property, and known for its Georgian architecture. Robert Adam designed a house there for the Earl of Derby in the 1770s. Additional information about the concept behind the silver design is available to us through the reprint of an Oneida company catalogue dating from the late 1920s, acquired by Tere Hagan, who reproduced several of its pages. The catalogue, intended for retail merchants rather than consumers, describes the pattern as follows: "The Grosvenor Design. Created in the finer mood of those great masters—the Brothers Adam. A fresh, spirited and charming interpretation of the vogue for rich simplicity in tableware. Bright Butler Finish."[7] The advertisement shows a photograph of a young bride wearing an eighteenth-century-inspired gown, with a four-piece place setting (dinner knife, dessert spoon, dinner fork, table spoon) in the advertisement foreground, highlighted against a background of lace. Aside from the oxymoron of "rich simplicity," the pattern's name and design appeal to British tradition, and "finer mood" suggests refined, classic taste.

The phrase "Bright Butler Finish" describes the surface texture of the metal as being reflective, rather than matte, and it also evokes the notion of household servants. This silver, however, was destined for buyers who were very far from having servants. Elsewhere in the same catalogue, the company describes the "Foursome Set," a twenty-piece service, with the copywriter's ellipses and italics:

It is built for people of good taste but small purse ... for people who want the best even if they have to take less of it ... for small families ... it recognizes *and turns to your advantage* the modern trend toward more intimate entertaining ... the bridge quartet, the small dinner.

The patterns for which the "Foursome Set" was available were listed as *Paul Revere* (1927), *Hampton Court* (1926), *Bird of Paradise* (1923), *Grosvenor* (1921), *Adam* (1917), and *Patrician* (1914). Out of six patterns, three relate to Colonial Revival style: *Grosvenor*, *Adam*, and *Paul Revere*. Since the latest of those patterns was issued in 1927, the catalogue must have been published no earlier than that year, and this suggests a general time period for the Adam-inspired patterns by Johnson Brothers.

The Invention of "Pareek"

At some point in the 1920s, Johnson Brothers added the term "Pareek" to some of its backstamps.[8] It is a common surname in India, deriving from a Sanskrit word meaning "examiner," but that has no logical connection to the British pottery industry.[9] What seems more likely is that it was an imagined combination of two words that were indeed familiar to British pottery: "Parian" and "Belleek."

"Parian" is defined as "a variety of unglazed, vitrified porcelain with a smooth, white surface, first made in the 1840s, and used especially for busts and figures."[10] The word is derived from Parian marble, that is, the marble statues of the Greek island of Paros. Parian ware in British pottery was so called in order to lend it the artistic eminence of Greek sculpture, as well as describing its particular surface texture. Belleek is a town in County Fermanach, Northern Ireland, founded in 1858, which began producing Parian ware in 1863. The connection between Parian and Belleek is reinforced by the Belleek Pottery's official history, which includes the following:

> By as early as 1865 the company had established a growing market throughout Ireland and England and was exporting pieces to the United States, Canada, and Australia. Prestigious orders were being received from Queen Victoria, the Prince of Wales, and the nobility. Porcelain was featured by Belleek for the first time at the Dublin Exposition of 1872. Their display was the largest in the Irish and English industrial areas. Among the pieces listed in the catalogue for the event are Parian china statues and busts, ice buckets, compotes and centerpieces.[11]

By combining the terms of "Parian" and "Belleek" into a new word, "Pareek," the Johnson Brothers company was appropriating the semantic fields of two words that were associated with British social status (used by royalty and the nobility) and aesthetic refinement (statues and centerpieces). The fact that Americans were significant purchasers of Belleek ware, and avid admirers of Victoriana in general, makes it plausible that Johnson Brothers sought to elevate the perceived desirability of its own products simply by adding the name "Pareek" to the backstamp.

An irony should be noted here, in that "Pareek" ware was not in fact white in color, but an off-white or ivory. The company did not seek to imitate the qualities that were associated with the name's inspiration, either in color or in the nature of the pieces made, because it was producing tableware, not decorative pieces for the parlor mantel. It was simply the name itself that defined the ware as being of superior quality to that which had been manufactured previously.

There were many patterns produced with the "Pareek" stamp, including numerous British-inspired names such as *Guernsey*, *Marlborough*, *Charlton*, and *Victoria*. There were also, however, "Pareek" patterns that ranged from the generically fanciful (*Springtime*, *The Rococo*) to the exotic (*Bermuda*, *Indian Tree*). In some examples, the quality of production is unremarkable, but in others the quality of production is quite high. This is notably true of one related group of six "Pareek" patterns, featuring a round shape with an orange band around the edge. The decoration on the rim and in the center of the plate is quite elaborate, and all share American-inspired names: *Mayflower, Columbus, Lincoln, Jefferson, Madison*, and *Garfield*.[12] The last four are names of American presidents, and it is rather unusual to see what appears to be a reference to James Garfield, who was assassinated in office on September 19, 1881, after serving only six months. As illustrated by Page and Frederiksen, *Jefferson* and *Lincoln* have an identical design but a variation in color, and this is also true of *Mayflower* and *Garfield*. The designs of *Columbus* and *Madison* are unlike the other two designs, although they may also have counterparts of different color that are simply unknown at present. An example of *Madison* (Plate 4A) features a relatively ornate pattern, with an unusual decoration of thick drops of red-and-yellow paint highlighting small round fruits. These three-dimensional highlights, found even in the center of the plate, would have been somewhat impractical for food service, since they were susceptible to damage from eating utensils.

The introduction of these designs, and their manner of decoration, may have been influenced by an American rival company, Lenox. That company was founded in 1889 in Trenton, New Jersey, a region described by the company as the "Staffordshire of America," with around 200 potteries in the nineteenth century.[13] Among the most celebrated of Lenox's designs was *Autumn*, introduced in 1918, which featured a deep, elaborate border with thick, hand-painted fruit accents. The Lenox factory later moved to Kinston, North Carolina, and a 2013 article in the *Raleigh News and Observer* described the *Autumn* pattern as requiring hand-painted dots of enamel in six different colors, originally applied with sharpened wooden dowels.[14] Designers at the Johnson Brothers company would certainly have been aware of their competition in America, and the elaborate patterns described above are very reminiscent of *Autumn*, although the patterns were simplified by using fewer colors of enamel dots. In characteristic fashion, however, this competition with Lenox was only a small part of the vast range of styles being produced, to accommodate every possible American taste.

One of the most interesting examples of "Pareek" is a design named *Petroushka* (Plate 4B). This is a very fanciful pattern of highly stylized flowers with a hand-drawn, hand-painted appearance (although the colors were not hand-applied), using bold primary colors. The backstamp has the name "Petroushka" written in sans serif capital letters set off by quotation marks. The pattern name appears to refer to the 1911 ballet composed by Igor Stravinsky, in collaboration with Sergei Diaghilev and others, which debuted in Paris under the title of "Petrouchka." (As a linguistic note, the French spelling combination of "ch" is pronounced as a soft "sh," whereas in English it is more fricative, as in "chair." In order to reproduce the correct pronunciation, the spelling in English was changed to "Petroushka." The title is now most commonly written as "Petrushka," since the English language does not have the French distinction between the vowel sounds of "u" and "ou.")

According to dance historian Natalie Shearer, the original production of the ballet featured very bright colors for the sets and costumes: "Red, green and blue are the prominent colors, and rabbits, palm trees and exotic flowers decorate the walls, along with a red floor [...] All the costumes are said to have been coordinated with the sets."[15] The pattern is highly creative, with a sense of dynamic energy that is both simplified and bold, as if echoing the unconventional physical and visual aspects of the ballet. The Russian theme is evident in the tiny buildings that form a background for the central floral motif, featuring little silo-shaped buildings with "onion" domed roofs, a cartoonish reference to St. Basil's Cathedral in Moscow. This design is impressively modernist, but was unlikely to have been a commercial success.

Art Deco Influence

While the date of the ballet "Petrouchka" was 1911, the series name "Pareek" places this plate in the 1920s. Furthermore, its bold colors and highly stylized forms suggest that it may have been created after the Paris International Exposition of Modern Decorative and Industrial Arts in 1925, the world's fair that launched the term "Art Deco." In honor of that fair, Johnson Brothers created a limited-edition pattern called *Les Fontaines* (The Fountains). This pattern is stamped "Pareek," and the backstamp contained the name "Les Fontaines" in quotation marks, with the words "Paris Exposition 1925" stamped underneath.[16] The plates have a plain round shape, and the central motif of a stylized "fountain" is formed by elongated half ovals, drawn in brown and green, against a background of black stippling and black-and-yellow stylized flowers. Variations of the central motif are repeated around the plate's edge, and the pattern is made to appear hand-drawn, with irregular lines, even though it is a transfer print. This "naïf" quality is shared by the pattern *Petroushka* described above, a trait that may further link the earlier design to the time period of around 1925.

This pattern is a simplified version of a textile wallcovering named *Les Jets d'eau* (Fountains), designed by Édouard Bénédictus for a reception room in the Pavilion of the French Embassy at the 1925 exposition. A panel of this wallcovering in the collection of the Saint Louis Art Museum (accession number 464:2018) shows several "fountains" of the same design, although the sprays of water are broken into smaller, mosaic-like geometric forms.

Bénédictus' wallcovering also inspired a competing design from the American company Lenox. The company history names *Fountain*, dating from 1926, as one of the most important designs by Frank Graham Holmes, who served as the company's chief designer from 1905 to 1954.[17] The Lenox *Fountain* pattern features a stylized spray of water similar to the fountain depicted in the original textile and in the Johnson Brothers pattern, although there are differences such as the addition of a pair of birds resembling Asiatic pheasants.

One Johnson Brothers pattern that was likely inspired by art deco style has octagonal plates, with a gilded edge that contrasts dramatically with a simple band of black lines and tiny squares (Plate 4C).[18] The backstamp features only a crown and "JOHNSON BROS ENGLAND" in sans serif capital letters. The Page and Frederiksen catalogue lists eighteen octagonal patterns made prior to the 1970s, when it was reintroduced, as will be discussed in Chapter 6. The catalogue also lists seventeen patterns in a dodecahedron shape that probably dates from the same period.[19]

Regina Lee Blaszczyk explained why art deco was not widely accepted by the American buying public:

> Price and prettiness shaped the product expectations of working-class women, for whom making do on small budgets mattered more than making appearances. Each social class possessed a distinctive material vocabulary for self-expression, but women in the upper echelons coveted the lifestyles of the rich and famous to a greater extent than did those who struggled simply to pay their bills. [...]
>
> Middle-class women had responded to extreme art-moderne styling with trepidation. Some felt that ultramodern accessories, like the spotted or zigzagged pottery designed for British manufacturers by Susie Cooper and Clarice Cliff, were ill suited to conventional decorating schemes, while others objected to cups and teapots with "decided angles and sharply contrasting surfaces," finding these objects "difficult to handle comfortably."[20]

This "trepidation" among American consumers undoubtedly explains why the majority of Johnson Brothers patterns in the late 1920s and 1930s continued to emphasize traditional floral motifs. The company's target audience was women who could not afford to replace sets of china easily, if the angular edges were subject to breakage.

Introducing Bill Norbury

The year 1927 would prove to be an important one for Johnson Brothers, because that was when Gordon Forsyth, the head of the Stoke School of Art, recruited a promising young student to train as an apprentice engraver for the Johnson Brothers company. This was William (Bill) Norbury, who was fifteen years old at the time. Norbury would remain at the company for fifty years, during which period he became the head engraver (Figure 2.2), overseeing design production not only for that company, but for several other companies acquired through the Wedgwood mergers in 1968 (see Chapter 6).

The work of an engraver was, in principle, to take a drawing produced by an artist and reproduce it on a copper plate, which would then be used to imprint the tissues used in the transfer printing process. It was skilled work in terms of learning how to manipulate delicate tools, but was generally viewed as "copying," and the work was not held in high regard. Gordon Forsyth was employed by Ernest Johnson, the company head at the time, to find young workers who could be trained to produce engravings at modest wages. Forsyth appears to have recognized, however, that the engraver's hand and eye made an enormous difference in whether or not the image would retain the visual appeal of the original, or would appear flat and awkward. He therefore looked for the most talented young artists, offering them the potential for steady work, even though it meant having virtually no artistic independence.

Figure 2.2 William Norbury, 1950s. Image courtesy of William Norbury.

Norbury's experience as an engraver has been documented by a personal unpublished memoir, *Designs on a Career as a Decorator*. It offers his recollections of a remarkable fifty-year career, with many comments about the design process and about his sense of identity as a creative artist.

Here is Norbury's description of his beginnings at the company:

> 15th February 1927—Invited by Sir Ernest Johnson's secretary to call on Johnson Brothers to see if I would like to learn to engrave, recommended by Mr. Gordon Forsyth, Head of all Art Schools in Stoke-on-Trent. So I started a six-year apprenticeship, and the very hard job of training hands and eyes, into fine control and the use of tools, etc. [...] My apprenticeship was a surprise to me. I had to be at work half an hour before the others to sweep the floor, clear out any rubbish and wash the tea cups. The foreman and Ted Evans, the engravers, Arthur Pedley, about five foot six, with a beery complexion who limped, 1917 war wounded Harry Lewis, who lived in a canal cottage at Endon, both were stolid workers. Mechanically doing engraving at work. Joe Jones, the apprentice before me, now looking for a better firm to work for, he went after two years. I think I learned the possibilities more by my own eagerness. I was top of my class at the art school, that gave me a lead about my potential and gave me pride in myself (9).

The Dawn *Series*

In 1929, the Johnson Brothers company launched a major new initiative: the pattern called *Greydawn* (Plate 4D).[21] Its distinguishing feature was that color was not applied only on the surface, but rather the color permeated the body of the piece, so that when chips occurred, they would be less noticeable. It was designed as hotel ware, and was described as such in advertisements of the period. The pieces were relatively plain in shape, with a simplified scalloped edge, and there was no decoration other than the color. A few pieces, such as teapots and sauceboats, had a molded grooved body that echoed the scallop theme.[22]

The color of *Greydawn* was not a true gray, but rather a muted pastel blue. According to David E. D. Johnson, the pattern was produced by several factories, and each one created a slightly different hue. The use of pastel colors, particularly in fashion, was linked by Blaszczyk to a shortage of dyes created by the First World War: "The feared dyestuffs famine became a reality after March 1915, when the British Royal Navy blocked German ships from the North Atlantic. American dyers increased their production of pastels."[23] Blaszczyk provides an illustration of fabric samples from the Bellas Hess & Co. catalogue of 1916, showing a swatch of "Blue" chiffon that appears very close to the shade of *Greydawn*.

Pastel shades were therefore popular in America, not only because of practicality (since strong dyes were hard to obtain) but also because of patriotism (to avoid reliance on foreign imports of dyes). This may help to explain why even though *Greydawn* was not produced until more than a decade later, its chosen hue was pastel. *Greydawn*'s simplicity of design and lack of ornamentation also kept the production costs low. There was, however, a marketing effort to promote the pattern as being not merely inexpensive, but also attractive and fashionable. The following is an advertisement for "Greydawn, for hotels, restaurants, clubs, cafés, canteens, institutions, etc.":

> Since the introduction of "Greydawn" in 1929 the demand for this beautiful ware has grown to a phenomenal extent, especially for HOTELS, CAFÉS, etc., where smart and distinctive appearance is valued. [...] It gives a valuable note of distinction to the Room and the Tables. The tint is in the Body, with transparent glaze which emphasises the beautiful texture and uniform color-tone. It is exceedingly durable, the composition being the finest Semi-Porcelain, while the glaze is prepared from a special formula to obviate crazing. Its artistic Pastel coloring enhances the effect of any Decorative scheme, either by harmony or contrast. For example—"Greydawn" ware on a Pink or Rose table-cloth is a vision of delight. The price is exceptionally low for ware of this class and character.[24]

The American spelling of "color" and "coloring" reveals this advertisement to have been intended for the company's marketing efforts in the United States.

In response to the success of *Greydawn*, Johnson Brothers soon introduced variations based on additional pastel colors: *Rosedawn* (peach pink), *Greendawn* (pale green), and *Goldendawn* (pale yellow). An advertisement for *Rosedawn*, probably from the early 1930s, waxes even more eloquent:

> The "roseate hue of early dawn" has fired the imagination of illustrious poets and painters throughout the ages, and now it has provided happy inspiration to the artist in Pottery. Made by Johnson Bros. (manufacturers of the famous "Greydawn") ROSEDAWN ware is a veritable symphony in form and colour. All the pieces are exquisitely modelled "en suite." The rich, transparent glaze which reveals the delicate pastel-rose tint of the body is smooth as velvet—a sheer delight to the touch. Experts in psychology affirm that colour exercises a very important influence upon appetite. Certain it is that a table laid with this [word unreadable] Rosedawn suggests a "feast set for Lucullus," and creates that atmosphere of good-cheer and happiness which is so eminently desirable within the family circle and so truly essential to the success of a party.[25]

The British spelling of "colour" makes the nationality of the intended consumer more ambiguous, but it is evident that the author of the advertisement is appealing to all of the buyer's senses ("poets and painters," "symphony," "velvet," "delight to the touch") as well as to his or her intelligence (references to psychology and classical literature) and positive emotions ("good-cheer and happiness"). The product itself is almost humble in comparison to this florid prose.

The marketing focus has also changed, in that this advertisement does not use the term "hotel ware," and it specifically refers to the "family circle" and a "party," suggesting that the pottery will be used in a private home rather than a public setting such as a restaurant. The intended buyer is therefore an individual consumer, rather than a hotel or restaurant purchasing in mass quantity.

The success of the *Dawn* series in combining a sense of modernity with traditional aesthetic values undoubtedly contributed to its impressive longevity, remaining in production for almost sixty years.[26] This design had no transfer decoration at all, and relied solely upon color and shape, which were simple but not plain, and could be adaptable to different types of table setting. Its appeal to the American buyer included the flexibility to combine the pattern with cutlery and linens of the buyer's choice, recognizing and promoting the individuality of each potential consumer rather than imposing a "standard" of good taste. The design's modernity also appealed to the American buyer's desire to be forward-thinking and contemporary, but without being too avant-garde or extreme.

"Series" Names and the Appeal of British Tradition

The popularity of Colonial Revival style indicated that many Americans were nostalgic for an earlier time of perceived prosperity and stability, when positive values prevailed and life seemed to follow a predictable course. The "old-fashioned" character of traditional decorative patterns may have been part of their appeal, constituting the heirlooms of a new generation rather than a reflection of fashion trends.

This was the likely inspiration for several names dated by Finegan as being "Pre-1930," which appear as "series" names in addition to individual pattern names. The "Victorian" series features pattern names such as *Old English Trellis*, which evokes a British-style garden with a trellis and flowering vines. Other "British" series names introduced in the 1920s or early 1930s were "Old English," "Old Chelsea," "English Oak," and "Old Staffordshire."[27] "Old English" includes the patterns *Belvedere, Chintz* (also produced as "Victorian"), and *Old English Clover*.[28] "English Oak" features a border that is not a transferware print, but rather a raised appliqué of oak leaves scrolling clockwise around the rim of a cream-colored plate. The leaves are the distinctive color known as "Wedgwood blue," and the design appears to emulate that company's similar pattern of raised blue grapes and grape leaves on a cream body.[29] "Old Staffordshire" includes names that are not British, such as *Dubarry, Rouen*, and *Ningpo*, but the series name refers to the home of the British pottery industry, and the foreign or exotic pattern names are an echo of French- and Asian-inspired patterns created before the turn of the century.[30]

These series and pattern names reinforce the British origin of the pottery, but beyond that, they emphasize the quality of being "old," that is, traditional and perhaps even of historical significance. The Victorian age was the era of the parents and grandparents of contemporary buyers, and by evoking that time period through the material culture of its textiles, tableware, and gardens, the company was offering its customers the opportunity to purchase "heirlooms."

Old Britain Castles

The successful strategy of appealing to the American market through traditional motifs and British pattern names led to a landmark design that came to be virtually synonymous with Johnson Brothers: *Old Britain Castles* (Plate 5A). This pattern was introduced in 1930, but was in development as early as 1928. The name itself combined several useful elements: a reference to Britain (the company's home), an evocation of historical tradition ("Old Britain"), and the romantic notion of castles (medieval history and legend combined). It should be noted that the pattern name is not *Old British Castles*, with two adjectives modifying the noun "castles," but *Old Britain Castles*, meaning the castles of Old Britain. The change from an adjective to a noun is significant, and may be seen as projecting the entire pattern into a distant, nostalgic past.

Even more important, this pattern featured landscape scenes, a different one on each piece of different shape, so that the entire set was a sort of pictorial tour of Britain. This was a parallel to the nineteenth-century Staffordshire production of "American" scenes, which had been extremely popular. Although several companies had continued to produce American historical scenes, as will be discussed in the next chapter, Johnson Brothers may have been the first one in the 1930s to invite American buyers to decorate their homes with scenes of Britain. Whether or not the company was the first one to introduce the idea, there is no doubt that *Old Britain Castles* became the most long-lived and successful pattern in the company's history.

The obvious reason why this design became so popular was that the artistic quality of the images was extremely high. In fact, these images were closely based upon actual historical engravings, transforming the tableware into a set of three-dimensional art objects. According to a letter written by a Johnson Brothers representative in 1981:

> The drawings for the patterns were done in 1928 by a Miss Fennel, the daughter of a Master Engraver, using book photographs of old steel engravings. It was her father's company who were commissioned to produce the engravings for us and involved a team of about 10 engravers working on the pattern for between 12 and 18 months. The engravings were started in 1929 and were completed during 1930, and although we are not absolutely sure, there were probably about 40 separate engravings involved in the initial item range.[31]

It is something of a mystery as to why this company anecdote describes an intermediate drawing having been produced by the engraver's daughter, since that intermediate step would not have been helpful or logical. The artist engraving the plate for the tissue transfers would have needed to see the original published artwork, in order to reproduce its fine detail. It is possible, however, that her role was to produce drawings that determined how elements of the original prints could be edited and reconfigured to fit on the piece of tableware for which it was intended. This was usually a necessary part of the process, especially for pieces of awkward size such as teacups. The engraver would then use those modified illustrations, in conjunction with the original print, to create the transfer image.

The "Master Engraver" of the series was Henry "Harry" Fennell, who did business in Mollart Street in Hanley; the first name of his daughter is to date unknown. Norbury recalled seeing Mr. Fennell for the first time, describing him as a character straight out of Dickens:

> As an apprentice, also a jack of all trades, as are all apprentices, I had to take a copper plate, to a Mr H. Fennil, just off Lichfield Street in Hanley. "Mollart Street" was where his shop was. What an amazing person he was. He could have been the very personification or in fact a reincarnation of Leonardo Da Vinci himself, at least it seemed so to my junior mind. The Engraving I was taking to him was "Old Britain Castles." [...] I saw him sometime later, walking down the street. He looked about 5 feet 6 inches tall, wearing on his head a very rakish Sombrero with a feather, very colourful character, he walked as if on velvet, a 3/4 length pinched-in waist, flared coat of rich light brown materials and a highly waxed walking stick. To me this seemed to be what I must aim for. How on earth did he achieve such shining shoes? He Looked a Splendid Creature. (p. 47)

It was not the practice for the engraver's name to appear on any tableware design, but an exception was made for Fennell, whose name was included below several scenes of *Old Britain Castles*. In producing these images, Fennell was a subcontractor for Johnson Brothers, and he would have wanted to promote his own business in any way possible. It is likely that he negotiated the right to put his name on these images, whereas no Johnson Brothers engravers were permitted to do the same. For example, "H. FENNELL" appears on a square covered vegetable dish, below the titles of images for "Oxford" (lid), "St. Woolstons Kildare" (outside bowl), and "Conway Castle" (inside bowl); on a teapot, "Farnham Castle"; on a sauceboat, "Rochester Castle & Bridge" on one side and "Runneymede [sic] or Magna Charta [sic] Island" on the other side; on a two-handled soup bowl, "Harlech Castle" (inside bowl) and its matching saucer, "Kenilworth Castle"; on a small plate, "Haddon Hall"; and on a small oval relish dish, "Warwick Castle." This unusual "artist's signature" is further evidence that the intent of the series was to present a series of artworks, decorative as well as functional.

All items of the *Old Britain Castles* series have a name on the lower right of the center image, giving the name of the castle followed by the words "in 1792." The source of at least some of the images for *Old Britain Castles* was a book published by the engraver John Walker in 1799, entitled *The Itinerant: A Select Collection of Interesting and Picturesque Views in Great Britain and Ireland, Engraved from Original Paintings & Drawings by Eminent Artists*.[32] One image used on a large oval platter, "Canterbury 1794," is a close reproduction of the "Canterbury" plate from *The Itinerant* (p. 43), with the castle on the left, the cathedral on the right, and a grouping of cows in the center foreground (Plate 5A). Another image used on a smaller oval platter, "Cambridge in 1792," is also from *The Itinerant* (p. 9), and it contains an unusual visual element, that is, horses that appear to be walking down the middle of the river (Plate 5B). Finegan identified a source that explained why: the riverbank was too soft for horses to walk along, pulling a barge, so a gravel causeway was built up in the middle of the river.[33] The faithful representation of horses seemingly walking on water is a surprise element that the engravers probably enjoyed.

Other sources were clearly more recent. The large platter features an image of Stafford Castle, a nearly exact reproduction of a drawing by Frederick Calvert, engraved by T. Radclyffe and published in 1830.[34] The image of Haddon Hall, which was used for a 6¼-inch bread plate (Plate 5C), was copied very faithfully by Harry Fennell from a print of "Haddon Hall Derbyshire," drawn by Thomas Hosmer Shepherd and engraved by Henry Winsor Bond, and published in Thomas Dugdale's *England and Wales Delineated* between 1838 and 1860.[35]

A document from Johnson Brothers company archives, providing historical background on many of the subjects used in the *Old Britain Castles* series, describes Haddon Hall in Derbyshire as follows:

> This famous manor house is a 20th-century restoration. The same basic materials were used as when the Hall was originally built. Devoid of brickwork or ornamental frills, the oldest parts of Haddon Hall date from the 13th century. [...] By the 18th and 19th centuries the Rutland family were using Belvoir Castle as their main country residence and Haddon Hall was abandoned. Detailed restoration, begun in the early 20th century, was not completed until the 1930's. The house is a fine example of change from an original fortified dwelling, although its battlements were never used by archers.[36]

The significance of this is that Haddon Hall was much better known in the 1930s than it would have been in 1792, when it was a minor residence no longer in use by its owners. Similarly, the scene selected for the all-important dinner plate was Blarney Castle in Ireland (Plate 5D), not one of the most impressive architectural or historical sites, but one that was familiar to many Americans, based on the fame of "kissing the Blarney Stone." Many Americans were also of Irish heritage, and could be expected to admire a plate reflecting the pride of their own "old country." "Blarney Castle" was also the motif found on a large square coffee pot with a capacity of 2.5 pints; Americans were known to enjoy drinking large cups of coffee. *Old Britain Castles* therefore reveals a marketing strategy aimed at the prospective American buyer of the modern era, highlighting a mixture of the recognizable and the unfamiliar, but all presented with a similar romantic appeal.

The decision to associate an earlier date with all of these images, regardless of when they were actually created, was probably made in order to lend them even greater historical importance. An actual date of the mid-nineteenth century would have been less than 100 years before the date of the series' production in 1930, and would not have been considered "old" by British standards, although most Americans would not be such high sticklers. In order to give these images the prestige of being truly antique, the British company directors who controlled all aspects of ceramic production must have believed that the images needed to transport the viewer further back in time.

The series featured a distinctive design for the rim of each plate, a highly decorative pattern of scrolls and flowers that seems Victorian in taste. The shape of the plate has four indentations and a molded rim with twelve indentations.[37] The backstamp was the familiar crown motif, above the words "Johnson Bros made in England." The "made in" is a new addition, in tiny capital letters above "England." The pattern name follows, written in a script identical to that which was used for many pattern names in the "Victorian" and "Old English" series.

Old Britain Castles was produced in blue, pink, green, purple (mulberry), and brown with splashes of green, red, blue, and yellow added by hand. The color blue was the most recognizably "traditional," resembling the Old Staffordshire discussed in Chapter 1, but other colors were also part of the pottery tradition dating back to the nineteenth century. The application of color to a brown printed image on tableware, however, was a twentieth-century innovation. Hand-colored engravings were highly admired in the eighteenth and nineteenth centuries, and the images of *Old Britain Castles* in what became known as "brown multicolor" are very evocative of that art form, although the quality of the color application was minimal, consisting of a few splashes that did not always stay within the lines of the engraving.

The *Old Britain Castles* series was a landmark in the history of tableware, produced from 1930 to 2014, a period of eighty-four years. It combined "fine arts" design with practical function, transforming the china cabinet into a display of engravings. It also invited its American buyers to become armchair tourists, making a scenic tour of a romanticized Old Britain, far removed from the daily realities of the Depression. And perhaps most important, this pattern did not condescend to its buyer, assuming that she would purchase any cheaply made pattern because of its price; on the contrary, the pattern treated its buyer as a person of education and sophisticated taste. It was still pottery, not fine bone porcelain china, but the quality standards of the illustration were far above what had been the previous norm.

Other British firms subsequently copied the concept, but none matched the quality or success of Johnson Brothers' original design. One of the rival patterns was *Historic Castles* made by Ridgway, which also had an image of "Conway Castle." It is very imitative of the images featured in *Old Britain Castles*, with a similar style of representing clouds, a border pattern featuring both flowers and heavily drawn rococo-style outlines, and a near-exact copy of the writing in script at the lower right. The subject of "Conway Castle" is also the same as one that was used in *Old Britain Castles*, as described above, but the view itself is different. Interestingly, the backstamp of this piece states "RIDGWAY Est. 1792," giving the same date as the engravings in *Old Britain Castles*, but referring to the founding date of the company. Sources differ as to this actual date; according to the website *thepotteries. org*, exhaustively researched by Steve Birks, the partnership of brothers George and Job Ridgway was apparently formed in 1782, taking over the production of pottery at the Bell Works in Broad Street, Hanley.[38] The Ridgway family, however, had a large number of branches involved in the pottery trade, at different locations, and it is possible that 1792 was a legitimate date associated with the founding of one of them.

Bill Norbury, from Apprentice to Manager

When Bill Norbury's apprenticeship ended in 1933, his life was changed in a significant way, as he relates:

> Soon after I completed the apprenticeship Sir Ernest sent for me, one of the managers had told him I was the best person to run the engraving shop, the others were not very interested anyway. So I became a manager, responsible for all new patterns and the existing ones and the quality of work. The older members had the difficult job, accepting how the situation had changed, but I carried it out, with some trepidation at first. Peter Johnson (nephew) saw I was keen and helped me to advance the quality of the patterns. (p. 9)

In order to understand why Norbury was promoted over more experienced engravers, at the relatively young age of twenty-one, it is important to understand the challenges of how transfers were applied to "biscuit," the unfired pottery. Norbury provides an explanation of the complicated process involved:

> Wrapping a sticky colour print around a piece of biscuit or on glazed ware, seems easy, looking at the description in words. On a glazed surface, accidentally touching the very colour on to the ware, can be easily cleaned off, but the same problem on Biscuit Ware may spoil the item, which would then be destroyed as useless. The Engraver executing the job must set out the Engraved pattern in such a way, that the girl who carried the responsibility of transferring it to the item can do so with a minimum of problems, or she will lose out on the payment or credit for the work. Some pieces of ware are awkward to decorate, and vary in shape according to the effect of heat upon the clay during the firing process. The pouring lip of a gravy boat can drop by almost a ¼ of an inch, altering the shape of the edge of the ware. And creases in the print leave a double impression of colour, which if very noticeable could spoil the item.
>
> [...] The overall sizes of items varies by a considerable amount, so the Engraver has to learn about pottery variations, the easy natural wrist and hand action, otherwise the transferrers' work will be impossible to fit a bulbous shape with an all-over pattern. It may only be made possible by the subterfuge of sectionising it into two or more pieces, to avoid creases in the print; it might

also require innovative changes in the design of either the design or in the ware, which again requires the Engraver to be in some measure a designer. (p. 40)

Given the difficulty of what is described, it is not surprising that with the introduction of a complex pictorial pattern such as *Old Britain Castles*, the responsibilities of the engraver became much more artistically demanding. Few engravers at the time would be up to that task, and Norbury's combination of engraving skill and artistic talent put him in a unique position to play a leadership role.

It was a proven market strategy to maintain sales of popular patterns by introducing new pieces, which would show new images and would add to the owner's existing "collection." This was certainly true in the case of *Old Britain Castles*, a fact that accounts for why there are relatively fewer images signed "H. Fennell," compared to the number of scenes that are unsigned, and were engraved by others. Norbury himself was responsible for several of those later pieces.

> I was now Engraving not practice, and Britain Castles gave me hope, Stafford Castle, Blarney Castle, were a new interest. I have a Ginger Jar which I am proud of, with its Castle printed in blue, on a difficult shape but minus the lid, I suppose by someone who shall be nameless, but the base is so good, applied as it was in four pieces, not apparent until looked at very carefully with a practised eye. 1949—Stafford Castle I put on a 12 inch dish, it looked so beautiful and proud. (p. 49)

The "ginger jar" was an Asian shape popularized in Britain in the eighteenth century, and while it was not a familiar item in America and would have been useless in a dinner service, it made an attractive decorative piece and was often sold with a carved "Asian" wooden stand. Norbury's image on the body of the jar features Ragland Castle, and the lid, which according to his account was done by someone else, features Kolich Castle.

Not only was Norbury asked to contribute illustrations to the company's most successful patterns, he was also able to design a few himself. This departed from the tradition that engravers were not allowed to create their own images, but were expected to copy from drawings provided by others who were hired as "designers." In Norbury's case, serving as a shop manager gave him a degree of control that enabled him to propose his own design, subject to the approval of his supervisor, Peter Johnson.

Norbury was actively involved in the design of a group of three patterns that are closely related to one another, and for which US patents were issued at about the same time: *English Chippendale*, *English Bouquet*, and *English Countryside*. The first pattern for which Norbury claimed significant credit was *English Chippendale*, which received the US design patent number 103232, issued in 1937.[39] This pattern features large flowers covering the entire surface of the plate, and it was much more stylized than the usual floral pattern (Plate 6A). The flowers and leaves are given depth of shading with dense stippling, and the pattern is all one color, with no hand painting required. The name alludes to the famous British furniture maker Thomas Chippendale, whose designs were extremely popular in America as well as Britain in the mid-eighteenth century. The pattern is also somewhat reminiscent of Asian decoration on the ceramics of that period, and may therefore have been inspired by the Colonial Revival movement.

Norbury dedicates a lengthy passage of his memoir to his thought process in developing this pattern, in regard to both design and production:

> "Chippendale"—This sketch came to me as a very amateurish copy in pencil. It appeared to be taken from a piece of embroidery or a simple type of tapestry. It also left me with a problem, how could I use this bold-looking idea on the small items of pottery? I proceeded with this conception in mind, I decided that it had to be an all-over type of pattern. I mean by this an edge to edge coverage; this would enable me to set up the pattern to be printed as a continuous strip, similar to the wallpaper industry. Large enough to cover the large items of ware when the excess print could be scraped off, using the edge of the biscuit ware, rather in the way of a steel edge of a blade. […] The excess tissue paper could fall harmlessly to the floor, better still if an empty container could be placed in an appropriate position. Now I would have enough print in one piece, coming off the printing machine, in a continuous strip like the wallpaper mentioned before. Nothing like it had ever been seen before. I carried on styling it, as I said before, rather bold in style, still with an antique look about it. The small items I would have to design a little differently. Then I had to fit in time and motion, and simplify the methods of transferring! Top Priority this one, but Quality remained as usual. It came out pretty successfully, a New Style, it would sit happily upon anyone's table. The name "Chippendale" came naturally. This was another totally on its own, just as Chippendale had been in furniture. I chose right in style, not easy for anyone to fault or copy. The whole service stood up proudly when I presented it formally to the Factory! Upon reflection at least 90% due to my skills, it sold for many years. No-one ever tried to imitate the style. (p. 62)

A related pattern is *English Bouquet*, which was issued design patent 108079 in 1938. Whereas *English Chippendale* was all one color, with no hand painting, *English Bouquet* is a red transfer print that features large flowers hand-painted in blue, red, and yellow, with some of the leaves painted green. A few of the leaves and small flowers are shaded by stippling, similar to the technique used throughout *English Chippendale*. In this case, however, the entire design is contained within the shape of the piece, unlike the manner in which the *English Chippendale* pattern was cut off at the edge of each dish. *English Bouquet* also features a molded "gadroon" edge, resembling a rope braid, that would be used by many Johnson Brothers patterns from the late 1930s through the 1950s.

According to Norbury, he developed *English Countryside* from 1936 to 1938, and its 1938 patent number was 108080, only one digit higher than the patent of *English Bouquet*, which suggests that both patent designs were submitted at the same time. This pattern was claimed by Norbury to have been entirely his own creation, in both design and engraving (p. 9). It features several large flowers, hand-painted to emphasize the shading of the petals, and these flowers in outline and color are almost identical to the ones featured in *English Bouquet*. The difference, however, was that these flowers were overlaid upon a background filled with a combination of tiny flowers and stylized swirls, with the spaces in between filled by fine stippling. This design was quite complex, creating a "mille fleurs" tapestry effect that was indeed innovative in comparison with other designs typical of the time.

It is interesting to note that all three of these patterns shared the term "English" as part of the pattern name. There was nothing specifically English about the visual images, and in Norbury's memoir, he in fact recalled the first pattern as "Chippendale," not "English Chippendale." As a marketing strategy, however, the company clearly wanted to emphasize the pottery's "English-ness" to the American buyers. This may have been partly as a result of competition with American companies, which had not yet risen to the same level of prestige as the English firms, but were continuing to emerge as serious competitors. If patterns were not recognizable as being "English" in origin, Americans might very well choose to purchase something just as pretty, but made closer to home. It was therefore important to emphasize English identity in every way possible.

The year 1938 was also the year of Norbury's marriage, on March 29. He and his wife, Phyllis, would be married for fifty years, with the day of her death falling on their golden anniversary, and the couple would have two children, Brian and Kathleen.

One strategy of marketing "English" appeal to Americans took a more personal approach, judging by two patterns dating from 1939 that share a clear association with popular members of the British royal family. The first is *Margaret Rose*, which features large roses in a complex, attractive border with a gadroon edge (Plate 6B), but the name is not merely a complement to the image. It would have been instantly recognizable in America, as well as in Britain, as the name of the younger daughter of King George VI and Queen Elizabeth, Princess Margaret Rose. Born in 1930, she would have been about nine years old when the pattern was issued, and her older sister Elizabeth about thirteen.

Another pattern associated with the year 1939 is *Queens Bouquet*, a traditional floral pattern on a white base with a gadroon edge.[40] The backstamp features the series name of "Old English" above an angular crown, but there is an additional inscription in bright red script writing: *"Queens Bouquet": A replica of a bouquet presented to H.M. Queen Elizabeth during the Royal Visit to Canada 1939. Reg*[d] *1940."* The double quotation marks around "Queens Bouquet" are an intentional nod to North Americans, particularly in the United States, who used that form of punctuation in preference to the single quotes that are the norm in Britain. King George VI and Queen Elizabeth made a royal tour of Canada and the United States from May 17 to June 15, 1939. Their visit to the United States included stops at Mount Vernon, the 1939 New York World's Fair, and a dinner at President Roosevelt's residence Hyde Park, during which the British royals were famously served hot dogs. There was a more somber motivation for the trip, however, as it was generally understood to have been intended to strengthen the alliance between Britain and its two American allies, in anticipation of possible war against Nazi Germany. This worry would prove to be well-founded, since Germany invaded Poland on September 1, 1939, and Britain declared war against Germany on September 3. Once again, a world war would have a profound effect upon the pottery industry, and Americans would be regarded as the key to survival.

After Britain declared war in September 1939, Bill Norbury enlisted in the Home Guard, although he continued to work at the company until his deployment to Egypt, leaving his wife Phyllis and infant son Brian living with her parents. Thanks to his skills as an engraver, he was assigned duties as a cartographer, but he did not return home until 1945.

The Johnson Brothers company, facing another drastic reduction in manpower and resources, had to scale back its production once more, and no decorated wares were allowed to be sold domestically. They could, however, be produced in order to generate revenue from the Americans. It was also possible to maintain the general standards of quality, because the vast majority of workers who applied transfers and did hand painting were women. This had traditionally been the case, because their smaller hands meant improved dexterity, although there was a physical cost. Norbury spoke of how "these women had to work really hard to earn their money and you could always tell a print shop worker by the hard calluses on their hands as large as a tennis ball. Sometimes they had calluses on their chests where the ware rubbed the skin as they rubbed the transfer on the coarse biscuit ware" (p. 34). Their continued employment, however, meant income for their families while the men of the family were away at war.

There were relatively fewer new patterns introduced during the war, and once more the lack of extant records limits our understanding of exactly what was produced and when. Fortunately, however, some patterns were printed with patent numbers. One of these was *Devonshire*, which received US design patent 118579, dated 1940 (Plate 6C). The pattern is a floral border transfer pattern, and the plate shape was circular with a gadroon edge. The service was offered in a variety of colors, including blue, green, red, and brown, and the red and brown versions were also offered in a "multi-color" variation, meaning that there were painted highlights of blue, red, yellow, and green. In this way, it was possible to offer a variety of choices without actually changing the design. *Devonshire* has some surprising design elements, including zig-zag bands that serve as perches for a pair of birds. It is familiar, however, in having a typically English place name.

The 1940s saw the introduction of a new Johnson Brothers series name: "WindsorWare." According to Finegan:

> "WindsorWare" is the tradename of a special range of Johnson Brothers patterns shipped to the Fisher Bruce Company of Philadelphia. This company was an importer/wholesaler that dealt mainly in patterns made exclusively for them. Occasionally, pieces in this line can be found with a U.S. Patent Office mark, presumably registered and obtained by the Fisher Bruce Company itself. A regular pattern name may or may not be included in the backstamp. The

"WindsorWare" line began in the 1940's and was discontinued in the 1970's after Johnson Brothers became a part of the Wedgwood Group. (p. 31)

It should be noted that while some examples of "WindsorWare" are imprinted with "F.B.&Cº" for the Fisher Bruce Company, many others are not, and the large number of "WindsorWare" patterns suggests that the series was not exclusive to one distributor. An example has also been found in which a dark-colored "WindsorWare" stamp was applied over an existing older backstamp of "Old English" with the angular crown.

The name "Windsor" was the family name adopted by King George VI's father, George V, in 1917. George V was a member of the royal house of his father, Prince Albert of Saxe-Coburg and Gotha, but because of anti-German sentiment during the First World War, he changed the family name to Windsor. This newly adopted family name honored Windsor Castle, a British royal residence with a history dating back to William the Conqueror. The new title of "Duke of Windsor" was subsequently created in March 1937, for the former King Edward VIII, who had abdicated in December 1936. There has been no other holder of this title since the duke's death in 1972.

The backstamp shown on pieces of "WindsorWare" reinforces the association with Windsor Castle (Figure 2.3). It shows a small sketch of the castle, with the words "WindsorWare" in a vaguely Gothic lettering above it and the words "Johnson Bros England" below. The words and image are framed by several scrolls that loosely form the shape of a shield.

The name "WindsorWare" served as a powerful reminder of the British royal family and the historic alliance between Britain and America. Although the United States did not enter the war until December 7, 1941, after the bombing of Pearl Harbor in Hawaii, Americans were sympathetic toward the British in their struggles against Germany. The purchase of British goods was considered by many Americans to be a form of extending support to that country, especially after the terrible physical damage and loss of life incurred during the Blitz of 1940–41. And it made perfect sense for Johnson Brothers to make practical use of that pro-British sentiment.

Most of the "WindsorWare" patterns have the same ivory color, plain round shape, and gadroon edge.[41] *Sheraton*, however, had no gadrooning, and instead of being round, it had a molded shape with twelve rounded scallops.[42] This new shape would be used very frequently in the 1950s, along with other variations with eight or six scallops, and it gave those later patterns a more contemporary feel. There was also an important innovation in terms of the backstamp. Instead of having a uniform "WindsorWare" stamp, *Sheraton* had its own motif, uniquely designed for that single pattern (Figure 2.4). This was the word "Sheraton" in a vaguely eighteenth-century-style handwriting, with curlicues added to the "S" and "n," encased in a "frame" with pineapple finials. The frame's quarter-round curves and finials suggest the design of eighteenth-century furniture and interior molding.

Although *Sheraton* was not the first Staffordshire pattern to have a unique backstamp, emphasizing visual or thematic aspects of the pattern on the front

Figure 2.3 Johnson Brothers WindsorWare backstamp, 1940s through 1970s.

side, this was a design element that would later become a Johnson Brothers signature.

Many of the "WindsorWare" patterns had a surprising longevity of production, which indicates that their visual characteristics fit well with contemporary American notions of what was attractive. *Garden Bouquet*, for example, was a delicate floral pattern with pastel-colored highlights that remained in production for thirty years, from 1940 to 1970, and *Sheraton* was a similar floral produced from 1944 to 1980, a period of thirty-six years. There are several patterns that seem

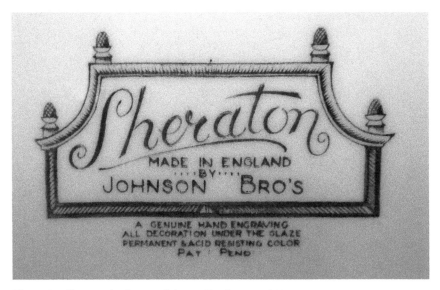

Figure 2.4 Sheraton backstamp, Johnson Brothers, *c.* 1944.

to share nearly identical floral elements, but in different configurations, including *The Marquis, Garden Bouquet, Sheraton,* and *Pomona. Pomona* also has a central bowl heaped with ripe fruit, including a pineapple and a pomegranate that is cut open to display its seeds. The significance of the floral motif is that it represents the continuity of tradition, which was an important notion during wartime, on both sides of the Atlantic. These designs filled the center of the plate with profuse arrays of blossoms and leaves, suggesting the bounty and resilience of nature. *Pomona*, named for the goddess of Spring, anticipates the return of abundance, including exotic imported fruit. Names such as *The Marquis* and *Sheraton* also evoked the historic British Empire, upon which the sun famously never sets.

Chapter 3

AMERICAN HISTORY (THE BRITISH VERSION)

Wedgwood Old Blue Historical

Around 1900, the firm of Josiah Wedgwood and Company introduced a series pattern that attempted to capitalize upon the popularity of flow blue, without actually having to undertake that complicated and unpredictable process. The series called "Wedgwood Old Blue Historical Plates," shortened to "Wedgwood Old Blue," was made by the standard transfer process, using blue ink. In addition to being much easier to produce, this series went back to the original concept of Staffordshire pottery made for export to America in the mid-nineteenth century, representing "American" scenes. This series was produced exclusively for the Boston firm of Jones, McDuffee & Stratton, and it would eventually expand to include an astounding total of more than 1,100 views.[1]

An advertisement for "Wedgwood Old Blue Historical Plates" was run by the Jones, McDuffee & Stratton company in a publication called *The Inter-Nation: A Journal of Economic Affairs*, in June 1907. This journal is not oriented toward a female consumer, and the advertisement contains language that suggests that it was aimed at a man who wanted to furnish his office or study with reminders of the deeds of great men of American history. There is an image of a plate with the portrait of George Washington, and below it is the following text:

GEORGE WASHINGTON, 1732–1799
  "Soldier and statesman, rarest unison: High-poised example of great duties done."

—JAMES RUSSELL LOWELL

  "America has furnished to the world the character of George Washington: and if our American institutions had done nothing else, that alone would have entitled them to the respect of mankind."—DANIEL WEBSTER at the completion of the Bunker Hill Monument.

  The cut represents one of seventy-three subjects of Wedgwood old blue souvenir plates (9 inch). The other subjects are, in part: The Washington Elm, Cambridge; under this tree Washington first took command of the American Army, July 3d, 1775—The Capitol, Washington—Mount Vernon, 1744—

Independence Hall, Philadelphia, 1743—Longfellow's Home, 1759; once Washington's Headquarters, Cambridge—The Old South Church, 1773—Faneuil Hall—The Old North Church, where Paul Revere hung out the lanterns in 1775—The Return of the Mayflower—The White House, Washington, 1792—The Landing of the Pilgrims—Priscilla and John Alden—Signing of the Declaration of Independence—Arlington House, home of Robert E. Lee—The Old North Bridge, Concord—Bunker Hill Monument—The Battle of Lexington—State House, Boston—Emerson's Home, Concord—Monticello, the home of Thomas Jefferson—Grant's Tomb, Riverside Drive—Yale College and the Old Fence—Elmwood, home of James Russell Lowell—The Chew House, Philadelphia—Carpenter's Hall, Philadelphia—Harvard College Gates—Lincoln—Roosevelt—Grant—Martha Washington—U.S. Frigate Constitution in chase.[2]

The advertisement begins by praising the character of Washington, and then proceeds to list the selection of scenes, in some cases explaining its significance through its association with an important man. Yale College and Harvard College are included, perhaps as places that might have been attended by some of the journal's readers, who could then acquire a plate as a souvenir of that prestigious *alma mater*. Interestingly, the list also includes commemoration of Civil War era figures, one on each side of the War Between the States (the Confederate General Robert E. Lee and the Union proponents President Abraham Lincoln and General, later President, Ulysses S. Grant). Priscilla and John Alden were made famous in "The Courtship of Miles Standish," the enormously popular poem published by Henry Wadsworth Longfellow in 1858, mythologizing the Pilgrims. Martha Washington may seem an unusual choice, but it was common to have side-by-side portraits of George and Martha Washington in many nineteenth-century American homes, and including her portrait allowed the decorative plates to serve a similar purpose. President Theodore Roosevelt had become president upon the assassination of William McKinley in 1901, and he was still president in 1907, the date of this advertisement. The inclusion of his portrait in this series, as a living president still holding office, recognized his widespread popularity at the time. And finally, there was an appropriately manly battle scene, involving a naval frigate "in chase."

The ad continues: "**A booklet of half-tone cuts of the series will be mailed free on request.** These pictures have been produced from engravings after etchings and paintings (at the famous pottery of Josiah Wedgwood & Sons, Staffordshire) of important subjects connected with American history." This reveals a marketing strategy of informing customers of the full range of possible items that could be obtained. This could operate in two ways: first, to give the purchaser choice in selecting scenes that were of greatest personal interest, and second, to encourage purchasers to become "collectors," owning the entire series. It is significant that the advertisement emphasizes the fact that these plates have been created from genuine artworks, "etchings and paintings." This phrasing, along with their description as "souvenir plates," suggests that they were intended for display, rather than for table service.

Jones, McDuffee & Stratton also ran an advertisement in a 1908 issue of *The Federation Bulletin*, the national publication of the General Federation of Women's Clubs. This advertisement, aimed at a female audience, has some interesting variations from the preceding one:

Wedgwood Old Blue Historical Plates

Seventy-five views on dessert plates (9-inch) engraved for us by **Wedgwood** from picturesque etchings of historical interest to all Americans, printed under glaze on **Old Blue Wedgwood** with foliage border, embracing scenes connected with the early struggles of the Revolutionary War, namely: Faneuil Hall; King's Chapel; Battle of Lexington; Washington Elm; Paul Revere's Ride; Old South Church; Old North Church; Old North Bridge, Concord; Washington's Headquarters, 1775; Harvard College Gates; Old State House; Bunker Hill Monument; Boston Tea Party; Also National Capitol; Mount Vernon; Independence Hall; White House, Washington; Landing of the Pilgrims; Birthplace of Whittier; Portraits of Washington, Lincoln, Grant, Cleveland, Martha Washington, and Roosevelt. The price is 35 cents each or $4.20 per dozen. A single plate of any subject will be mailed in a safety mailing box to any post-office in the United States on receipt of 60 cents, post-office order or stamps. *A Booklet of half-tone cuts of the series will be mailed free on request.*[3]

The first significant difference between the two advertisements is that the plates are not described as "souvenir plates (9 inch)," but rather as "dessert plates (9 inch)." This change identifies the intended consumer as being female, since women were assumed to be more interested in using plates for food service. The plate depicted has also changed; instead of showing a portrait of George Washington, accompanied by two quotations praising him, it shows "Bunker Hill Monument, Dedicated June 17, 1843, Height 220 feet." There is another quote underneath, this time in homage of the monument:

"Let it rise! Let it rise, till it meet the sun in his coming. Let the earliest light of the morning gild it, and parting day linger and play on its summit."—Daniel Webster, 17th June, 1825.

The apparent conflict of dates above may be explained by the fact that Webster's poem was written prior to the actual construction of the monument, which occurred between 1827 and 1843. This advertisement seems to appeal to a general sense of patriotism, rather than encouraging an identification with the heroic (and male) *persona* of George Washington.

Another evident change is that "Longfellow's Home" in Cambridge, Massachusetts, previously mentioned and described as Washington's Headquarters, has been replaced by the "Birthplace of Whittier." John Greenleaf Whittier (1807–92) was a Quaker poet and abolitionist, and his birthplace in Haverhill, Massachusetts, had only become open to the public as a museum in 1893. Although it is hard to see a difference between two houses associated with poets, Longfellow's home had a military connection that was lacking in the case of Whittier's birthplace. It may have been presumed by the writers of the advertisement that the female readers of the journal, many of whom resided in Boston, would share Whittier's abolitionist views and be admirers of his poetry. Whittier's death in 1892 was also more recent than Longfellow's death in 1882, making him a subject of more timely interest.

In the previous advertisement, there was no noticeable priority of geography, with the first four items located in Cambridge (Massachusetts), Washington, Virginia, and Philadelphia. In this version, however, the first grouping of thirteen names (through "Boston Tea Party") emphasizes scenes that are localized to the area around Boston, the city where Jones, McDuffee & Stratton was located and where *The Federation Bulletin* was published. Sites in Virginia, Philadelphia, and Washington are only mentioned in the "Also" listing; this may suggest that the primary intended audience of the advertisement resided in Boston. The address of the Jones, McDuffee & Stratton company is given as a street address, without mention of any city, whereas the previous notice in the male-oriented publication stated "Boston, Mass."

The list of post-Revolutionary War portrait subjects in *The Federation Bulletin* advertisement adds the name of President Grover Cleveland, who served two terms in 1885–89 and 1893–97; his inclusion is somewhat mysterious, except for the fact that he was a Democrat, whereas Roosevelt was a Republican. It is possible that the company wanted to offer a choice to buyers who happened to be members of either political party. The year 1908 was also the year in which Cleveland died, and there may have been a wave of sentiment in his honor that could inspire a purchaser to acquire a plate bearing his image, or so the company may have hoped.

One example of the Wedgwood "Old Blue Historical" series may be seen in Plate 6D. It depicts the White House in Washington, DC, as seen from a wide, curved roadway, with a tiny horse-drawn carriage. The view is almost identical to one in a photograph taken in 1892,[4] which does not feature the carriage; that may have been added to indicate the building's scale. The photograph features a flagpole behind one of the chimneys; in the plate, the flagpole is moved closer to the center of the image and doubled in size, with a flag completely unfurled in the wind. The addition of this patriotic detail reinforces the building's symbolism.

The backstamp of this plate features not only information about the makers, but a brief history lesson about the building. This was an element of the series evident in other examples seen, sometimes with very lengthy explanations. In this case, the backstamp information includes the following, all in small capital letters:

(upper left of backstamp) "copyright 1900 J.McD.&S.C^{o}"
(upper right of backstamp) a circle with a lion rampant and the words "Sole Importers, Jones McDuffee & Stratton Co. Boston"
(center of backstamp) **The White House** Erected during President Washington's term 1792. First occupied by President John Adams. Partially destroyed 1814. Restoration completed 1818. Wedgwood Etruria England

The strong similarity between the photograph, taken in 1892, and the plate image, copyrighted in 1900, suggests that the designers of the "Old Blue

Historical" series were not in fact attempting to re-create the past. Instead, the "historical" buildings featured were so named because of their historical importance, not because the scenes themselves were supposed to be from many years ago.

Another example from the "Old Blue Historical" series highlights a house that was mentioned in the 1907 advertisement: "The Chew House, Philadelphia." This was the home of Judge Benjamin Chew, and it played a role in the Battle of Germantown during the Revolutionary War. The Chew family had evacuated the property, leaving a few servants behind, and during the conflict, it was used as a retreat by the British commanding officers. It was said to have withstood attempts to set it on fire, and the British officers remained safe inside. Ironically, however, this battle was lost by the American forces. Perhaps for that reason, the Chew House is not a household name among Americans, although the Jones, McDuffee & Stratton company in Boston considered the house to be worthy of commemoration in the "Old Blue" series. This may be a case where a plate was targeted at a specific audience, in this case residents of Philadelphia who would recognize this building and appreciate it as a relic of the colonial period, even though it was associated with a British victory.

The image on the plate is virtually identical to an engraving of the Chew House, by artist Thompson Westcott and published in *The Historic Mansions and Buildings of Philadelphia* in 1877.[5] The same illustration was reproduced in *Ancient and Modern Germantown, Mount Airy and Chestnut Hill*, published by Rev. S. F. Hotchkin in 1889, with permission from Westcott's publishers.[6] It is not known exactly when the Chew House plate was issued, but since it was listed in the 1907 advertisement, no more than thirty years could have passed between the date of publication of the original illustration and the appearance of the plate. As in the case of the White House plate, the image does not seemingly attempt to evoke a long-distant past, but rather simply to depict the architectural features of the building as it existed in the contemporary present.

The backstamp has the circle motif identifying the company and the words "Wedgwood Etruria England," but the rest of the text is quite unexpected:

> The Chew House (Built 1763)/Germantown Philadelphia/Scene of the battle Oct. 7, 1777/"The old village was then a long broken line of small grey stone houses, set in gardens on each side of the highway, with here and there a larger mansion like the Chew House, Cliveden, or that of the Wisters."/"Hugh Wynn" (Weir Mitchell)

This inscription does not actually describe the house's inhabitants, or its historical role in the battle; instead, it quotes from *Hugh Wynne, Free Quaker*, a novel published in 1897 by Dr. Silas Weir Mitchell.[7] That book is a fictional memoir of a young man from Philadelphia who joined General Washington's revolutionary forces and became a military hero. Thanks to its historical detail, action scenes, and a happily resolved romance between Hugh and his sweetheart Darthea, this book was very popular and was reprinted many times, most recently in 2016.[8]

It is quite unusual for a backstamp to contain a quote from a popular novel, and this is even more unexpected when one considers that the "Old Blue Historical" series was intended to provide a documentary record of the most notable icons of American history. Instead of facts about the house and its inhabitants, the backstamp has Silas Weir Mitchell's fictional description, elevated to the status of a "true" historical account. The only rationale for this seems to be a commercial one, that is, to capitalize upon the novel's popularity and thus promote sales of the plate, in the sense of a modern merchandising tie-in.

The success of Wedgwood's "Old Blue Historical" series inspired many imitations, although most rival companies could only aspire to the production of a small number of plates, often issued for a specific anniversary. One example is a plate honoring the bicentennial of George Washington's birth in 1732, made by Copeland Spode as early as 1930, based on an impressed date mark on a plate seen by the author. The front of the plate is a faithful reproduction of the Washington family crest, as it was printed on a bookplate dating from around 1772.[9] In place of the coat of arms in the center, there is an oval frame with a profile of Washington, wearing a laurel wreath on his head. Below the frame is a banner with Washington's personal motto, *Exitus acta probat*, often translated as "the outcome justifies the deed," but since that implies a rather questionable morality, Washington's intentions may have been in keeping with a more literal translation, "success proves the value of actions." The backstamp reads: "Spode's contribution to the George Washington Bicentennial 1932, produced in a limited edition of 2500, each piece numbered."

Another example is a series of "George Washington Bicentenary Memorial Plates 1732–1932," made by Crown Ducal Ware, an imprint of A. G. Richardson and Co., Ltd., of Tunstall and Cobridge, England.[10] There are twelve scenes in this series, including "Mount Vernon," "Washington and his family," "Washington and his mother," "Washington at Valley Forge," "Washington and Lafayette at Mount Vernon," "Birthplace of Washington at Wakefield" (Virginia), "John Adams Proposing Washington for Commander-in-Chief of the American Army," "Washington at Trenton" (New Jersey), "Washington's Headquarters," "Washington Crossing the Delaware," the "Surrender of Cornwallis," and a view of the "Washington Ancestral Home, Sulgrave Manor, Banbury," emphasizing his family's link to the mother country.

Johnson Brothers' Historic America

The most important successor of the Wedgwood "Old Blue Historical" series would be the pattern called *Historic America*, created by Johnson Brothers (Plate 7A). This pattern would combine the appealing subject of American history with the practicality of the company's most successful pattern to date, *Old Britain Castles*. Instead of concentrating on dinner-sized plates, as Wedgwood had done, Johnson Brothers' new pattern would offer a wide variety of types of pieces, each one featuring a different image.

The design was patented in 1938 (US design patent number 111255). It had been in development for several years prior to that date, and according to Bill Norbury's account, when the idea was proposed, the company director Ernest Johnson contracted with an independent engraver instead of using the company's own staff:

> I knew Harry Latchford, Engraver, had been called in to see Sir Ernest's offices to talk about a new pattern "Historic America". Ted Evans had said it was too difficult for him to tackle. Harry Latchford had been given four engravings to do, so I went in and said to Sir Ernest Johnson, that pattern should be ours, why haven't we been given the chance to demonstrate our skills to the company? He replied, Do one and show me the quality. Let Latchfords set it up and you prove yourself. I did this and found an unexpected bonus. Latchford had made some glaring errors which I corrected and having done so pointed them out to Sir Ernest. Having proved my point, my share of the pattern was total control of the pattern and I was given the job of instructing Latchford. (p. 49)

Bill Norbury's memoir was still in unedited draft form when he died in 1999, and there are several passages that repeat similar content. Another passage describing the origins of *Historic America* is found ten pages later, and it provides additional details:

> The initial engraving of this pattern was commenced by "J.H. Latchford, Engravers and designers", Honeywell Lane, Stoke-on-Trent. I heard about this just before I became Manager one month previously [1936].[11] Apparently the guy that was then the manager of the Engraving Department, had told Sir Ernest Johnson that this pattern was beyond the powers of the existing department to complete, either in the time available, or to the technique required. I did not agree with this and didn't mind saying so [… I was] gradually to take charge of the pattern, and the development of what was to be a Major Pattern in the industry. I engraved quite a lot of it myself, whilst also finding out how to be completely capable, in control of engravings from start to finish, plus all the artwork. (p. 59)

The Johnson Brothers pattern drew inspiration from the characteristics that had made *Old Britain Castles* a success. The first such element was to have images rendered as fine art by a master engraver. Norbury identified another engraver who produced many images for *Historic America*, Claude Whittingham, whose "forte lay in illustrating with very fine work only superseded by a few […] he was notorious for his 'Claude's' Finework, minute detail, and clean work, almost perfect but sometimes lacking in window appeal" (p. 78). As for Norbury's own work, he stated, "I always tried to develop patterns, checking their impact from 10 feet distance as an arbitrary measure, posing the questions, Does it look good at this distance or better at a closer distance. I personally felt that it should have the same impact at all distances" (p. 78). The image quality therefore equaled or exceeded that of *Old Britain Castles*, and was intended to create a similar effect of having an art display in the china cabinet.

The second critical element was the authentic "historical" character of the images. In contrast to the Wedgwood Old Blue Historical series, which used many views that were contemporary with the plates' production around 1900, the scenes of *Historic America* were all drawn from nineteenth-century engravings, intentionally evoking a more distant historic past. This was similar to *Old Britain Castles*' use of illustrations from 1792, and allowed customers of the mid-1930s to escape into a romanticized past. Many of the *Historic America* images were taken from images published by the celebrated firm of Currier & Ives, founded in New York in 1834 by the American engraver Nathaniel Currier. He became successful creating and selling prints of American scenes, some of which were based upon paintings, and in 1857 he entered into partnership with another engraver, James Merritt Ives. The firm did not survive long beyond the deaths of the two partners, and was liquidated in 1907, but during the company's existence it is believed to have created over 7,500 lithographs, selling more than 1 million copies.[12] By choosing subjects that American customers could recognize from prints hanging in their parents' or grandparents' homes, Johnson Brothers was able to confer instant "heirloom" status upon these plates, even though they were being produced in the late 1930s.

According to Bernard F. Reilly, Jr., former curator of historical prints at the Library of Congress in Washington, DC:

> From the viewpoint of the 1920s, a world drastically changed during the preceding three decades, the progress, innovation, and enterprise of the Victorian period marked a heroic era. Viewed through the prints of Currier & Ives, it was a vital time, a time of fleet, graceful sailing vessels, prosperous farms, and westward expansion. These prints projected a sense of optimism and simple values. The joys of domestic life, the tranquillity of the home, the rewards of temperance and morality, must have been attractive to the twentieth-century person ... Straightforward and literal, these earlier views, portraits, and genre scenes seemed to embody a distinctly American approach to art.[13]

In addition to the prints of Currier & Ives, it has been possible to identify other sources of nineteenth-century published illustrations that inspired the images of *Historic America*. These included Nathaniel P. Willis's *American Scenery: or Land, Lake, and River Illustrations of Transatlantic Nature*, with illustrations by the British artist William Henry Bartlett, published in London in 1840,[14] and *Picturesque America; or, The Land We Live In*, edited by the famous orator William Cullen Bryant and published in New York, 1872–74.[15] Other scenes were taken from individual prints that were specific to a single location. "St. Louis/Missouri," featured on a tab-handled soup bowl, is taken directly from a view of St. Louis in 1846, drawn by Henry Lewis.[16] "Stage and Mail Coach/View of Mount Shasta" [California], featured on an ash tray, was copied from an illustration by Aaron Stein, created for the California & Oregon Stage Company in the early 1870s.[17]

In order to demonstrate the accuracy with which the *Historic America* scenes reproduced the images upon which they were based, the scene of St. Louis,

Missouri, will be analyzed in detail (Plate 7B). In the original illustration, St. Louis is viewed from the east bank of the Mississippi River, looking westward from Illinois. The scene on the bowl shows only the central part of the entire original engraving, but it is very accurate in depicting distinctive roofs of the cityscape, two steamboats, a barge with a sail, and a foreground showing a hillside with a man, woman, and covered wagon. On the bowl, the placement of some details has been altered, presumably to simplify the engraving for reproduction and to better fit the piece, but other details are perfectly accurate, such as the direction of the smoke billowing from the boats, and the visible tail end of the horse. (The horse is not in harness, in front of the wagon; being released from the hitch means that the horse is resting, adding to the peaceful mood of the scene.)

There are numerous other images in which some details of the source have been altered in their proportions, in order to fit the pattern to the piece, but in all cases where source images have been identified, there are very specific points of similarity that indicate the artist/engraver was working from the original print. Such points include the shape and placement of trees, architectural details, and human figures. In some cases, the scene has been edited, removing details that would make the image appear cluttered in its smaller size. One example is the oval bowl featuring "Tow Path/Erie Canal," in which the original engraving had foreground figures of a man herding a large pig and several small piglets.

Historical authenticity of another sort is found in the border of each piece of *Historic America*. The border pattern is a careful reproduction of an earlier pattern made by Ralph Stevenson & Williams of Cobridge, on plates of American scenes made between 1825 and 1840. The pattern is very distinctive, having large oak leaves of a variety with rounded edges, intertwined with acorns; the background is a series of small circles creating a net-like effect, and both the outer edge of the plate and the inside of the border are banded with a white scallop pattern. Johnson Brothers' *Historic America* reproduced this same oak leaf and acorn pattern on all of its pieces. Since Stevenson & Williams plates were noted examples of "Old Staffordshire" that might be seen in American museums, the person who originally came up with the concept of *Historic America* (and who is unknown to us) may have felt that copying that border would be a clever way of reinforcing the pattern's "genuine" historical origins. Bill Norbury, however, was not impressed with this motif, believing that the oak leaves looked a lot more like cabbage leaves.[18]

The choice of images also reflects a strategy of selecting scenes that appealed to a broad market of potential consumers. The original Staffordshire marketed in the early nineteenth century had represented scenes from the east coast of the United States, but not the westward expansion and urban development that occurred later in the century. For example, of the 796 examples in Ellouise Baker Larsen's compendium of *American Historical Views on Staffordshire China*, there is not a single view of Chicago, Illinois.[19] The Johnson Brothers pattern rectified such omissions, adding scenes of cities like Sacramento, which was only founded in 1848 but played an important part in the California Gold Rush and was named the state capital in 1854. St. Louis, Missouri, was also an obscure river settlement in the early nineteenth century, but gained much wider recognition as the site of the Lewis and Clark Centennial Exposition, better known as the 1904 World's Fair.

Adding scenes from across the expanse of the United States made it possible for the series to appeal to twentieth-century buyers who lived in those locations.

The final innovation of *Historic America* was the backstamp, which showed a stylized American eagle (Figure 3.1). In the backstamp's center are the words "Historic America," in a hand-lettered serif that suggests colonial-era type. Above and below, two banners offer space in which the image can be identified, also in hand-lettered serif. The use of banners suggests that these images are heraldic in importance, and the eagle reinforces the symbolism of American national pride.

On examples of the pattern issued after the popularization of automatic home dishwashers, around 1950, the backstamp added the phrase "all decoration under the glaze permanent & acid resisting colors," with the American spelling of "colors." There is another addition, however, either above the eagle or added to the "all decoration" text: the phrase "A Genuine Hand Engraving." This phrase offsets

Figure 3.1 Historic America backstamp, Johnson Brothers, *c.* 1939–74.

the practical consideration of durability with a reminder that this is a work of fine art, originally engraved by hand.

Two advertisement brochures obtained by Mary J. Finegan are dated from the series' launch in 1939.[20] Finegan received these from separate antique dealers, in Bend, Oregon, and Clarksville, Virginia, and each one had different introductory matter, but they were followed by identical lists of items with brief descriptions. The first advertisement makes reference to the Frederick & Nelson department store, which was founded in Seattle, Washington, in 1890 by Donald E. Frederick and Nels B. Nelson. In 1918, the store moved to a six-story building at Pine Street and Fifth Avenue, and it became known as the premier retailer in Seattle.[21]

In some instances, there is a discrepancy between the name listed and words actually printed on the backstamp of the piece. This suggests that the advertisement may have been issued when the pattern was still in production, and the final names for the item had not yet been determined. For example, the 12-inch platter named as "Broadway" in the advertisement was actually produced with a backstamp that reads "Barnum's Museum, Broadway, New York"; the creamer "R.R. Valley of the Mohawk" actually reads "Railroad, Little Falls/Valley of the Mohawk"; and "The Rocky Mountains" actually reads "Covered Wagons/and the Rocky Mountains." One reason for the modification may have been that the backstamp was designed to have two banners, one above and one below the words "HISTORIC AMERICA," so more words may have been added to create visual symmetry.

These advertisements will be reproduced in their entirety, because they are very informative about the manner in which they sought to appeal to the emotions of American buyers. National pride, admiration of heroes, and even future financial security are among the incentives offered to the potential purchaser. The list of items will reveal the British designers' selection of subjects that they believed merited inclusion, for different reasons.

The text of the advertisements is not written in an anonymous third person, but is rather presented as a monologue spoken by another American, who speaks of "our history on china."

[first advertisement introduction]

HISTORIC AMERICA—1839-1939

A NEW-OLD DINNER WARE FASHION THAT REVIVES THE ROMANTIC SCENES OF EARLY AMERICAN HISTORY! A FASHION OF THE PAST ... AND THE FUTURE!

As far back as 1839, historic decorations made their first appearance on the English china that came to be known as "Old Staffordshire." Now in 1939, historic designs appear again! This time on a new series of English dinner ware called "Historic America."

Turning back the years to a century ago, we find the new world's beloved Hudson River, the majestic Mississippi ... the "wild" and unknown West, being reproduced by artists who made special trips to the New World to accomplish this feat. Now we find America's own famous designers using "Old Staffordshire" motifs for inspiration and bringing forth this new historic series. A series that without doubt will be as cherished in years to come as "Old Staffordshire" is a century after its birth. For example, since 1830 the price of Staffordshire has soared from something like an English sixpence to $1,225 ... a sum recently paid for an "Old Staffordshire" platter at a New York auction.

So it is with pride that FREDERICK & NELSON presents the new "Historic America" ... a dinner ware fashion destined to be treasured in the world of tomorrow.

SETS AND OPEN STOCK PIECES IN DELFT BLUE! THIRTY HISTORIC SCENES ARE REPRODUCED ON THE VARIOUS PIECES/For detailed information of the designs see inside this sheet.

[second advertisement introduction]

RELEASE ON HISTORIC AMERICA 1839-1939

Our own designer hearked [sic] back to that day one hundred years ago, when England, the mother country, was at once affirming a faith in the New World colony and enriching her already profitable trade with the States, which were to become the American Republic.

At the forefront of this trade were the potteries which sought to emulate American names and American places by putting views of principal scenes in our history on china. Often at great expense, artists were commissioned to tour the country and return with suitable illustrations of the Hudson, the Mississippi, the "Wild West" and such famous dates and events as had made our industrial development a conspicuous one.

These designs, reproduced on earthenware which has since become famous as "Old Staffordshire" were at first invariably done in blue. After 1830 when the discovery of lithography cheapened the transfer process, this "Dutch Delft blue" was joined by paler tints, particularly light pink, green and mulberry. (Towards the end of the century, of course the common tableware in popular use became white.) But the early ware distinguished itself by a rise in price from something like an English sixpence in its own day to such current prices as the $1225 which an old platter entitled "New York from Weehawk" brought at a recent auction.

We thought that a similar series of "Historic America" scenes, again manufactured by a famous English house, would be an interesting tribute to the memories of early America which are being revived so pleasantly and so dramatically today. For its sources, the designer selected over 30 different scenes all about 100 years ago, from which copper engravings were made, and from which the designs in turn were impressed under the glaze on a complete china service. To lend unity to the series, the famous over-all "oak and acorn" design was used as the pattern for the border of each piece. Many interesting examples of this design are to be seen today in the American wing of the Metropolitan Museum and also at the Philadelphia Museum. A distinguishing backstamp bears the American Eagle and the title of each scene.

The more detailed information which research provides for the Various design back grounds employed are appended herewith.

Both introductions include several direct references to the history of British pottery, as well as a number of statements intended to affirm the bond between England and America. England is portrayed as the "mother country," originally "affirming a faith in the New World colony" and today paying "tribute to the memories of early America." The illustrations were commissioned "often at great expense," as though that conferred greater value on the end result, and the buyer is reminded that those historical wares command astronomical prices, as though *Historic America* may attain a similar value in the future. Since the new series would produce hundreds of thousands of mass-produced pieces, however, such a result would be highly unlikely.

The scenes are said to be taken from ones "all about 100 years ago" (i.e., 1839), although that would prove to be inaccurate, as will be noted later. The so-called "famous" oak and acorn border was also not particularly famous, except among a handful of scholars of Old Staffordshire, but it was true that some examples could be found in American museum collections. The buyer is therefore being offered the opportunity to acquire not just her own collection of fine artworks, but ones that are actually "museum pieces."

Both advertisements included an identical list of items available, which will be reproduced below. In cases where the source image has been identified by this author, that information will be provided in a note.[22]

HOME FOR THANKSGIVING—Turkey Platter[23]
Adapted from the Currier and Ives print and truly American in feeling. These great print makers depicted their life and times in their prints.

RICHMOND, VIRGINIA—Round Vegetable Dish[24]
Was founded in 1733 and named Richmond for a similar site on the Thames River in England. In 1779 it was made the state capitol and in 1861 was made the capitol of the Confederate states. The capitol building was built from plans brought from France by Thomas Jefferson.

CAPITOL AT WILLIAMSBURG—Cream Soup Cup and Saucer
The first capitol, recently reconstructed by Rockefeller, was built originally in 1705. The second capitol burned down entirely in 1832.

SAN FRANCISCO—Teacup and Saucer[25]
In 1848, when gold was discovered at Colma[26] ... a city of tents and shanties mushroomed into growth and swelled the existing population of 800 inhabitants of San Francisco. Fortunes were won and lost and the cost of living was fantastically high.

R.R. VALLEY OF THE MOHAWK—Creamer[27]
The first steam engine was called "*The Best Friend of Charleston*." It made its appearance in 1830 and resembled a catsup bottle on wheels. Peter Cooper, using musket barrels for boiler tubes, produced, later, an engine which would take curves. The first transcontinental railroad was completed in 1869.

THE CLERMONT—Sugar[28]

America, over many years, was the maritime power of the world. Clipper ships, during the gold rush to California, were greatly in demand. In 1807, Robert Fulton, artist, and dilettante, ran the first steamboat on the Hudson River. Steam vessels were used at first for travel only.

THE FLYING CLOUD—Chop Dish

Clipper ships, so named for the clip which they attained, were the fastest ships afloat. In 1851, *The Flying Cloud*, designed by the famous ship designer, Donald McKay, established the record for all sailing vessels. He reached San Francisco from Sandy Hook in 87 days.

LOW WATER IN THE MISSISSIPPI—Sauce Boat[29]

Discovered by De Soto in 1541, the "father of waters" was for many years the main artery for north-south traffic. Early transportation was by barges and keel boats, which seldom attempted a return trip. The first steamboat made its appearance on the Mississippi four years after Fulton made his memorable journey down the Hudson. The next 30 years marked a great era of steam-boat navigation, an era that was colorful and romantic.

WALL STREET—Luncheon Plate[30]

Owes its name to a palisade which was built by Peter Stuyvesant. The street became famous after the revolution. Government offices of city, state and nation were located there. At the Federal Hall, on the site of the present Sub-treasury building, George Washington was inaugurated first president of the United States. Today Wall Street is one of the famous financial centers of the world.

BROADWAY—Platter, 12 inch[31]

By 1831, New York was a financial and industrial center. The Broadway theatres helped to crowd the busy street. Barnum's Museum was purchased in 1841 by P. T. Barnum, who made it a great success by showing his celebrated midget, Tom Thumb. Below the Museum were St. Paul's Church and the Astor House.

CENTRAL PARK, GRAND DRIVE—Mug[32]

In 1853 a stretch of land in the center of Manhattan Island was purchased for a park. In 1858 Calvert Vaux and Frederic Law Olmstead won a prize of $2,000 for the best proposed plan. In 1859 the first band concert was on the Mall. The drive was thronged by fashionable carriages and riders at all times.

BROOKLYN FERRY—Cream Soup Bowl[33]

Ferry boats have always played an important part in the commerce of Brooklyn. The first ferry was established across the East River from the present foot of Fulton Street by the Dutch settlers. This settlement was known as "The Ferry."

NEW YORK CRYSTAL PALACE—Cake Plate[34]

Built to house the first International Exhibition of Industry of all nations. It was made of iron and glass and was located on Reservoir Square, where Bryant Park now stands. A celebration was held there when the Atlantic cable was laid. Like its replica in London, the New York Crystal Palace burned.

THE ROCKY MOUNTAINS—Bread and Butter Plate[35]
During the 19th century, many families piled all they owned in covered wagons and began to push westward. With unbelievable hardships to overcome, they finally reached the Rockies and eventually crossed to the Pacific coast.

THE MAIL AND THE STAGE COACH—Ash Tray[36]
Stage coaches which traveled on the California and the Oregon stage route carried Wells Fargo express and the U.S. mails. Mt. Shasta is shown in the background.

NIAGARA FALLS—Platter, 11 ½ Inch[37]
Attracts more visitors and honeymooners than any other single natural phenomenon. In 1750 a fort was built here and called "Little Niagara." With the construction of the hydraulic canal, and the development of power from the falls, the little village grew rapidly. The first bridge over the island was built in 1855. Goat Island separates the American and Horseshoe Falls.

THE WHITE HOUSE—Demi-Tasse Cup[38]
Closely follows the plan of the seat of the Dukes of Leinster, near Dublin. In 1814 when Madison was President, the White House was burned by the British.

THE CAPITOL AT WASHINGTON—Square Plate[39]
Was planned by l'Enfant under the supervision of President Washington. Public buildings, memorials and parks make this one of the most beautiful cities in the world. Until the Civil War progress in building the city was slow, but it then became a great attraction for both sides. Throughout the war it was the center of military operations.

MT. VERNON—Teapot[40]
The former home of our first President was built on the Potomac River by Washington's family. In 1761, when Washington came into possession, he enlarged and beautified the estate according to his own specifications.

MONTICELLO—Jug[41]
Was planned and built by Thomas Jefferson, on top of his "Little Mountain." His natural instinct for what was good and appropriate, helped him to build this classic home at the age of 27. Monticello overlooks the Blue Ridge Mountains.

HANCOCK HOUSE—Cereal[42]
The home of the first signer of the Declaration of Independence. John Hancock was extremely active in politics during the revolution. He was a wealthy man of fine social position … liberal and public spirited.

INDEPENDENCE HALL—Platter, 16 inch[43]
Philadelphia's most famous building is Independence Hall, designed by Andrew Hamilton. It was built between 1732 and 1741. The Liberty Bell is housed here. The first Congress sat in the hall at the corner of Sixth and Chestnut.

BOSTON, MASS.—Dinner Plate[44]
The Capitol building on Beacon Hill has dominated the landscape ever since the revolutionary war. In the Boston Harbor was held the famous tea party and

from the belfry of Christ Church on Copp's Hill lanterns were hung to warn Paul Revere of the route the British were taking to Concord. Boston is indeed the seat of the American Revolution.

SACRAMENTO CITY, CALIFORNIA—Tea Plate[45]
The capitol city of California, taken from the foot of J Street. The first gold nugget which started the rush to California was discovered in this vicinity. In 1859 the Sacramento Valley Railroad joined with the Central Pacific from the East.

THE ALAMO—Coffee Cup
In 1836 a small band of Americans were surrounded in this fort by the Mexican general, Santa Ana. They held out for 13 days. Under the slogan, "*Remember the Alamo.*"

NEW ORLEANS, LA.—Pickle Dish[46]
Named for the Duc d'Orleans, was purchased by the United States in 1803. This had a beneficent effect upon trade especially with advent of steam navigation. The levee was the scene of bustling business as commerce increased.

FORT DEARBORN—Egg Cup[47]
Was built on the Chicago River in 1804, as defense against the Indians. It is a famous historical landmark of Chicago.

WEST POINT—Soup Plate[48]
The United States Military Academy located on land formerly the property of the British Crown. Washington occupied headquarters here during the revolution and urged the establishment of a military school.

KANSAS CITY, MO.—Covered Vegetable Dish[49]
Is called the Gateway to the Southwest. It was established by fur traders in 1821, then called Westport. Before 1850 it was practically the only eastern terminus for the Santa Fe trade, and a great outfitting point for emigrants to California.

THE ERIE CANAL—Oval Vegetable Dish[50]
After 1825 the construction of the Erie Canal greatly contributed to the growth and power of New York. The railroad put an end to the era of the economic value of canal construction.

In the above list, no hyperbole was spared in praising America as the country of magnificent natural wonders and beautiful cities, and praising Americans themselves, in the form of their leading citizens, as benevolent philanthropists or prodigies. Thomas Jefferson had a "natural instinct for what was good and appropriate," and John Hancock, despite his wealth, was "liberal and public spirited."

There appear to be a few places where a British cultural viewpoint makes a subtle appearance. The reference to the Staffordshire platter's value in both introductions states that it was originally worth an "English sixpence," instead of giving its value in American currency (which would have been used in 1839 as well as in 1939). A "tea plate" (Sacramento City) was not a familiar part of an American table service, since Americans did not commonly have afternoon tea. The plate is somewhat superfluous as an element of the table service, since its center (excluding the rim) is virtually identical to the center area of the square plate, approximately 5 inches in diameter. It is noticeable also that the description of the White House mentions its having been a copy of "the seat of the Dukes of Leinster" (in Dublin, Ireland, and today the home of the Irish Parliament), a fact that no American was likely to have learned in school, and may not have been something Americans would be pleased to learn. This may also be a debatable point, since there are architectural differences between Leinster House and the original White House, before the portico was added on the north side. The fact that West Point was located on land "formerly the property of the British Crown" seems rather odd to mention, given that all of the American colonial territory could be described in that manner.

It is also of interest that of these thirty designs, nine referred to New York City or New York State: Wall Street, Broadway, Central Park, Brooklyn Ferry, New York Crystal Palace, Valley of the Mohawk, Niagara Falls, and West Point. This may have been because New York City was the largest population center in the United States, and therefore represented the biggest commercial market. "Barnum's Museum/Broadway New York" (Plate 7C) is an interesting selection, because it represents a tourist attraction known on both sides of the Atlantic for generations. Originally founded in 1790 as the "American Museum" by members of the fraternal Tammany Society, it was later acquired by the naturalist and taxidermist John Scudder. In 1841, the famous showman P. T. Barnum purchased Scudder's Museum and added living attractions such as a dwarf named General Tom Thumb.[51] "Scudder's Museum" was sufficiently well known to be chosen as the subject of a plate by Ralph Stevenson, the same Staffordshire designer of the oak leaf and acorn border,[52] but it was as "Barnum's Museum/Broadway, New York" that it was commemorated in the *Historic America* series.

In the case of Wall Street, the British designers may have misunderstood the site's associations to an American audience. Wall Street in New York City was the subject of an historic print dated *c.* 1850,[53] but the name became synonymous with the stock market crash of October 24, 1929, also known as the "Wall Street Crash," which precipitated the Great Depression. Fewer Americans living in the late 1930s would probably want to buy a plate bearing a name that was a reminder of the hardships faced by the middle and lower classes, following the failure of thousands of banks across the nation in the early part of the decade. Confidence in banks would be somewhat restored in 1933, when President Franklin D. Roosevelt created the Federal Deposit Insurance Corporation (FDIC), but by then, many people had lost their savings.

The *Historic America* series was also innovative in seeking subjects that were based upon the experience of pioneering the American West. The bread plate named in the advertisements as "The Rocky Mountains," which actually bears the backstamp of "Covered Wagons/and the Rocky Mountains" (Plate 7D), exemplifies the movement of westward expansion, without identifying a specific locality. In the foreground of this image, a small caravan of three wagons drawn by teams of oxen meanders along the bank of a river, with two small figures on horseback representing what may be Native Americans. The mountains are seen in the distant background, in the upper half of the image. Similarly, the ash tray motif "The Mail and the Stage Coach," which was named on the actual piece as "Stage and Mail Coach/View of Mount Shasta," shows the northern California natural landmark only faintly in the background, with a stagecoach pulled by six horses occupying the horizontal foreground. The galloping horses are literally pointed westward to the viewer's eyes, in the act of pulling the coach from right to left across the plate. The "Flying Cloud/Clipper Ship," "Railroad Little Falls, Valley of the Mohawk," and "The Erie Canal" celebrate modes of transportation and routes of American commerce, leading to economic prosperity in the nineteenth century. In that sense, these designs celebrate the notions of entrepreneurship and freedom of movement that are often stereotyped as part of the American spirit.

Another subject calculated to appeal to the American purchaser was the Thanksgiving motif, employed in the series' largest single piece, the oval serving platter "Home for Thanksgiving." That "signature" item was the first one named in the 1939 advertisements. The image, taken directly from a Currier & Ives illustration, shows a family welcoming guests to a farmhouse, in a snow-covered setting with a live turkey. The presence of snow suggests a New England locale, evoking the legend of the first Thanksgiving at Plymouth, Massachusetts. In that region, snow falls infrequently on the fourth Thursday in November, the holiday's official date established by President Lincoln in 1864. The use of snow, however, increases the scene's marketing appeal, since it could also be used for the December holiday of Christmas.

Historic America remained in production for many years, from 1939 to 1974, and new designs were added over time to this original list. Existing designs were used again, as in the motif of "The Hancock House/Boston Massachusetts," originally on a cereal bowl, which was put on a small round plate of 7-inch diameter. The image on the 7.5-inch diameter soup plate, "View of the Hudson/from West Point," was reused on a 7-inch diameter square soup bowl, and a large cup and saucer (referred to by Replacements Ltd. as a "joke cup") reused the mug's image of Central Park on the cup and the ash tray's image of the "Stage and Mail Coach/View of Mount Shasta" on the saucer. The image used for the dinner plate, "View of Boston/Massachusetts," was reproduced on the lid of a 9-inch round tureen and on the saucer of a "colossal cup and saucer set," which had the Central Park image on the cup. "Am Kai (Levee)/New Orleans," used on the "New Orleans, LA.—Pickle dish" described in the 1939 advertisement, was later used again on a gravy boat with an attached underplate. There were two sizes of jugs made with the "Monticello" image, with a 24-ounce or 32-ounce capacity (which one came first is unknown), and the image was later used on a tall coffee pot.

In other cases, historical images not previously used were placed on newly designed pieces added to the service, such as a 14-inch platter illustrated with a "View of the City of Washington D.C." from *c.* 1833.[54] A small bowl with a 5-inch diameter, known as a fruit, dessert, or "berry" bowl, was made with an image of "The Natural Bridge/Virginia."[55] These two items were listed in another advertisement seen by this author, produced by the R. H. Macy & Co. department store in New York.[56] This advertisement was a trifold single-sheet flyer, and the back page stated "*Grateful Acknowledgments to* THE NEW YORK PUBLIC LIBRARY/ THE LIBRARY OF THE METROPOLITAN MUSEUM OF ART/THE MUSEUM OF THE CITY OF NEW YORK." It is unknown whether the illustrations for *Historic America* were indeed all obtained from these three sources.

A later variation of the popular "Home for Thanksgiving" motif was not listed in any of the three advertisements mentioned above, and therefore was created at some point after their publication. It was a large buffet plate based upon another Currier & Ives image, "Frozen-Up,"[57] which shows a farmhouse in a snowy landscape (Plate 8A). The plate has significant alterations to the original image, which were not necessitated by having to adapt the scene to an odd-sized piece such as a teacup. In the Currier & Ives print, on the left, a team of oxen is hitched to a sleigh loaded with bundles in front of the house, and to the right, a man is driving another sleigh, drawn by a horse, across a small bridge in front of a water mill. The image on the plate shrinks the scene, eliminates the oxen, and moves the horse-drawn sleigh directly in front of the house. Most important, there has been an artistic addition not present in the original engraving: a live turkey in the foreground. The backstamp banner added the word "Thanksgiving" to the upper banner, putting the original title of "Frozen up" in the lower banner. The changes are clearly intended to reinforce the "Thanksgiving" appeal for American purchasers, and the large plate size was undoubtedly chosen because the American Thanksgiving meal typically includes a large number of traditional dishes served at once.

Another later design, a soup plate depicting "Michigan Avenue/Chicago," seems to have been based upon the familiarity of the site to an American consumer in the twentieth century. Upper Michigan Avenue was only widened and developed into a commercial district between 1909 and 1920, and some of its most prominent buildings were constructed from 1920 to 1929, including the Wrigley Building, Tribune Tower (built as headquarters for the *Chicago Tribune* newspaper), and the Drake Hotel.[58] Upper Michigan Avenue did not have the nickname of "The Magnificent Mile" until the term was coined by a retail developer in 1947. Since this plate is not listed in the advertisement of 1939, and the pattern remained in production until 1974, it is likely that this item was introduced later on, after Michigan Avenue had acquired its famous nickname.

There is another instance of an image being chosen for its recognition value to American purchasers of the 1930s. "The Capitol/Williamsburg Virginia" was depicted inside the bowl of a two-handled bouillon cup, and it is described in the advertisement as follows: "The first capitol, recently reconstructed by Rockefeller, was built originally in 1705. The second capitol burned down entirely in 1832." The first capitol burned in 1747, and it was replaced by another building of a completely different design. That second building was in turn used as the capitol only until 1779, when the state capital of Virginia moved to Richmond, and the building was then used for a variety of other purposes until it was destroyed by fire in 1832.[59] There was nothing at all on the site from that time until the 1930s, when John D. Rockefeller, Jr. decided that the first building would be the one reconstructed, based on its historic associations with America's "founding fathers." This means that the "Capitol/Williamsburg" does not show America of "about a hundred years ago," but rather of about two hundred years earlier. The *reconstruction* of the first capitol, however, was completed in 1934, and this was the building that was very recent and timely in the minds of the consumers of 1939.

Wedgwood Old New York

The year 1939 was notable not only for the launch of Johnson Brothers' *Historic America*, but also for a new series by Wedgwood, called *Old New York*. This series was created to commemorate two events of 1939: the 150th anniversary of George Washington's inauguration and the 1939 New York World's Fair. Because the timing of the two patterns was so close, it is impossible to know whether or not one design may have directly inspired the other. The Staffordshire potteries were very close to one another geographically, with different potteries often employing members of the same families, and it would have been hard for any pattern to have been kept a "trade secret."

An undated advertisement for "Old New York Macy-Wedgwood Service Plates" credits the same sources listed in the Macy's brochure for *Historic America*, but in a different order: the Museum of the City of New York, the Metropolitan Museum of Art, and the New York Public Library.[60] The Wedgwood company had had great success with the "Old Blue Historical" plates produced around the turn of the century, and the Macy's company had an incentive to commission an exclusive item that could be sold to visitors at the World's Fair, many of whom would be native New Yorkers. *Old New York* was therefore an extension of that previous series, but with a different sponsor: instead of being produced for sale by Jones, McDuffee & Stratton in Boston, it was produced for Macy's in New York. The pattern is described as consisting of twelve large "service" plates, each one featuring a different historical scene. A service plate is a base plate or charger, not used directly for food but intended to occupy a place setting in a decorative manner, while other, smaller plates were placed on top during the meal. Some other pieces such as demitasse cups and small plates were also produced, although they were not listed in the advertisement.

The advertisement copy begins on a strikingly jaunty note, but even so it appeals to the buyer's respect for tradition:

> Are you one of those disappointed souls who didn't have a foresighted forebear? A Great-great who bought Staffordshire Ware for a song … Sandwich glass for a drink?
>
> Now you can repair that thoughtless strain in the family and become a haloed ancestor. Behold the general edition of our famous first edition service plates (the first set is deposited as a Gift in the hospitable custody of the Museum of the City of New York). They were made in commemoration of Washington's inauguration, April 30th, 1789, and the New York World's Fair, 1939.

The engravings are just like the originals; only the backstamp is different. Views of old New York printed under the glaze. Our artist evolved the designs from prints of the years 1626 to 1861. They are authentic and beautiful. Sold in sets of one dozen. Choice of pink, blue, or mulberry.

The scenes included were: "South Street Waterfront, 1855"; "The Heere Gracht (Early 17th Century)"; "Broadway from Bowling Green, circa 1826"; "Nieuw Amsterdam, 1626"; "The Stadhuys, 1676"; "Fort George and New York City, 1740"; "Fraunces Tavern (circa 1783)"; "City Hall, 1791"; "Second City Hall, 1822"; "Castle Garden, 1825"; "Wall Street, Second Trinity Church, 1829"; and "Iron Bridge, Central Park, 1861." Each one of the names is followed by a brief and sober description of the subject, in contrast to the humorous tone of the main text. It is interesting to note that one scene, Fraunces Tavern, is admitted to be imaginary: "No authentic print of the tavern of this period exists. The print on the plate is therefore conjectural. Here Washington said farewell to his officers after the Revolution."

The backstamp of the series is also reproduced in the ad, and it features a bust of George Washington, in profile, above the words: "OLD NEW YORK/ Commemorating the inauguration of George Washington at Federal Hall New York April 30, 1789 and the New York World's Fair 1939." The "s" in Washington appears in an antiquated type style, resembling an "f," but the "s" in World's Fair is a modern "s." For one actual plate of the series seen by the author, the backstamp is different from the one in the advertisement. The "Iron Bridge, Central Park, 1861" plate has the same language, beginning with "Commemorating the inauguration …," but instead of showing the profile of Washington, it includes a small illustration of a classically inspired pavilion, under which a small group of figures presumably represents Washington being inaugurated.[61] The plate of "City Hall, 1791," however, identifies that as the place where Washington took his oath of office.

Following in the footsteps of "Old Blue Historical," Wedgwood *Old New York* was clearly intended to celebrate a romanticized version of American history. Unlike the earlier series, it had more historical depth, using images from the seventeenth, eighteenth, and nineteenth centuries instead of images that were roughly contemporary to the plates' production. At the same time, however, it had more limited geographical appeal, since only New Yorkers would recognize and care about such scenes as Canal Street ("The Heere Gracht") or the Battery ("The Stadhuys"). It also had a limited temporal appeal, and would be forever centered on the year 1939. The date when the pattern was discontinued is unknown.

Imitations and Reimaginings

In contrast to Wedgwood's *Old New York*, Johnson Brothers' *Historic America* was not linked to a specific location, historical anniversary, or contemporary event. This is very likely the reason why the pattern remained in continuous production for a very long time period, from 1939 through 1974. During this thirty-five-year span, there were many attempts to imitate its success, by manufacturers in Britain and in the United States, facilitated by the fact that there were no copyright protections for Currier & Ives prints. A few of these many imitations will be described below.

In 1941, the Homer Laughlin China Company of East Liverpool, Ohio, under the supervision of its art director Frederick Hurten Rhead, undertook the creation of a series based on paintings by the artist Joseph Boggs Beale. These illustrations were put into production in late 1942, and the pattern, originally called *Liberty*, was launched as *Historical America*.[62] The similarity between this pattern title and the one used by Johnson Brothers is unmistakable, and in this case, the Johnson Brothers pattern takes precedence. Beale (1841–1926) was a Philadelphia-born artist who trained at the Pennsylvania Academy of Fine Art, and later specialized in creating lantern slides, featuring scenes of American history.[63]

The *Historical America* pattern remained in production until the 1960s, and its subjects included "The Arrival of the Mayflower," "The First Thanksgiving," "Purchase of Manhattan Island," and "The First Steamboat, The Clermont, 1807." Some were based on patriotic stories from colonial times, such as "Franklin's Experiment" and "Betsy Ross Showing the First Flag," and another scene featured a cowboy on a galloping horse, honoring "The Pony Express."

The British pottery William Adams & Sons created a series based on Currier & Ives sometime before 1955, according to the company mark used on the backstamp.[64] The images were copied directly from prints that included some of the scenes used by Johnson Brothers, such as "Frozen Up" and "The Rocky Mountains, Emigrants Crossing the Plains," and other scenes not used by other known manufacturers, such as "A Midnight Race on the Mississippi."[65] It featured an unusually detailed backstamp, intentionally imitating the style of a nineteenth-century advertisement. Within an ornately scrolled rectangular border resembling a picture frame are the following words, with each line in a different typeface: "COLORED ENGRAVINGS FOR THE PEOPLE PUBLISHED BY N. CURRIER LITHOGRAPHER, 2 SPRUCE STREET NEW-YORK. FOR SALE HERE." Adams's choice of reproducing a real or imaginary nineteenth-century backstamp is quite interesting, as it reinforces the plates' identity as not only showing images from the past, but being themselves "authentic" relics of American history.

In the United States, many companies issued patterns inspired by Currier & Ives, including Homer Laughlin, Monarch, Taylor Smith Taylor, and Anchor Hocking, with drinking glasses made by companies such as Libbey.[66] Among the most successful of these was the *Currier & Ives* pattern by the Royal China Company of Sebring, Ohio, produced between 1950 and 1986. Its popularity was partly based on the fact that not only was it sold in department stores, but it was also given away or sold at a very low price as a premium for purchases at A&P grocery stores.[67] Even a free gift, however, would not have been continued for so many years if the pattern did not have widespread appeal to the consumers of that time period.

The Royal pattern featured a border that imitated wood grain, embellished by a scattering of scrolls and with a printed edge suggesting bands of wicker. There was a different image on each piece, and there were also multiple scenes available for the dinner plates, encouraging the buyer to collect a "complete" set. The scenes of this pattern were for the most part based on sentimental scenes of nineteenth-century rural life, such as "The Old Grist Mill," "Harvest," "The Schoolhouse in Winter," and "Maple Sugaring." It did, however, include a few specific subjects such as "The Birthplace of Washington," "Fashionable Turn-Outs in Central Park," and "The Clipper Ship Dreadnought Off Tuskar Light." Scenes that overlapped with images used in *Historic America* included "The Rocky Mountains," "Low Water in the Mississippi," and "Central Park, The Drive."

In 1965, Royal China made a pattern called *Memory Lane* that featured Currier & Ives images, but had a border that clearly imitated the oak-and-acorn border of *Historic America*. The artist of Memory Lane also decided to "improve" upon the original, by making the acorns more recognizable than the bullet-shaped versions in the Johnson Brothers pattern. The entire pattern, including the border, was less skillfully drawn, and the stippling technique is more obvious, but a buyer who had never seen a comparable example of *Historic America* would not notice the difference of quality. This visual appropriation acknowledges the historical precedent of the Johnson Brothers pattern, which itself had appropriated that same border from Ralph Stevenson's pattern of the 1840s. The pattern name of *Memory Lane* refers to the expression "taking a walk down memory lane," but in this case, there would be no one alive in 1965 with actual memories of these nineteenth-century scenes. Instead, it refers to a kind of shared cultural memory, based on a nostalgic ideal.

In the late 1950s, Wedgwood decided to reissue its own series of "Old New York," but with some contemporary updates. This relaunch was produced for the New York department store of B. Altman & Co., a company founded around 1865 by Benjamin Altman. The flagship store at 361 Fifth Avenue opened in 1906, and for decades it was considered one of the most prestigious department stores in the city, until its closure in 1989.[68]

This new series was called *Scenes of Old New York*, and individual plates had designs such as "City Hall Park" and "Harris' Point with Gracie Mansion" (the home of the mayor of New York City). In the backstamp, references to Washington's inauguration and the New York World's Fair were eliminated, and only the series title and scene are mentioned, followed by the phrase "Designed especially for B. Altman & Co." Two circular maker's marks appear, one stating "WEDGWOOD of Etruria & Barlaston, Made in England," and the other with a striped diamond and two crossed engraver's tools, surrounded by the words "Engraved by the Wedgwood Studios." The former mark was introduced in 1940 and was very commonly used on Wedgwood made for the US market[69]; the latter mark is unusual, but was used on a bowl made for the Bailey, Banks & Biddle store in Philadelphia in 1959.[70]

The new *Scenes of Old New York* was less expensive to make than the earlier *Old New York*, since it appears to have only included large plates, cups, saucers, a teapot, and a coffeepot. The series used a ribbed molded form called "Edme," which according to the Wedgwood company was introduced in 1908. The "Edme" shape was most popular from the 1940s through the 1960s, although a new version was advertised in 2017.[71] Only the plates of *Scenes of Old New York* featured decoration, and those images were much less detailed than in the original *Old New York*. It is not known how long this pattern was in production.

Another British manufacturer that drew inspiration from Wedgwood *Old Blue Historical* and Johnson Brothers *Historic America* was the Enoch Wedgwood Company of Tunstall, named for one of its original founders, a distant cousin of the more famous Josiah. In 1976, Enoch Wedgwood created *Liberty Blue* in honor of the Bicentennial of the American Revolution. It was commissioned as a promotional item by the Benjamin Franklin Federal Savings and Loan Association, based in Portland, Oregon, which was celebrating its own 50th anniversary.[72] After a brief sales run of only one year, it became a purchase premium for Grand Union and other grocery stores for five more years.[73]

Advertisements from this period demonstrate that the series' value was believed to derive not only from its visual re-enactment of American history, but also from its creation by English pottery makers. In one such advertisement, the Grand Union grocery exaggerates its own role in the series' creation, among other forms of hyperbole:

> **Fourteen historic American scenes on a superb set of English dinnerware.**
> In early 1973, Grand Union commissioned a special set of dinnerware. It was to be the most extensive and exciting collection of blue-printed Staffordshire glazed ironstone since 1860. It was to be authentic in every detail … in every step of its manufacture. And it could only be made by the potters of Staffordshire.
> **Liberty Blue Dinnerware**
> The results exceeded even our expectations. From the original copper etchings, created exclusively for this collection … to the absolutely authentic Wild Rose border … (created circa 1784) … here is dinnerware that recreates an age and an art thought long gone.
>
> It took the potters of Staffordshire to create Liberty Blue. It took a tradition of craftsmanship, passed from generation to generation, to duplicate each step in the original process. And it took Grand Union to bring you Liberty Blue in all its glory and loveliness … to use, to treasure, to pass on to future generations … See the complete selection.[74]

In this advertisement, there is no direct reference to this tableware as being related to the American Revolution Bicentennial. Instead, it is presented as an heirloom to be acquired for future generations, which is an ambitious destiny for a grocery store promotion priced at fifty-eight cents per place setting, with a five-dollar purchase.

Liberty Blue was only in production for about five years. *Historic America* had already been phased out by Johnson Brothers in 1974, perhaps as sales dropped because of so many competing American patterns. And by the end of 1976, Americans had become weary of the endless celebration of the Bicentennial, and the marketing hype that had overtaken it. The once-innovative notion of using tableware to present a visual history of America had finally run its course.

Chapter 4

COMMEMORATIVES AND SOUVENIRS

Long before the Second World War, British potteries had already understood the potential American market for items that promoted a particular destination or event. It was profitable to create a limited run of items, often restricted to plates or cups and saucers suitable for display, and these patterns were often sponsored by individual merchants or organizations, which would advertise the items in exchange for being credited on the backstamp. The audience would also be targeted to a specific, interested group of customers, thus making the anticipated sales more predictable. A relatively small number of items could be produced, and if these sold out, more could be produced without incurring new costs for creating the transfer designs.

There was also a more subtle component to these souvenirs, which one might consider cultural or even psychological. The American sponsors and British suppliers were banking on what they expected their customers to consider worthy of commemoration, and this was reflected in the nature of the design. If the souvenir was based on the pleasure of having visited a specific location while on vacation, the plate might represent an accurate image of that, as it would be seen under ideal conditions. If it was based on an experience involving many sights, such as visiting a fair, the plate might have multiple views of memorable "highlights." If it was based on the buyer's emotional attachment to an entity such as a university or a church, it might have images that not only represent the architecture accurately, but also evoke the high status that made that institution a source of pride. This chapter will discuss several types of commemorative wares and will consider how each one sought to tap into the psychology of why one purchases a souvenir.[1]

American World's Fairs

In 1851, London presented "The Great Exhibition of the Works of Industry of All Nations," housed in the newly constructed Crystal Palace in Hyde Park. In imitation of this, New York built a Crystal Palace of its own in 1853, intended to host exhibitions of the industries of all nations. The New York building was poorly constructed, however, and it was an unpopular destination, destroyed by fire only four years later.[2] It is interesting to note that the *Historic America* series featured a

"New York Crystal Palace" cake plate, even though that site was very short-lived and was probably unknown to most Americans in the twentieth century. Since the London Crystal Palace was very famous, however, having been relocated to a suburb in 1854 and still extant until 1936, this may have been a case in which the British designers overestimated the importance of that particular American site.

The earliest successful American "World's Fair" was the Centennial Exhibition in Philadelphia in 1876, celebrating 100 years since the beginning of the American Revolution. Souvenirs were created for sale at the fair, but according to Frank Stefano, Jr., "additional items were produced and sold throughout the United States. You did not have to go to the exhibition to obtain some souvenir of it."[3] An example of a Philadelphia Centennial souvenir was a small creamware pitcher (7½ inches high) produced by Wedgwood. This had not only a transfer image of the fair's main building, with the words "July 4th 1876" underneath, but an unusual molded band around the pitcher's neck, resembling a Roman fasces on which the encircling bands featured abbreviations for the thirteen original colonies (e.g., "VERM[ONT]," "MASS[ACHUSETTS]").[4]

The next major American World's Fair was the World's Columbian Exposition in Chicago in 1893. Wedgwood produced items for this fair also, as did many other companies. This was followed by the Pan American Exposition in Buffalo, New York, in 1901, at which Thomas Edison introduced his wireless telegraph.

A vast number of commemorative items were designed for the 1904 World's Fair in St. Louis, originally known as the Louisiana Purchase Exposition in honor of the centennial of Thomas Jefferson's purchase of territory from France in 1803. (The fair was supposed to have been in the centennial year of 1903, but as in the case of the 1893 Columbian Exposition, the organizers missed that date by one year.) One such item was a plate made by an unknown pottery in Staffordshire, commissioned by the Rowland & Marsellus Company of New York City, a firm of importers and wholesalers, and sold by the Barr & Company department store.[5] It features the bust of Thomas Jefferson in the center, and the border is filled with oval vignettes of principal buildings of the fair, clockwise from upper left as follows: "Palace of Machinery," "Palace of Varied Industries," "Palace of Art," "Palace of Liberal Arts," "Palace of Electricity," and "Cascade Gardens." An inscription on the bottom of the plate reads "The World's Fair St. Louis Mo. U.S.A." This plate was most likely intended for display.

Another plate imported by Rowland & Marsellus and sold by Barr & Co., of approximately the same vintage and of similar design, is entitled a "Souvenir of St. Louis Mo" (Plate 8B). This plate was also commissioned by Barr's department store. Its central image is City Hall, which was completed in 1898, and the images from upper left are identified on the backstamp as follows: "Eads Bridge," "Old Court House," "Music Pavillion [in] Forest Park," "Washington University" (University Hall, now known as Brookings Hall, completed in 1902), "Union Station" (completed in 1894), and the "Columbus Statue [in] Tower Grove Park."

There was other commemorative ware designed for food service, as well as for display. Johnson Brothers created a pattern for the 1933 Chicago World's Fair, "A Century of Progress," which celebrated the centennial of the city's incorporation as the Town of Chicago. This pattern, named *A Century of Progress 1833–1933*, was commissioned by the Marshall Field & Company department store in Chicago, and was made in blue, pink, and lavender (mulberry).

The medium-sized plate (8¾ inches in diameter) presents a scene of "The First Fort Dearborn," founded in 1803 (Plate 8C). One might think that a better way to commemorate a "century of progress" would be to depict a new building, but instead, this plate reminds us of the historical origins of the city. The view of Fort Dearborn was not the same one later used for the egg cup of *Historic America*, which is actually of one guard tower. This scene is a bird's eye view of the entire fort, with several buildings enclosed by two rows of wooden palisade fencing and two guard towers, surrounded by grassy fields and rolling hills. Including the fort in this series is a way of extending the city's historical roots back another thirty years, and thus legitimizing Chicago as being equal to the older cities of the east, like Boston and New York. The plate was produced with careful attention to detail; the scalloped edge has fine ridges accented by the same color ink as was used for the transfer scene, and the center image, an artist's engraving of high quality, is bordered by a halo of ridges and a molded pattern of daisies and leaves.

The teacup and saucer illustrate how these souvenir items were intended to appeal to cultural values. The saucer depicts the Art Institute of Chicago, with a throng of people approaching it; these Chicagoans are obviously well educated and sophisticated enough to value their art museum as a major treasure. This "beaux-arts"-style building had been constructed for the Columbian Exposition of 1893, and it subsequently became the home of the Art Institute, a school founded several decades earlier. The fair of 1933 was the fortieth anniversary of the Art Institute's move to its new home, and the same image was used on a small berry bowl.

The teacup is embossed on the exterior with a different flower pattern, perhaps cherry blossoms, and the image is found on the inside of the cup, on the side where it would be seen by a right-handed drinker. The picture portrays a statue of Abraham Lincoln by the sculptor Augustus St. Gaudens, which stands in Chicago's Lincoln Park. Underneath the pedestal is an inscription, "The Gift of Eli Bates." Eli Bates was a prosperous lumber merchant in Chicago, who died in 1881. In his will, he left funds for two sculptures, the Standing Lincoln and the Fountain in Lincoln Park; both were executed by St. Gaudens and installed in 1887. The selection of these images for the souvenir series is a statement about the importance of art in defining the city's stature as world class. It also defines the visitor and purchaser of these items as someone who wants to bring representations of high art into their home. The backstamp of the teacup makes particular mention of the artist, "St. Gaudens' Statue of Lincoln," enhancing the value of the artwork by identifying its much-admired American creator.

Other items created for *A Century of Progress 1833–1933* included a small plate featuring the "Chicago Court House," an oval platter with the "Field Museum," and an oval bowl with "The Forks—Joining Two Rivers."[6] The Cook County Courthouse depicted was built in 1853, but was destroyed in the Great Fire of 1871. It may have been included because it was the location where the body of Abraham Lincoln had lain in state after his assassination in 1865. The Field Museum also dated from

1893, as the "Columbian Museum of Chicago," but it was renamed as the Field in honor of a prominent donor, and became the Field Museum of Natural History in 1905. A new building was constructed in Grant Park to house the museum's growing collections, and this was opened in 1921. That made the Field Museum the most recent building to be commemorated in the Johnson Brothers series, and this choice of subject celebrated the civic promotion of science and education, an attribute of any city with a claim to greatness.

There was also a practical aspect to this pattern, not commonly found in other tableware patterns. All of the pieces are small in size and relatively light in weight, restricting its use to serving afternoon tea or dessert. The advantage, however, was that a traveler could more easily pack the items in a suitcase when returning home.

Universities

Perhaps among the earliest plates honoring a university was also a commemoration of a royal visit there. In 1884, the Prince of Wales (the future King Edward VII) visited the University of Toronto, and a plate was issued by the Staffordshire firm of Wallis Gimson & Co. of Fenton.[7] This was a 9.5-inch-wide octagonal plate inspired by the aesthetic movement, with a spray of irises, cherry blossoms, and a butterfly, and two off-center vignettes, featuring an oval portrait of the prince, framed by a delicate laurel wreath, and a rectangular view of the university building, framed with sticks of "bamboo." The image of the university is more than twice as large and more centrally positioned than the image of the prince, suggesting that the primary buyers of this plate would be citizens of Toronto and/or students, faculty, and alumni of the university. Most of the surface of the plate is given over to the floral spray against a blank background, so that the first impression from a distance is of the flowers, with the vignettes indistinguishable except upon closer inspection. This, combined with the plate's unusual shape, would have made it attractive for display.

In the period between the two world wars, Wedgwood was the dominant supplier of commemorative wares for academic institutions. This practice had begun before the first war, but was greatly expanded afterward, in part because so many American universities were "coming of age," celebrating centennials. A university commemorative pattern typically featured a series of plates, depicting prominent buildings that would be recognizable to former students, and they followed the visual model of the "Old Blue Historical" series, with deep borders ornamented with flowers, leaves, and fruits. Borders could also be white, embossed with molded floral motifs. They were most often issued in blue and white, but could also be offered in a variety of colors such as pink and green, to suit the decorating scheme of the household. Such plates were evidently profitable, because an internet search on any given day may identify dozens of patterns, made for large public universities (such as Universities of Michigan, Pennsylvania, and Iowa), large private universities (such as Yale, Cornell, and Brown), and small private colleges (such as Williams, Earlham, and Denison).

American's oldest institution of higher learning was Harvard College, originally founded in 1636 in Cambridge, Massachusetts. It has been described as "undoubtedly the leader in the ceramic pictorial field, having had four separate series of twelve items each produced through Jones, McDuffee & Stratton Co. and Wedgwood."[8] Based on internet searches, the dates of those series appear to be 1927, 1932, 1936, and 1941, and they were issued in red, a color suggestive of the school's official color of crimson, and also in Staffordshire blue. The 1927 series had twelve dinner plates, each one with a different scene; the 1936 series was issued in honor of Harvard's Tercentenary, and included not only twelve plates but also teacups with saucers, demitasse cups with saucers, a punch bowl, and an ashtray.

The buildings featured on the Harvard commemorative items are exemplary of other university plates during this time. They show a mixture of current and former buildings, such as "The First Gore Hall 1838," which was Harvard's first library building, demolished in 1913 for the construction of Widener Library. Gore Hall, as depicted on a demitasse cup, had an elegant neo-Gothic design strongly resembling that of a northern European church of the late medieval period. This image therefore bestows even more prestige upon the university, even though its subject no longer existed. Among the more modern buildings depicted was "Memorial Church 1932," but that was deliberately designed in an eighteenth-century colonial style, to look at home in the Boston of Paul Revere or the Williamsburg of Thomas Jefferson. One interesting feature of the demitasse cups is that the image is intended to be seen by the person drinking from the cup (if holding it in the right hand). What is seen by other diners is a logo with the dates "1636 1936" inside a cloud of calligraphic swirls. The image could have been repeated on both sides, but the decision to put the dates on the "outside" could be seen as a form of one-upmanship; many people could have tableware with university images, but only Harvardians could boast of their *alma mater* having existed for 300 years.

The plates commissioned by Duke University in Durham, North Carolina, have archival documentation that suggests the manner in which many such patterns came into being. The following summary is provided by the Rubinstein Library:

> In 1937, planning for the 1938–1939 centennial celebration of Duke University was well underway. The Alumni Association contracted with the famed English firm of Josiah Wedgwood & Sons to produce a set of commemorative china plates. The first edition, three hundred sets of twelve plates, bore the signature of William Preston Few, Duke's President, on the back. A second unsigned edition was also produced. The plates are no longer made.[9]

There is also a promotional brochure for "The Duke University Plates," distributed by the university Alumni Association in 1936.[10] The language of this brochure appeals to the buyer on several levels, first as a knowledgeable collector of antiques: at the top left of the cover page, it proclaims "*Like OLD STAFFORDSHIRE*." Underneath the image of a plate and the title of "*The* DUKE UNIVERSITY PLATES," it states "Fashioned from hand engraved copper plates on Queensware by Josiah Wedgwood and Sons Ltd., Etruria, Staffs., England." The reader, presumably someone worldly and well traveled, is expected to recognize the British abbreviation of "Staffordshire."

Inside the brochure, the text continues:

> The purpose of the Alumni Association in sponsoring this series of Duke University plates is: To commemorate the charm of Duke University in a beautiful and useful manner; to commemorate the Centennial of the origin of Trinity College; and to create a fund to be administered by the Alumni Association for scholarships or fellowships. [...] The design for the embossed white border, which is the same on all the plates, has been inspired by natural forms characteristic of the two campuses. Its basis is a scroll motif of conventionalized oak leaves and acorns combined with branches of pine. Medallions of dogwood blossoms set off by contrast the simplified seal of the University, which surmounts the plate.
>
> Precedent for the fluted shoulder, effecting the transition between the center scene and border, is found in the cream-colored ware created for Queen Charlotte in 1762, which won for Josiah Wedgwood his appointment as Potter to the Queen. The plates will be dinner-service size, measuring about ten and one-half inches. The official choice of the committee as to the color of the center scenes is Duke blue; however, the plates may be ordered in rose-pink, green, or mulberry.

This text is notable for the manner in which it attempts to present the plates as being created specifically for this university. Although oaks, pines, and dogwoods can be found in many regions of the United States, not just North Carolina, the writer describes them as "natural forms characteristic of the two campuses." The preferred color is not "Staffordshire blue," but "Duke blue." The text also plays up the prestige of Wedgwood as a purveyor to the British royal family, even though the above-mentioned Queen Charlotte was the wife of King George III, who was usually portrayed as the "villain" in the teaching of American history.

Royal Milestones

The writer of the 1936 brochure for the Duke University plates made the assumption that the anticipated purchasers were fans of the British monarchy. This was an entirely safe assumption to make, because members of that royal family had become celebrities as famous as any Hollywood movie star. There were countless ceramic souvenirs, including but certainly not limited to tableware, of every British royal wedding and coronation celebrated in the twentieth century. No attempt will be made here to catalogue the variety of such wares produced, but one example will be analyzed, as being representative of how tableware design attempted to rise to the occasion of a royal coronation.

In 1953, the coronation of Queen Elizabeth II on June 2 was commemorated by Johnson Brothers with a plate, appropriately printed on the "Old English" series already in production. This series featured a round shape with a molded gadroon border. The base of the design was a pattern called *Chadwell*, which had a beige body color and a border design of gold-colored transfer scrollwork, accented by two dark blue bands.[11] This body shape was also used for the *Queens Bouquet* pattern of 1939, mentioned in Chapter 2, as well as many other patterns from the 1940s and 1950s,[12] but its previous use for a royal commemorative made it a logical choice for this subject. The backstamp carries the "Old English" name and angular crown motif, with the words "Johnson Bros Made in England" confirming that it was intended for export. In addition, it has the capital letters "E II R" surmounted by a crown, the initials of "Elizabeth II Regina," and an oval Union Jack motif framed by the words "Official Design/British Pottery Manufacturers Federation."

In place of the center floral bouquet, this plate has a profile portrait of the young queen, framed by an oval motto of *Honi soit qui mal y pense*, the motto of the Order of the Garter, topped by a crown and the words "CORONATION June 2nd 1953." To the left is a flag bearing the Royal Standard, in use since 1837, and to the right is a British flag. There are gold flowers and leaves beneath the flags and the central oval, as well as a banner that reads "H.M. QUEEN ELIZABETH II." The flags are designed with careful attention to detail; the Royal Standard on the left is correctly seen from the "reverse" side, with reverse images of the English arms, three gold lions on a red field, and glimpses of the Scottish arms, a red lion on a gold field, and the Irish arms, a gold harp on a blue field. The profile of the queen is also done by hand, with realistic representation of her features on a natural skin tone, and a flattering view of her hair in a complicated braid with golden highlights.

The use of color and gold accents makes the plate suitable for display, but the central decoration is small in size and does not cover the entire center of the plate. The effect is therefore one of tasteful modesty, which was appropriate at a moment when the British economy had not yet recovered from the effects of the war. The naturalistic image of the monarch as a youthful and attractive woman, rather than merely a profile, reflects the queen's status as a popular celebrity of her day, and not just a symbol of national unity. It is interesting to note that the portrait depicts her hair as light brown with blonde highlights, although she was famously a dark brunette. Perhaps the artist meant to suggest that even though America might have its Grace Kelly, Britain had its Queen Elizabeth.

This exact same motif appeared on a large number of commemorative items that were sold by different companies. While Johnson Brothers had its mark on the plate described above, and used a plate of its own design from the *Chadwell* pattern, the same motif has been found on plates, mugs, and other items stamped by companies including A.J. Wilkinson Ltd., Furnivals, Wood, and others.

Cities and Civic Pride

Another important category of commemorative was the souvenir of a place, not an event. This was typically commissioned by the site itself, for sale to visiting tourists, or by a commercial enterprise such as a department store. Once again, the number of such souvenirs was enormous, with examples produced by nearly every pottery in existence, and the practice is continued today. The least expensive items to produce would involve taking a preexisting plate or cup and adding a stamp, such as "Souvenir of […]" in a convenient spot. In cases where an item was specially designed for that site, however, it may be seen to reflect ideas about why the site was worthy of being so honored, and what the sponsor wanted the purchaser to remember about the visit.

In one example, Johnson Brothers received a commission from the Marshall Field & Company department store for a plate of the city of Chicago, Illinois (Plate 8D). This plate is an imaginative composite image of several scenes that in real life could not be viewed from a single vantage point. Instead, it compresses together a variety of landmarks representing the city's history, arts, and commerce. The plate dates from the 1950s,[13] but all of the landmarks depicted are from earlier time periods. The two oldest elements are seen in the foreground: on the left, one of the bronze lions that have greeted visitors at the entrance to the Art Institute of Chicago since 1893, and on the right, an ornamental clock that symbolized the Marshall Field flagship store since 1897.

The backstamp has an outline of the clock, containing the words "Chicago Plate made exclusively for Marshall Field & Company by Johnson Bros England" (Figure 4.1). Underneath, there is a schematic outline of the landmarks visible on the front. Five of those landmarks have printed names, and the others have numbers, which correspond to two columns of names on the right and left. The named features are "Art Institute Lion," "Michigan Randolph Colonnade," "Soldiers Field" (actually called Soldier Field), "Chicago Natural History Museum" (actually called the Field Museum of Natural History), and "Marshall Field and Co Clock."

The numbered landmarks are listed as follows: "1-Nation's Rail Center, 2-Industry, 3-Conrad Hilton Hotel, 4-Michigan Avenue Bridge, 5-Board of Trade, 6-Sheraton Hotel, 7-310 So. Michigan Bldg., 8-Buckingham Fountain, 9-Wrigley Building, 10-Grant Park and Shell, 11-Daily News Building, 12-Old Water Tower, 13-Civic Opera Building, 14-LaSalle Wacker Bldg, 15-Pure Oil Building." It is interesting to note that the first two items are not the names of specific landmarks, but rather they are generalized references to the city's economic prosperity. Items 3 and 6 are the names of prestigious hotels: the Hilton Hotel, which opened in 1927, and the Sheraton Hotel, which opened in 1921. The latter was depicted in the plate with considerable artistic license, being shown as far taller than its actual size.

There is considerable prominence given to landmarks of culture, such as the Art Institute (fine arts museum), the natural history museum, the band shell, and the civic opera building. Equal attention, however, is given to skyscrapers, including the corporate headquarters of the Wrigley Chewing Gum company, built in 1920–24; 310 S. Michigan Avenue (now known as the Metropolitan Tower), built in 1923–24; the Pure Oil Building, built in 1926; and the Board of Trade and LaSalle Wacker Buildings, both built in 1930. Modern skyscrapers were not tourist "sights" in the usual sense of buildings of historic significance or architectural beauty, but they were symbolic of modernity and progress. The landmarks of "Nation's Rail

4. Commemoratives and Souvenirs

Figure 4.1 Chicago backstamp, Johnson Brothers, *c.* 1951.

Center" and "Industry" are of even less visual interest; the "Rail Center" shows four rail cars winding around a curve of silos, and "Industry" is represented by a group of smokestacks, complete with trails of dark smoke fortunately blowing toward the left, away from the city. The inclusion of these two items, however, was clearly a means of proclaiming the city's economic power. These items were also intentionally listed at the top of a list of twenty, making "Nation's" the very first word in that list. Finally, the planes flying overhead metaphorically represent the city itself, modern and moving forward into the future.

Another commemorative design was created in honor of New York City, commissioned by the Empire State Building for sale on its premises, and created by Johnson Brothers in 1959 (Plate 9A). Not surprisingly, the plate featured the "Empire State Building" in its center, with surrounding vignettes of "The Public Library" in the top center, followed clockwise around the plate by "George Washington Bridge," "Rockefeller Center," "United Nations Building," "Washington

Square," "The Coliseum," "The Statue of Liberty," and "Central Park." The most recent of these landmarks was the Coliseum, a convention center that opened in 1956, but no longer exists, having been demolished in 2000.

The backstamp highlighted the Empire State Building with a smaller version of its image on the front, surrounded by various interesting bits of information about it. Starting at the top one finds "TV Antenna," with "1472 Feet Above Street" below it on the left and "Used by All 7 New York Stations" on the right. Moving clockwise, the snippets read: "Visibility 80 Miles, 86th Floor Observatory 1,050 Feet, 74 Elevators, 16,000 People Work in Building, 1,860 Steps Street Floor to 102nd Floor, 60,000 Tons of Steel, 1,500,000 Visitors Annually, 6,500 Windows, 102nd Floor Observatory 1,250 Feet." The reference to each observatory is positioned approximately next to where it was located in the building.

The Empire State commemorative also had a demitasse cup and saucer, featuring a very clever design (Figure 4.2). The saucer depicts the cityscape, similar to what is on the front of the plate but not identical to it, as it includes more detail. The words "Empire State Building" appear unobtrusively in the bottom center border. The building is shown rising up from that label, and extending to the midpoint of the upper border. The demitasse cup has straight vertical sides, and has another cityscape view running continuously around the bottom of the cup, with the Empire State Building placed in the center (as seen by the drinker). Another image of the building is on the far side of the cup, where it would be seen by someone

Figure 4.2 Empire State Building demitasse cup and saucer, Johnson Brothers, c. 1959.

Plate 1A Sugar bowl, Johnson Brothers late Pankhurst, *c.* 1883.

Plate 1B Pattern 131486 sauceboat, Johnson Brothers, *c.* 1889.

Plate 1C Wisconsin plate, William Brownfield & Sons, *c.* 1871–91.

Plate 1D Aesthetic-style butter pat, Minton (?), *c.* 1860.

Plate 2A Rolland covered vegetable bowl, Johnson Brothers, *c.* 1890.

Plate 2B Vienna pitcher, Johnson Brothers, *c.* 1898.

Plate 2C Savannah sugar bowl, Johnson Brothers, *c.* 1890.

Plate 2D Florida plate, Johnson Brothers, *c.* 1890.

Plate 3A Oxford covered vegetable bowl, Johnson Brothers, *c.* 1890.

Plate 3B Watteau plate, unknown Staffordshire maker, *c.* 1910.

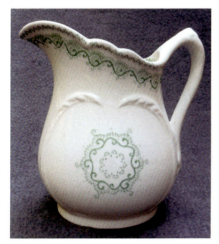

Plate 3C Franklin milk jug, Johnson Brothers, *c.* 1909.

Plate 3D Davenport sauceboat, Johnson Brothers; Grosvenor spoon, Oneida Ltd., *c.* 1921.

Plate 4A Madison plate, Johnson Brothers, *c.* 1920.

Plate 4B Petroushka plate, Johnson Brothers, *c.* 1925.

Plate 4C Untitled art deco-style plate, Johnson Brothers, *c.* 1925.

Plate 4D Greydawn bowl, Johnson Brothers, *c.* 1929.

Plate 5A Old Britain Castles "Canterbury Castle," Johnson Brothers, *c.* 1930.

Plate 5B Old Britain Castles "Cambridge," Johnson Brothers, *c.* 1930.

Plate 5C Old Britain Castles, "Haddon Hall," Johnson Brothers, *c.* 1930.

Plate 5D Old Britain Castles, "Blarney Castle," Johnson Brothers, *c.* 1930.

Plate 6A English Chippendale, Johnson Brothers, *c.* 1937.

Plate 6B Margaret Rose, Johnson Brothers, *c.* 1939.

Plate 6C Devonshire, Johnson Brothers, *c.* 1940.

Plate 6D Old Blue Historical, "The White House," Wedgwood, *c.* 1900.

Plate 7A Historic America, "The Capitol," Johnson Brothers, *c.* 1938.

Plate 7B Historic America, "St. Louis Missouri," Johnson Brothers, *c.* 1939.

Plate 7C Historic America, "Barnum's Museum New York," Johnson Brothers, *c.* 1938.

Plate 7D Historic America, "Covered Wagons and the Rocky Mountains," Johnson Brothers, *c.* 1938.

Plate 8A Historic America, "Frozen Up," Johnson Brothers, *c.* 1938.

Plate 8B Souvenir plate of St. Louis, *c.* 1904.

Plate 8C A Century of Progress, "First Fort Dearborn," Johnson Brothers, *c.* 1933.

Plate 8D Chicago, Johnson Brothers, *c.* 1951.

Plate 9A Empire State Building, Johnson Brothers, *c.* 1959.

Plate 9B Williamsburg Restoration, "The Governor's Palace," Wedgwood, *c.* 1950.

Plate 9C Piranesi Series, "Basilica of St. Mary Major," Wedgwood, *c.* 1950.

Plate 9D Pennsylvania German Folklore Society, Johnson Brothers, *c.* 1960.

Plate 10A The Oregon Plate, Johnson Brothers, *c.* 1957.

Plate 10B Mount Rushmore, Johnson Brothers, *c.* 1965.

Plate 10C Mount Vernon, Johnson Brothers, *c.* 1954.

Plate 10D Floating Leaves, Johnson Brothers, *c.* 1955.

Plate 11A Day in June, Johnson Brothers, *c.* 1954.

Plate 11B Old Flower Prints, "Rose," Johnson Brothers, *c.* 1949.

Plate 11C Game Birds, "Partridge," Johnson Brothers, *c.* 1951.

Plate 11D Fish, Johnson Brothers, *c.* 1955.

Plate 12A Olde English Countryside, Johnson Brothers, *c.* 1957.

Plate 12B Barnyard King, Johnson Brothers, *c.* 1950.

Plate 12C His Majesty, Johnson Brothers, *c.* 1959, detail.

Plate 12D Merry Christmas, Johnson Brothers, *c.* 1959.

Plate 13A The Old Mill, Johnson Brothers, *c.* 1951.

Plate 13B The Friendly Village, "Village Street," Johnson Brothers, *c.* 1953.

Plate 13C Apple Harvest, Johnson Brothers, *c.* 1954.

Plate 13D Dream Town, Johnson Brothers, *c.* 1956.

Plate 14A The Road Home, Johnson Brothers, *c.* 1954.

Plate 14B Coaching Scenes, "The Coach Office," Johnson Brothers, *c.* 1963.

Plate 14C Jamestown, Johnson Brothers, *c.* 1965.

Plate 14D Fruit Sampler, Johnson Brothers, *c.* 1965.

Plate 15A Alice in Wonderland, Johnson Brothers, *c.* 1974.

Plate 15B Neighbors, "Band Concert," Johnson Brothers, *c.* 1974.

Plate 15C Petite Fleur, Johnson Brothers for Laura Ashley, *c.* 1976.

Plate 15D Heritage Hall, "Georgian Town House," Johnson Brothers for Sears Roebuck & Co., *c.* 1977.

Plate 16A Heritage Hall, "Spanish Hacienda," Johnson Brothers for Sears Roebuck & Co., *c.* 1977.

Plate 16B Eternal Beau, Johnson Brothers, *c.* 1981.

Plate 16C Summerfields, Johnson Brothers, *c.* 1985.

Plate 16D Historic America II, "The Capitol," Johnson Brothers, *c.* 2002.

across the table. When the cup sits in the saucer, however, the building appears to begin on the saucer and end at the top of the cup.

The artwork for the *Empire State Building* was created by Bill Norbury, who wrote: "I remember working on souvenir plates, all were perfect in presentation. 'The Empire State Building' was one of them; the first order was for seven thousand plates. Each one was a work of artistic beauty finer than anything ever produced before. Others followed in quick succession" (p. 17). In another passage of his memoir, he wrote: "I took on a task, a souvenir plate it was to be, depicting 'The Empire State Building' U.S.A. 'New York'. Very, very prestigious with good expectancy with regard to sales figures. The finished ceramic plate was brilliant from a perfect engraving, it made me feel really proud" (p. 60).

Norbury's pride was well justified. The images have depth and perspective, with subtle shading that suggests morning sunlight. The composition is well balanced, with the geometric shapes of buildings and bridges anchoring the upper and lower left and right, and the two "human" figures of the Statue of Liberty and Rockefeller Center's Atlas in center left and right. The Empire State Building in the center is majestic, towering above the surrounding cityscape and shown against a backdrop of white clouds. The transfer design is inked in a gray-brown, not black, which gives the images a lighter quality, and touches of paint were added by hand, a light turquoise blue for the sky and a pale yellow-green for trees. And in keeping with company policy, the colorist who probably spent less than a minute adding those highlights was entitled to paint her initial on the back, but the name or initials of Norbury, the engraver, could not be placed anywhere on the plate, front or back.

Another plate commemorating New York City was commissioned by "Enco National Inc., New York, N.Y.," and produced after 1966. Enco National was a company that imported souvenirs for sale in the United States, and they are known to have been active from the 1950s to the early 1970s. This plate was actually made in England, according to its backstamp: "Fine Staffordshire Ware" (in Gothic lettering), "Made in England/Underglaze-Detergent Proof." The backstamp also has a banner on which is written "Fabulous New York City of Wonders," and a "scroll" upon which the following lengthy passage is printed:

> First viewed by Verrazano in 1524. Discovered by Dutch Henry Hudson in 1609. Settled in 1613. Manhattan Island purchased from Indians for $24.00 by Peter Minuit in 1626. Peacefully occupied by British in 1664. Recovered by G. Washington in 1784 during Revolutionary War. Greater New York founded Jan. 1st, 1898 which includes the counties of New York (Manhattan), Bronx, Kings (Brooklyn), Queens, Richmond (Staten Island).

None of this extended history lesson is reflected by the scenes chosen for the front side, even though one might expect to see at least the Verrazano-Narrows Bridge, which was the world's longest single-span bridge when it opened in 1962. Instead, the scenes include the Statue of Liberty in the center, flanked on the left by the Empire State Building and on the right by the tower of Rockefeller

Center, even though of course those three were nowhere near each other. There are four vignettes: "Lincoln Center" at top center; two jet planes (somewhat disconcertingly pointed on a collision course) with the phrases "John F. Kennedy International Airport" and "La Guardia Airport" at center right; "United Nations" at center left; and "Times Square" at bottom center. Like the Johnson Brothers plate of New York, this souvenir highlights landmarks of modernism, such as the United Nations building, and the arts, represented by Lincoln Center. Like the *Chicago* plate, it features modern jet planes and the fact that the city has not one but two major airports. It also, however, includes a view of Times Square, lined with movie houses, and the scene contains such mundane details as parked cars and even a trash bin.

The building on the right is a movie house, and it has "THE BIBLE" in bold letters, with the director's name of John Huston above. This identifies the date of this plate, because a movie was released in 1966 entitled *The Bible: In the Beginning*. It was directed by John Huston, produced by Dino De Laurentiis, and featured a number of prominent actors including Richard Harris, Franco Nero, Ava Gardner, George C. Scott, and Peter O'Toole. What this plate tells us is that for the tourist of 1966, visiting a big, state-of-the-art movie house in New York City was an exciting prospect. The traveler might arrive on a plane, though perhaps not a jumbo jet; he might see the United Nations building, though he was unlikely to enter it; and he might walk past Lincoln Center, but was unlikely to buy an expensive ticket for a performance there. Those vignettes recognize the city's importance as a center for culture, international politics, and transportation. But the fourth vignette represents the real-life experience of the traveler, who was very likely to visit Times Square and see a movie.

At the height of the genre, in the 1950s and 1960s, the travel souvenir plate was intended to provide a visual record of the tourist's visit, but it also sought to reinforce positive cultural values, by providing a little history lesson or giving prominence to certain things that the visitor/viewer was supposed to admire. In an artistic sense, it also created an idealized experience of perfect weather and vantage point, even to the point of a heightened reality that could not actually be seen, but that spoke to the imagination.

Wedgwood's Historic Sites

The Wedgwood company, which had relaunched the popularity of commemorative plates with its "Old Blue Historical" series at the beginning of the twentieth century, continued to produce many such plates on commission after the Second World War. Wedgwood enjoyed the highest level of prestige among American patrons, and it was selected by Williamsburg Restoration Inc. to produce a series of plates with scenes of Williamsburg, Virginia.

Colonial Williamsburg was the first capital of Virginia, but by the early twentieth century most of its buildings had become dilapidated or significantly altered. Thanks to the persuasive efforts of the Rev. William A. R. Goodwin, the rector of Bruton Parish Church, the wealthy industrialist John D. Rockefeller, Jr., funded the restoration of the entire city, beginning in 1927.[14] The first restored buildings were opened to the public in 1932, as a "living history museum," and additional buildings were added over the next several decades.[15] In 1942, a US federal trademark was registered for Williamsburg Restoration Inc., to appear on souvenirs of Williamsburg, including reproductions of eighteenth-century items such as brass trivets.

The first edition of Williamsburg plates made by Wedgwood included scenes of specific buildings, based on drawings by the American artist Samuel Chamberlain (1895–1975).[16] The plates had a cream-colored, scalloped body with very delicate transfer imagery, including sprays of flowers and two coats of arms on the border. The arms at the top, with a small image of the Capitol building, bear Rockefeller's motto given to the 1920's Williamsburg Restoration project, "that the future may learn from the past." The arms at the bottom represent a 1757 insignia for the then-British colony of Virginia.[17] The round image in the plate's center is surrounded by a "frame," including multiple rococo-style scrolls.

One example depicts *The Governor's Palace*, seen at a distance, with a foreground including large trees at left and right (Plate 9B). In the center lower foreground, two cows are facing away from the viewer, looking at the mansion from a thicket of shrubs and flowers. The scene also includes small figures of two women and two horse-drawn carriages pulled up in a circular drive.

The plate's backstamp (Figure 4.3) bears the impressed date of 1949, and two circular stamps, stating "Wedgwood of Etruria & Barlaston/Made in England" and "Williamsburg Restoration First Edition 1950." Two rococo scrolls decorate the top and bottom center of the plate's reverse side. The backstamp also includes both a written credit to the artist, Samuel Chamberlain, and a reproduction of his signature, confirming the plate's authenticity as an original work of art.

This plate communicates a subtle elegance, through the delicacy of the transfer decoration, and the bucolic elements contribute to a sense of tranquillity. The display of such plates would mark the owner as a person of good taste and refinement. The stately architectural beauty of the palace, in the Georgian style, also establishes the American colonial capital as a worthy rival of contemporary cities in England. Although the plate could easily have reproduced the building alone, reflecting how it could be seen to the tourist of 1950, it preferred to depict an idealized view of how the building might have appeared in the days of the country's founding fathers. The purchasers of these plates were not seeking connections to their own personal history or visitor experience. Instead, they were commemorating the history of their country, and a time period that most likely preceded the immigration of their family to American shores.

After the first edition was produced, Wedgwood issued later versions of Williamsburg plates, and although they had similar subjects, the presentations were very different. A series with an impressed date of 1956 used other illustrations by unnamed artists, and had a border crowded with other small

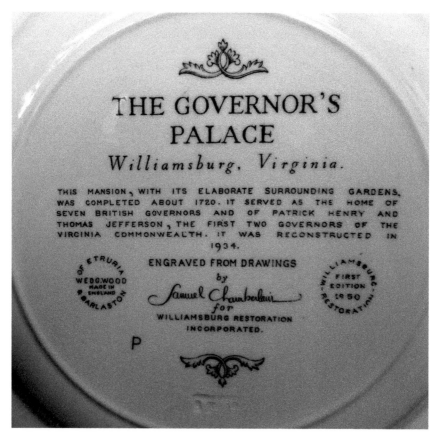

Figure 4.3 Williamsburg Restoration backstamp, Wedgwood, c. 1950.

scenes. The backstamp has different text from the first edition, and one of the circular stamps says "Williamsburg Commemorative Ware." These plates lack the artistic quality and rococo-inspired elegance of the first series, and are designed to resemble the type of tourist souvenirs that might be found anywhere. One might speculate that as the number of visitors to Williamsburg increased, the Wedgwood company decided that the potential purchaser was more likely to want to display the plate alongside trophies of other vacation sites. The company may therefore have aimed toward a lower common denominator in regard to design.

Another Wedgwood series of around 1950 was commissioned by the Archdiocese of Boston, as a fund-raiser for charitable support of poor children. These plates were produced on the cream-colored "Edme" body, but the images reproduced engravings of *Views of Rome* by the eighteenth-century artist Giovanni Battista Piranesi. The connection between poor children in Boston and the city of Rome might be very tenuous, but it appears that the intended purchasers were devout Catholics, who would be interested in views of historic Catholic churches near the site of the Vatican, the home of the Pope.

One example of this series features the church of "Sta Maria Maggiore," as the name appears in script under the image in the plate's center (Plate 9C). The backstamp reads as follows:

BASILICA OF ST. MARY MAJOR
The largest and most famous church in the world dedicated to Mary the Mother of God—this dedication commemorates the great Council of Ephesus (431) at which Mary's prerogatives were emphasized. After many architectural additions and changes it is the principal feature of the Esquiline Hill, one of the "Seven Hills" of ancient times.

These Piranesi Plates were Selected by and are Distributed under the Auspices of The Most Reverend *Richard J Cushing* Archbishop of Boston. A Substantial Portion of the Proceeds will Benefit Physically and Mentally Deficient Children of the Poor Irrespective of Race, Creed or Color.

The name of Archbishop Cushing (who later became a cardinal) is his actual signature, and two circular marks state "Wedgwood of Etruria & Barlaston/Made in England" and "Jones McDuffee & Stratton Co/Boston."

The use of Cushing's signature and the extensive discussion of the church's significance to Catholicism identify the target audience as Boston Catholics. At the same time, however, the fact that these views were originally composed by a famous Italian artist would make them even more desirable, and potentially interesting to a wider group of purchasers. These plates were truly "works of art" for display in the home, and the price of a plate would be far less than the price of an actual Piranesi engraving.

Churches and Private Societies

Frank Stefano, Jr., noted that decorated ceramics were widely used as a fundraising vehicle by many American churches and other local institutions, and although most of these were produced by US manufacturers, some were imported from other countries, including England and Germany.[18] A few examples of this type of commemorative will be discussed here.

In light of the major commitment made by Wedgwood to the commemorative market, it is not surprising to find that they produced many plates for churches. One example is a plate produced for the modern Gothic cathedral of St. John the Divine in New York City. "The Font in the Baptistry of the Cathedral Church of St. John the Divine, New York" is printed on the backstamp of a cream-colored plate, with stamps reading "Wedgwood of Etruria & Barlaston/Made in England" and "Engraved by the Wedgwood Studios," the latter mark encircling a square (suggesting a copper plate) and two crossed engraving tools. An impression mark dates the plate to 1957. The image on the front of the plate appears to be based on a photograph; the stone-carved figures of the font are shown in outline, leaving white space to suggest the white color of the stone, and the gothic-inspired stone walls are depicted as shadowed, created by very fine stippling. Breaks in the stippling pattern create a suggestion of light from stained glass windows, falling on the left-hand wall and on the base of the font. The overall mood is contemplative, as befits the subject, and there is a highly artistic quality to this image, which makes it more conducive for display than for use in a table setting.

Although Wedgwood enjoyed the highest prestige, the greatest volume of commemoratives featuring churches was produced by American companies. Mark Gonzalez studied many examples from the 1950s and 1960s, and found that smaller companies would purchase "blanks," unprinted in the center, from large manufacturers. They would then add their own image and sell the item. This was far less costly than producing the ceramic base. According to Gonzalez:

> During the 1950s there were several small decorating companies which would purchase dinner plate blanks and put special treatments with churches. These blanks include Harker Pottery's Gadroon, Steubenville's Adam Antique and Mt. Clemen's Vogue. Most of the blanks came from the Homer Laughlin shapes Theme Eggshell, Georgian Eggshell, Rhythm and Nautilus. The Theme Eggshell church plates are by far the most common with Georgian next and Rhythm and Nautilus being a little harder to find.
>
> The churches featured are from all over the United States with no region being more common than any other. Church plates have been found from almost every one of the 48 contiguous states with several different denominations such as Presbyterian, Methodist, Church of Christ, Nazarene, Episcopal, Lutheran, Baptist and Catholic.
>
> The treatments themselves are very simple: a single color and sometimes with gold or silver trim. The most common colors are black, brown, red, blue and purple. The name of the church and its location are also featured on the front of the plate, and many times a brief history of the church is given on the reverse.
>
> More often than not, a church plate will have the added marking of the decorator. The vast majority of church plate treatments were made by World Wide Art Studios of Covington, Tennessee. […] While most of the plates by these companies featured churches, some show other buildings such as courthouses, college buildings, hospitals and schools.[19]

An example of a commemorative plate made for a private society is one by Johnson Brothers, commissioned by the Pennsylvania German Folklore Society of Ontario, Canada (Plate 9D). The society was established in 1951 "to research and record the contribution of the early settler families from Pennsylvania who began arriving in Upper Canada beginning in 1786. Many of these families were of the Mennonite faith."[20] This plate was a compilation of scenes based on photographs by David Hunsberger, and is dated to 1960.[21] David L. Hunsberger (1928–2005) was the son of a Mennonite preacher, and he took many photographs of his home village of St. Jacobs; the collection now resides in the University of Waterloo, Ontario.[22] This plate features six scenes, clockwise from upper right: "First Log Cabin near Jordan/Built about 1777/Preserved by W.E. Troup"; "Covered Bridge over Grand River at West Montrose Ontario"; "Balls Mill at Balls Falls near Jordan/Built about 1800"; "First Mennonite Burying Ground 1798/Located at Vineland Ontario"; "Pioneer Memorial Tower near Doon Ontario"; and in the plate's center, "Original Covered Wagon Visiting Niagara Falls 1952/Made the Trip to York County Ontario 1797."

In keeping with the society's historical focus, the scenes depict landmarks of the late eighteenth century that were still standing when Hunsberger took his photographs in the 1950s, as well as a covered wagon, which was not only still used by some Mennonites at that time, but also was an icon of pioneer life. Even the more recent Pioneer Memorial, which was built in 1926, was constructed of local fieldstone. The imagery therefore has a timeless quality, as though very little changed from 1777 to 1952. The scenes overlap unobtrusively, tied together by an imagined foreground of a rocky hillside with three tall trees. Two of the trees balance the plate's composition, at far left and far right.

The plate's backstamp reads as follows:

Made for the Pennsylvania German Folklore Society of Ontario/A Genuine Hand Engraving from Photographs by David Hunsberger/Made in England by Johnson Bros/All Decoration Under the Glaze Detergent & Acid Resisting Colour/Pat Pend

America the Beautiful

The postwar period in America saw an increase in disposable family income and a reduction in working hours that often included paid vacation time. This, in conjunction with advancements in automotive technology and the expansion of the national highway system, meant that more families could enjoy taking road trips. And these vacations often led to a destination catering to the tourist trade, complete with gift shops selling a variety of items that could serve as mementos of the trip. Such items included nearly anything on which the name of the site could be inscribed, and items that were lightweight and cheap, such as salt and pepper shaker sets, were in high demand, but there was also a demand for attractive plates worthy of display. British potteries were only too happy to meet this demand.

From the late 1950s through the 1960s, Johnson Brothers produced a number of high-quality commemorative plates for American states, promoting their history and tourism. An early example is "The Oregon Plate," dated 1957 (Plate 10A).[23] It was commissioned by the Meier & Frank Co. of Portland, which according to the backstamp was "Established in Oregon in 1857." Although only a few people would care about the store's centennial, many more would be interested in the 1959 centennial anniversary of Oregon becoming a state, and the plate was undoubtedly used for special sales promotions during that year.

The Meier & Frank Co. was originally a dry goods business that evolved into a major department store. Its 1932 flagship store covered an entire city block and was followed by large new stores in Salem, opened in 1955, and Portland's Lloyd Center in 1960.[24] The scenes selected for representation begin with a nineteenth-century view of the "Oregon City" settlement, in the center. As was the case with the images of *Historic America*, this one is based on a real painting of the time period, made by Henry James Warre around 1845.[25]

The border contains small vignettes, with the seal of the "State of Oregon" at the plate's top center, and moving clockwise: the State Capitol building in Salem; a portrait of William Clark in an oval frame; the Bonneville Dam (completed in 1938); the state fish, a Chinook salmon; a side view of the side-wheeler "Lot Whitcomb" (built in 1850 and considered the first steamboat built in Oregon); the state bird, a Western meadowlark; a view of Crater Lake; a portrait of Meriwether Lewis in an oval frame; a view of a group of "Celilo Indians" fishing near a waterfall; and a beaver sitting on a log. The backstamp provides a history lesson that spans the period from 1778 to 1859, with "Data by Oregon Historical Society."

These images combine history (the early settlement, Lewis and Clark of the famed expedition to explore the territory purchased by Thomas Jefferson) with modern progress (Bonneville Dam). It also promotes, however, the magnificent scenery of Crater Lake as it would be seen by the contemporary tourist. The group of three Celilo Indian fishermen is also wearing modern American dress; one man has a buttoned shirt with a pointed collar and rolled-up sleeves, and a fedora-style hat. The tourist, who is presumably white and middle class, might therefore hope to catch a glimpse of "real" Indians during a visit to what might be Klondike Falls.

Another Johnson Brothers plate dating from 1963 is "The Arizona Plate." This is similar in design to the Oregon plate, including a backstamp with a history lesson based on "Data by Arizona Library & Archives." It was commissioned by Diamond's, a major department store in Phoenix. The images on this plate include a center image of Arizona's most famous tourist attraction: the Grand Canyon. In the top border there is the Great Seal of the State of Arizona, with the date of 1912 marking when it became a state. Moving clockwise, one sees a large ball of cotton (a major element of the state's agriculture); a view of a building labeled "State Capital Phoenix" (which should perhaps have more properly been written as "Capitol"); Roosevelt Dam (the Theodore Roosevelt Dam northeast of Phoenix, completed in 1911); a scene of "Arizona Cattle"; a Kaibab squirrel, a species with tasseled ears and a white tail, found only in Grand Canyon National Park and Kaibab National Forest; the state flag; the state bird, a cactus wren; a scene labeled "Navajo Indians," which features an Indian woman wearing traditional dress and weaving a rug on a loom; a view of a sparsely populated town labeled "Jerome"; a view of the San Xavier Mission; and a desert scene with "Saguaro Cactus," embellished with a giant cactus flower seen head-on. The town of Jerome requires explanation: it was a copper mining town that at its peak in the 1920s had 15,000 inhabitants. The mines closed in 1953, however, and it became a virtual ghost town with as few as fifty residents. After this plate was made, in the late 1960s, it became a hangout for hippies, and the town was named a National Historic Landmark in 1976. It eventually became known as a colony for writers and artists. Since all of that occurred after 1963, however, we can only assume that Jerome was a tourist site at the time, as a copper mining boomtown that had become an abandoned relic.

In contrast to the Oregon plate, every image on the Arizona plate was something that could be seen by the contemporary tourist. This reinforces the plate's function as a travel souvenir. The central image of the Grand Canyon also features an unusual use of color. Both the Oregon and the Arizona plate have touches of color; Oregon has patches of blue, applied to areas of water or sky, a few green touches on grass, trees, and leaves, and four red splashes on buildings in the early settlement scene. Arizona, however, has blue, green, and yellow, not necessarily in places that make sense; for example, a patch of yellow is on the Navajo rug and another is on the grass next to the cattle, and there is a green stripe highlighting one of the rows of cotton. What is most striking is that the Grand Canyon scene has rocks colored with bright yellow, sky blue, and deep purple. This unlikely combination of colors may have been intended as a way of suggesting the famous "Painted Desert," an Arizona attraction with rock formations that have horizontal striations that appear as different colors, even though the Painted Desert is not the same location as the Grand Canyon.

The plate examined still carries a price sticker, which indicates that it was sold in a Fred Harvey establishment for a price of two dollars. In 1875, Fred Harvey opened his first café, and he would eventually found a chain of American hotels and restaurants catering to travelers. The Harvey Hotels were typically near railway stations, and the company also provided catering for train dining cars. In 1905, the Fred Harvey Company opened the El Tovar Hotel on the south rim of the Grand Canyon,[26] and in 1908, the company opened the Fray Marcos Hotel in the Santa Fe Railroad Depot in Williams, Arizona, which was the railway stopping point for visitors to the Grand Canyon.[27] Harvey Hotels typically had gift shops, and the Fray Marcos, like some other Harvey establishments, had a so-called "Indian Room" where souvenirs were sold.[28] This plate might have been sold at either one of these locations, or even at other tourist stops along the famous Route 66 to the American Southwest.

The last "state" plate to be described, dating from 1965, is not identified on the backstamp merely with the state's name. It proudly proclaims itself to be "The Great State of California." The images on the front are labeled, starting with "Yosemite Falls" in the center, and then clockwise from upper right: "Golden Gate" (Bridge), "Lake Tahoe," "Hollywood Bowl," "Giant Redwoods," "Sutter's Fort," "Fisherman's Wharf," "San Diego Mission," "Monterey," "Disneyland," and "Capitol—Sacramento." At the top center of the plate's border, there is "The Great Seal of the State of California," framed by a "Calif Poppy" on the left and a branch of "Citrus Fruits" on the right. At the bottom center of the border, there is the state flag, featuring a star and a grizzly bear.

Unlike the plates previously described, the explanations on the backstamp correspond to the eleven images represented on the front. Of these images, only three refer to the state's history: "Sutter's Fort—commemorates the discovery of gold in 1848," "San Diego Mission—oldest mission founded in 1769," and "Sacramento—state capital since 1854." The third item is correctly labeled on the front as "Capitol," since it represents the capitol building completed in 1874, which was modeled after the U.S. Capitol in Washington, DC. All other scenes are contemporary, and the backstamp description emphasizes their appeal as tourist sites: "Yosemite Park—famous for its giant Sequoias, mountains, high waterfalls"; "Golden Gate Bridge—nearly a mile long with towers 746 feet high"; "Lake Tahoe—6225 feet above sea level, famed for its beauty and resorts"; "Hollywood Bowl—world's largest natural amphitheatre"; "Giant Redwoods—over 200 feet tall and thousands of years old"; "Fisherman's Wharf—San Francisco—famous for seafood restaurants"; "Monterey—oft painted scenic beauty is world renowned"; "Disneyland—'The Happiest Place on Earth.'" The first image in the above list is actually of "Yosemite Falls," and is labeled as such on the front of the plate.

Several of these images are not just scenic views, but they also contain images of people enjoying the visitor experience. Fisherman's Wharf has several people standing on the pier; Lake Tahoe has a man in a boat; Disneyland has a line (but not a crowd) of people crossing the moat on the approach to Sleeping Beauty's Castle; and the giant redwood tree has a car driving through an opening hollowed out at its base, a "drive-through" gimmick that predated the era of environmental consciousness. These images are explicit about promoting California as a visitor's paradise, including the state's history, government buildings, concert arenas, vacation resorts, wildlife, dining destinations, and wonders both natural and man-made. It is particularly telling that instead of giving a description of Disneyland, the world-famous theme park that opened in 1955, it offers the park's own advertising slogan, "The Happiest Place on Earth."

In Bill Norbury's memoir, he speaks about Johnson Brothers commemorative plates with a special kind of pride. As the head engraver, he worked personally on these plates, and the format of multiple vignettes enabled him to showcase his artistic skill in a variety of genres, including the two of which he was most proud, landscape and portraiture.[29] One particular example stood out in his memory as being one of the most difficult, and also most successful: a plate of Mount Rushmore, South Dakota. The plate has one single image covering its gently curved surface: the faces of the four American presidents in a landscape of craggy rocks, gravel, and trees (Plate 10B). The backstamp description is as follows:

> Mt. Rushmore National Memorial/Shrine of Democracy/Black Hills, South Dakota Picturesque Mt. Rushmore National Memorial, where the busts of four great American leaders, George Washington, Thomas Jefferson, Theodore Roosevelt, and Abraham Lincoln, are sculptured in heroic proportions, is the largest monument ever carved. It was executed by the late Gutzon Borglum who carved these busts 450 feet high in a granite mountain 6000 feet high. Imported exclusively for the Burgess Company, Keystone, South Dakota, from Johnson Bros. England.

The words "shrine, picturesque, great, heroic, largest" leave no doubt about this being more than merely a tourist site; it is a monument to American patriotism and national pride.

Bill Norbury recalled this plate with an unusual degree of enthusiasm and humor:

> The pottery engravers [put] three dimensions into their scenic work, producing skills, as painters-in-oils did, line work used to its ultimate possibility. [...] "Mount Rushmore," so well-done and so commemorative. No pottery print had ever reached this level in quality and one guess who produced it? Yours Truly the still humble Me That's Who! [...] "Mount Rushmore" was up to the required Presidential Standards, at least as a souvenir and certainly as engraving standards are assessed by us. (pp. 17, 89)

Although a photograph was certainly used in creating this image, Norbury was able to reproduce the recognizable likenesses of the four presidents, a very difficult task for any artist and almost impossible for the vast majority of pottery engravers. As a single image, with the four faces illuminated by sunlight against the shaded landscape, it has a painterly quality, and no printed words interfere with the reception of this image as a work of art.

Another commemorative commission that Norbury recalled with particular satisfaction was from the Hudson's Bay Company in Canada. This firm was originally established in 1670 as a fur trading company and eventually became a major chain of department stores throughout Canada, the first of which opened in Calgary in 1913.[30] At least two Hudson's Bay Company plates by Johnson Brothers are known to exist, and although their exact date is unknown, they most likely predate 1965, when the company adopted a shorted version of its name and marketed itself as "The Bay." Norbury recalls the circumstances of this commission in considerable detail:

> I had a call from Bill Hall. He had the difficult task of being the halfway man, in that he was a glory hunter representing the company as head salesperson and representing the customer's interests to our directors. "Bill," he said, "I have a problem. The Hudson Bay Company require a presentation plate, all I have at the moment are some photographs and postcards from them, what can we do?" Intrigued and somewhat amused, I said, "Let me have what you have plus their logo, and come up to the studio and we'll discuss what you think the Canadians would like!" How to get one plate to encompass the spirit of Canada, items such as:
>
> 1. The Klondyke Lakes including Louise, Saskatchewan, Ontario.
> 2. Wolfe, and the Battle of Quebec.
> 3. Native Indians, Cree, Navahoe [sic], Shoshonee, Apache, Etc.—the list is endless.
> 4. Totem Poles, Wigwams, Buffalo Hide Shields, Bows and Arrows.
> 5. Buffalo Hunts, Tribal Dances, Costumes, Etc.
> 6. Mounted Police, Moose, Bear.

All of the above to go on one 8 inch plate. (You mean one service per subject, don't you, Bill!). (p. 77)

The two known plates have the backstamp of "Made Expressly for the Hudson's Bay Company, incorporated 2nd May 1670/by Johnson Bros of England, all decoration under the glaze permanent & acid resisting colors/a genuine hand engraving." One of the plates has an additional title of "Souvenir of Vancouver Canada." Both plates have an image of a winged bird totem in the upper center, and the bottom features a beaver sitting on a garland of maple leaves. Both plates also include the busts of an Indian chief with full feather headdress, at lower left, and a member of the Royal Canadian Mounted Police, nicknamed a Mountie, at lower right.

The Vancouver plate has four scenes identified by name, with "Lions Gate Bridge" at top center, "Stanley Park, Vancouver" at right, "The Lions [a mountain range] 6500 Ft. Vancouver" at bottom center, and a view of the city "Towards North Shore Mountains" at left. The "Stanley Park" view gives a noticeable nod to tourism, because the most prominent element of the scene is a divided six-lane highway, with cars and a bus (which may be filled with sightseers).

The other plate, which lacks a title, appears to highlight the beauties of the province of Alberta. The scene at the top is the "Banff Springs Hotel," founded in 1888 and redesigned in 1928. This site, located at a natural hot spring, is a famous vacation and honeymoon destination. At right is the "Bow River Valley"; the bottom center is "Mount Rundle"; and at left is "Lake Louise."

The most unusual feature of both plates is that instead of having a central image and vignettes around the border, each plate is a composite of four scenes that blend into one another through the device of overlapping trees, mountains, and clouds. Bill Norbury recalls how he came up with this composition:

> How to arrange them on a plate with enough impact in each case, maybe in framed sections, "No," not good, cold, impersonal. A border in sections, Cloud sections, Maple Leaves, I made a start, jumping in at the deep end drawing a circle plate size. I started on a rough idea, avoiding a dated look but giving a regal flavour instead, using free thought which I have found to be important. I produced what was enough to make people take a second look, or even a third! Interesting enough to make them examine the detail and to visualise in the mind's eye what it would appear like if it was engraved. I took it to show Bill Hall who did the same to his Directors, who could only approve quite categorically the option I had derived. (p. 78)

More than thirty years later, Norbury remembered his work with deep feeling:

> Only in this medium was it possible. Looking rather searchingly over the engraving some time later I felt that I had visited these places, I had met the Indian chiefs, had the pow-wow […] To put it mildly it was simply bloody Marvelous! The maple leaves were captivating. I could see the glory of the "BIG SKY." The wide expanse of Canada. […] Not with pride, I prefer the word

humility, and a revelation of how beautiful it is, filled my mind. If I could spend the remainder of my career just doing this, I would feel that my life had been more than worthwhile. (p. 78)

Norbury's passion for his art helps to explain why many of the Johnson Brothers commemorative plates are so visually compelling. He did not treat this work casually, and neither did the people who admired and ultimately purchased them. At its most basic level, the travel souvenir was intended to provide a visual record of the tourist's visit, but it also sought to reinforce positive cultural values. This was done not only by giving prominence to those things that the viewer was supposed to admire and providing a history lesson on the backstamp. In addition, it created an artistically heightened reality that could not actually be seen, but could be imagined. At its best, the plate could transcend the actual travel experience, and become an emotionally and spiritually uplifting celebration of national pride.

Chapter 5

PROSPERITY AND NOSTALGIA

The Allied victory at the end of the Second World War brought peace to Britain, but economic recovery would lag far behind. Many cities had suffered extensive bombing damage, and those communities struggled with rebuilding their economies. Restrictions on British potteries' sale of decorated ware to the domestic market were still in place, and as late as May 1952, such sales were no longer prohibited, but had to come out of a manufacturer's "home market quota."[1] As described by Patrick J. Maguire:

> Constantly increasing production for exports was crucial. As in the immediate aftermath of the First World War this was, largely, not a problem of discovering markets but one of supplying them. [...] In the case of British exports this was further facilitated by the initial absence of German and Japanese competition which would begin to re-emerge at the end of the decade. The problem from the perspective of the government was, therefore, twofold: it needed to increase the supply of goods for export and to direct, as far as possible, those goods to the most financially strategic markets.[2]

Unlike Britain, America had not suffered damage to its physical infrastructure, and the end of the war brought a rapid upsurge of economic prosperity. The irony was that Britons who were still living in stringent circumstances were creating images of this prosperity for the benefit of the Americans. As resources previously dedicated to the war effort were redirected to the private economy, and manufacturers once more had sufficient manpower, many American women who had been employed during the war were dismissed, so as not to take a "man's job." The American social climate of the late 1940s and 1950s emphasized women's domestic role as wives and mothers, and many households now had sufficient resources to rely on one income, that is, the husband's. While financial prosperity was not universally enjoyed, and the idealized "nuclear" family was perhaps more of a social construct than a reality, many tableware designs in the 1950s celebrated a nostalgic ideal of the "simple" life of past times.

Tried and True

At first, Staffordshire pottery factories being reconverted from wartime production to peacetime manufacture of goods for export did not have time to invest in the creation of new designs. Instead, they relied upon patterns that had proven to be good sellers in the past. A clear example of this is Johnson Brothers *Winchester*, a pattern of 1947 that copied the same transfer design and color scheme as the *Dorchester* pattern of 1931, and the same round body shape with gadroon edge as *Devonshire* of 1940. Even the pattern name of *Winchester* differed only from *Dorchester* by the first syllable.

Many Johnson Brothers patterns of the early 1950s are virtually indistinguishable stylistically from patterns of the late 1930s and 1940s, reflecting the fact that American decorative taste in the postwar period continued to be shaped by conservative and traditional values. *Bird of Paradise* of 1951 used the same body shape as *Pomona* of 1941, plain round with a gadroon edge, and the pattern was very similar, featuring a basket of fruit surrounded by sprays of flowers, but with the addition of two Asiatic pheasants. The backstamp of *Bird of Paradise* even featured a version of the Johnson Brothers angular crown used widely in the 1920s and 1930s, although it was in an unusual position, to the right of the words that state that "all decoration under the glaze permanent & acid resisting colors." The use of language asserting the plate's durability in an automatic dishwasher and the American spelling of "colors" identify the target consumer.

Rose Chintz was a pattern with a name similar to the earlier *Chintz*, but its design patent number is 160783, dating it to 1950. The name also refers to a textile originally from India, but manufactured in English mills from the eighteenth century onward, used for household furnishings such as draperies and upholstery and usually featuring traditional floral motifs. A similar pattern by Spode, *Rosebud Chintz*, was introduced in 1954, and it has a more compact, dense design, but both patterns clearly seek to appeal to feminine taste in household decoration.

One feature that distinguished many postwar patterns was the use of the new body shape that had been used for *Sheraton*. This form had no gadroon edge, and had not only a gently scalloped edge but also slight curved ridges impressed into the rim.[3] The shape gave these patterns a decorative but modern feel, and it lent itself equally well to patterns with floral motifs and pictorial scenes, even if they were asymmetrically arranged on the plate.

Another original feature of postwar patterns was a backstamp specially designed to be unique to each pattern. In some cases, the backstamp was decorated with versions of motifs featured on the front side; *Bird of Paradise* (1951) has a flying bird that appears to be exactly the same as another bird on the front, and may have been made with the same transfer pattern. *Rose Chintz* has a smaller version of a motif on the front, a single rose stem with several leaves, but the engraver has added a few small cross-hatch marks, to suggest the texture of woven cloth. That cross-hatching is not present in the actual pattern on the front. In other cases, the motif was inspired by the front image but is noticeably different. *Harvest Time* (1951) has assorted fruits and leaves on the front, but in the backstamp image, fruit is overflowing a footed bowl that is not featured in the pattern. The pattern name is also rendered in a hand-lettered style that may have been designed solely for that backstamp, which was the case for *Bird of Paradise*'s fanciful cursive lettering.

In 1950, Johnson Brothers introduced a new pattern called *Haddon Hall*, based on different images from the view previously engraved by Harry Fennell for *Old Britain Castles*. In order to understand why that particular subject was chosen, it is important to know that the house's history included a romantic anecdote about the owner's daughter, Dorothy Vernon, who eloped with a suitor named John Manning. The dinner plate had three scenes: a center view of the courtyard inside the walled gate, with the house seen in the left background; an upper left view of deer in the wooded grounds; and an upper right view of what was known as "Dorothy Vernon's Postern," with a small female figure at the foot of the staircase by which she presumably escaped. In order to keep the production cost low, all of the various pieces in the set featured one of those three views, with the perspective view of the house appearing most frequently. The body shape of *Haddon Hall* was the same one used for *Old Britain Castles*,[4] and the backstamp reinforced the association with Dorothy, showing a larger version of the female figure appearing in the staircase view on the front.

The story of Dorothy Vernon was the subject of several American fictionalizations, including a 1902 historical novel, a 1903 play, which ran for forty performances on Broadway, and a 1924 film starring the matinee idol Mary Pickford,[5] but it is questionable whether any American women in the 1950s would still be familiar with the anecdote or its fictional versions from decades earlier. The *Haddon Hall* pattern would remain in production, however, from 1950 to 1974, demonstrating that buyers still liked the pretty scenes on the front, even if the figure of the woman on the backstamp had little or no meaning for them.

There were other patterns that had been introduced many years earlier, which were still being produced in their original form. When Queen Elizabeth II visited the Johnson Brothers factory in Hanley, on November 2, 1955, she was photographed in the showroom, wearing a fashionable mink coat.[6] Although there are several patterns visible on the shelves, which are from the 1950s, including *Barnyard King* (1950) and *Harvest Fruit* (1955), the queen is looking at a tureen of the *Willow* pattern, which dated back to the 1920s. It was the custom to offer the monarch a free service of her choice, even though such gift services were never actually used by the monarch, but were normally put in storage or passed along to members of the royal household staff. Her selection was *Hampton*, a pattern with a simple round shape and a gadroon edge that Finegan dated to c. 1930.[7] *Hampton* had a delicate motif of beige scrolls and potted floral sprays, and featured an unusual turquoise-colored background on the flat rim. The flowers also had hand-painted coral-colored dots, and the edge was painted in gold. The queen's selection was perhaps influenced by the popularity of American Navajo silver and turquoise jewelry in the mid-1950s. Her choice may also have been influenced by the fact that this traditional, dignified pattern bore the name of Hampton, associated with the royal palace of Hampton Court. That palace was the residence of King Henry VIII, whose daughter was Elizabeth's famous predecessor as queen.

The Sincerest Form of Flattery

Postwar pottery design at Johnson Brothers gradually expanded to include some modest risk-taking, in the form of new patterns that retained some similarity to what had proven to be successful in the past. As usual, the American market was directly targeted, as can be seen with the pattern *Mount Vernon*, introduced in 1954. This was a "WindsorWare" pattern, and it had a novel shape of eight scallops with a raised molded line around the edge of the rim.[8] Unlike other "Windsor" patterns with English associations, *Mount Vernon* was a serial pattern with images of George Washington's historic plantation home in Virginia. Like *Old Britain Castles* and *Historic America*, it featured several scenes, in order to entice the customer to collect all pieces in the set. This was done more timidly than before, however, as there were fewer scenes, and these relatively few scenes were used on multiple pieces. "View Over the Potomac—East Front" was the scene for the dinner plate (Plate 10C) and oversized saucer; "Main Entrance—West Front" was used on the salad plate, the 14-inch oval platter, and rimmed soup bowl; "Garden House" was on the bread and butter plate, regular saucer, lugged cereal bowl, and fruit/dessert bowl; and "Ancient Entrance" was on the creamer, sugar bowl, oval vegetable bowl, and relish/gravy underplate.

The image on the 12-inch and 16-inch oval platters has an identifiable source image, an American print based on a drawing by George Isham Parkyns and published *c.* 1855.[9] The grounds seen in the print have been significantly altered on the platter, but the Johnson Brothers engraver reproduced very specific human figures in the foreground, including a man and woman on foot, at the left center of the image; a man on horseback in the center, tipping his hat; and another man on horseback to the right.

It is interesting to note that the *Mount Vernon* body shape is somewhat reminiscent of the scalloped shape used by Wedgwood for its *Williamsburg* series in 1950 (Plate 9B). Most of the Staffordshire potteries were aware of what the others were doing, and eager to jump on whatever bandwagon was successful at the time. The *Williamsburg* pattern has six scallops with a raised molded edge, and instead of a continuous band of decoration around the rim, there is a separate decal placed in the center of each scallop. *Mount Vernon* has eight scallops, with a raised molded line just inside the plate's edge, and the border pattern is separated into eight sections. Both patterns feature scenes with architectural elements seen at a distance, framed by trees and including human figures. While the Wedgwood pattern is noticeably superior in terms of the fine detail of the engraving by artist Samuel Chamberlain, the Johnson Brothers pattern could be considered a creditable effort. And the Johnson Brothers pattern had the advantage of including a range of pieces, making it appeal to a purchaser in need of a functional service, rather than a collector of souvenirs looking only for plates to display.

Johnson Brothers was also not above seeking to capitalize on the success of another company's product in more blatant fashion. The American company Homer Laughlin of West Virginia had had great success with its colorful *Fiesta* pattern, introduced in 1936. Designed by Frederick Hurten Rhead, this pattern had a ribbed body and a plain round shape, but its distinguishing feature was the use of a very brightly colored glaze. Its heavy weight made it suitable for everyday use, and the solid colors lent cheer to any table. When the series was first launched, services were available in red, yellow, cobalt, light green, and ivory; turquoise was added in 1937. In 1951, cobalt, light green, and ivory were discontinued, and rose, chartreuse, gray, and dark green were introduced.[10] In 1955, Johnson Brothers advertised a pattern called *Carnival*, solid-colored plain ware in six "exquisite colours": jasmine yellow, dove gray, lime chartreuse, peacock blue, peony maroon, and forest green.[11]

There was another case in which a Johnson Brothers pattern was clearly intended to copy a successful American product line. In 1940, the California-based company of Gladding, McBean & Co. introduced a hand-painted and embossed earthenware pattern called *Franciscan Apple*, followed by *Desert Rose* in 1941.[12] The motifs of apples or flowers and twigs were in a rustic style, as if painted with a thick brush, and the colors were bright and cheerful. These patterns were extremely successful, since they appealed to Americans looking to break from the tradition of a formal table, and wanting to emulate the casual, outdoor living of sunny California.

The *Franciscan* patterns sparked numerous imitations, including a pattern by the European company Villeroy and Boch, originally founded in Luxembourg in the eighteenth century. Their pattern was named *The Delicious Apple*, and it was introduced after 1946. Clearly inspired by *Franciscan Apple*, the Villeroy and Boch pattern had a yellowish-colored base, embossed decoration, and hand painting. Its major variation was the addition of a motif in the plate's center, a large apple on a leafy stem. There were two versions of this pattern, one with red apples and another with fruit that had the unlikely color combination of half red, half yellow.

In 1955, Johnson Brothers introduced its own California-style pattern, *Peachbloom*. This pattern did not have a motif in the center of the plate, but its leaves and stems were very similar to the border motifs used by both the *Franciscan Apple* and *The Delicious Apple* patterns, and it had a virtually identical body in terms of color and weight. This was the known only pattern produced by the company in this high-relief hand-painted style, and it had a very short production life of only five years (1955–60). It is possible that the pattern was shut down after protest by Gladding, McBean & Co., although there was an ironic ending to the story. In 1979, over a decade after Wedgwood had acquired Johnson Brothers, it acquired Franciscan Ware. In 1984, the Franciscan factory in Glendale, California, was closed, and the production of Franciscan patterns was moved to the Johnson Brothers factory in England.[13]

Introducing Louise Flather

Louise Gemley Wall Little Flather (1905–90) was the artist of numerous patterns produced by Johnson Brothers in the 1950s and 1960s. She worked for Macy's for around forty years, prior to her retirement in 1978,[14] and for many of those years she was a designer of ceramic and glass tableware. She was born in Cleveland, Ohio, in 1905, to William and Anna Wall, and married James Lovell Little, Jr., the scion of a wealthy Boston family. That marriage produced a daughter, Mary Lee, but it ended in divorce, and she later married H. Shepherd Flather, with whom she was listed in the 1940 census as living at East 78th Street in New York City. She may already have been working at Macy's at that time.

There is very little information about Flather's life or artistic training, because for most of her life she was estranged from her daughter, the child of her first marriage, and was not close to any of her grandchildren. One of them, Leonora Vance Stulz, received a portfolio of Flather's papers after her death in 1990 and shared them with this author.[15] Those papers include photocopies of advertisements for several Johnson Brothers tableware designs, and sketches in her own hand. There is also a photocopy of an exhibition catalogue for "Contemporary American Glass, Lent by the Corning Museum of Glass," published by the National Gallery of Art in Washington, DC, in 1956, and describing a decanter and a liqueur glass "designed by Louise Flather for the Imperial Glass Corporation."

The significance of Louise Flather's contribution to Johnson Brothers tableware design is that it confirms the company's reliance upon American consumers, to the extent that they hired an American woman artist who could presumably understand and anticipate what other American women wanted to buy. In some cases, this would mean a delicate "feminine" pattern that nevertheless had elements of surprise, giving it a more modern look.

Some of the sketches in Flather's portfolio reflect a distinctive artistic trait of stylizing small leaves as tiny loops, and scattering small snippets of leaves and stems to create an asymmetrical overall design. One of the earliest patterns on which this type of design appears is *Rose Chintz* of 1950, described earlier in this chapter, and a later example is the imaginatively named *Floating Leaves* of 1955 (Plate 10D). This pattern features a repeating design such as would typically be used for wallpaper, formed of disconnected individual leaves ranging from very detailed (a seven-lobed grape leaf[16]) to very stylized (heart shapes). There are also tiny sprigs of two or three loop-shaped leaves. The pattern's name transforms the ivory background into a still pool of water, in the viewer's imagination. Another pattern of 1955 was *Lace*, a highly stylized design of loop-shaped leaves on a continuous serpentine stem, highlighted with stylized tulip-shaped flowers. The pattern is unpredictable but still calming, and while there is no visual resemblance to the textile familiarly known as lace, there is a conceptual association in the sense of the elements being interconnected, delicate, and "feminine." *Autumn's Delight* of 1960 had plump, colorful fruits similar to those of the earlier design *Harvest Time* (1951), but with the addition of Flather's characteristic sprigs of loop-shaped leaves, in this case with pointed tips.

The imaginative character of many of Flather's pattern names is also evident in the case of *Day in June*, introduced in 1954 (Plate 11A). This was a floral pattern with three sprays, and two small sprigs of flowers and foliage were scattered around the rim of the plate, extending toward the center. It is the pattern name, however, which evokes a time of day (daylight hours), location (outdoors), and season (early summer). A "day in June" does not describe the flowers, but rather evokes a temporal and sensory experience.

The Plate as Botanical Art

There was a significant category of tableware patterns that aspired to the role of art, and that was the botanical illustration. Floral motifs had been popular for a very long time, but in this instance, the purpose was to represent individual flowers with scientific accuracy. A botanical illustrator would take a dried specimen on a sheet of paper and transform it into a living example, retaining every detail of how the flower, leaves, and stems were configured. On tableware, the designer would represent an accurate example of that plant species, on a plain white or ivory field.

Numerous Staffordshire companies followed this trend, and among the earliest was Cauldon Potteries Ltd. in Hanley, which had a botanically inspired flower series with a backstamp dated to the period of c. 1920–30.[17] That pattern was not named, but it was a series, with about twelve different flowers represented on the dinner plates. The plates had a rim of eight scallops with a gadroon edge, and just inside the gadrooning there was a thin line of green, harmonizing with the bright green color of the leaves. Another version of the series had a very decorative molded rim, but with no coloration, making the floral image in the center stand out.

Johnson Brothers created its own botanical pattern, *Old Flower Prints*, in 1949 (design patent number 155423). This was sponsored by Macy's in New York, and Louise Flather's portfolio contained numerous drawings related to it, establishing that she was involved in its design. Flather's New York connection was instrumental in the creation of this pattern, because according to an advertisement brochure in her portfolio, the "Sources For The Prints" were taken from the New York Botanical Garden library. Eight specific sources are listed in the brochure of which four were British and four were French, including three books by the famous illustrator Pierre-Joseph Redouté (1759–1840), who taught art to Marie-Antoinette.

The brochure listed thirty-five individual pieces in the set, with only one pattern repetition: "Rose" is featured on the 10-inch "dinner plate," the "turkey platter," and the "tureen." Another piece not listed in the brochure is a 10¾-inch buffet plate, also with "Rose" on the backstamp, but the actual image is different from the one used on the smaller dinner plate, and the transfer motif is larger, extending from the center portion onto part of the plate rim (Plate 11B).

The Johnson Brothers pattern had a plain round body with a gadroon edge (and thus it may have been directly inspired by the earlier Cauldon pattern). Its floral designs, however, were very precise, which was by now an expectation of the company's highly accomplished engraving staff. In the advertisement brochure, Macy's promoted the plates as "engravings" by stating: "Macy's presents OLD FLOWER PRINTS Engraved by hand on copper plates Entirely hand painted by the famous firm of Johnson Brothers England." The name "Macy's" is printed in a cursive typeface, as it was used in advertisements of the period, but the names of the pattern and the Johnson Brothers company are written in a unique, highly embellished, nineteenth-century-style type. The rest of the words, "Engraved by hand ...," are in a Gothic typeface, undoubtedly to lend them even more "historic" prestige. The backstamp of the plates also included the phrase "A Genuine Hand Engraving," which had been featured a decade earlier in the backstamp of *Historic America*.

This pattern was clearly promoted as a work of art, carried out by the "hand" of a real engraver. The brochure even included illustrations of several groupings, with plates and bowls shown vertically, to demonstrate how different pieces could be arranged in a display cabinet. Each illustration, as well as the cover of the brochure, was framed by a rococo-style border of scrolls. Even more impressive was the presentation of "The Backstamp" (also in Gothic type), which was surrounded by a draped, fringed curtain hanging from a curved support framework. That framework was in turn topped by three groups of triple ostrich feathers, the traditional symbol of the British Prince of Wales. Macy's was clearly pulling out all the stops in presenting this tableware pattern as the epitome of high art and good taste.

There were subsequent Johnson Brothers patterns that were probably inspired by *Old Flower Prints*, but were based on a single motif: *Azalea* (1951, design patent number 164122) and *Camellia*. The latter was described in a May 1951 issue of the trade journal *Pottery and Glass*, in the following caption above a photograph of an oval platter and covered sugar bowl:

> "Camellia" design on rimless plate styled for the U.S. market. It is made in an underglaze engraved print in monotone "Silver Sage" colour; also printed in brown and painted in enamel colours. A present-day application of engraved decoration by Johnson Brothers (Hanley) Ltd.[18]

The *Camellia* pattern was engraved by Norbury, and he described the meticulous process it involved:

> The first sketch produced was initially round, but in that form displeased me, so I took it upon myself to make it into an oval shape, which seemed more fitting, for the overall effect. When I started in on the stipple punching beginning with the shadow areas, I tried to imitate the delicacy of the shadows, like the mists brought on by the fluctuations of the nuances in temperatures. The dots appearing gently at first without a definitive pattern, then gradually getting firmer as they approached the center of the flower, becoming ever more graceful and beautiful in formation. The line work I carefully fed into the punching almost imperceptibly at first, then getting more and more visible as it got nearer to the depth of shade as required by the curvature of the flower in its deepest parts. The portrayal of a flower in this respect demands all of the skill of the engraver to portray all of the subtleties of nature. (p. 51)

These botanically inspired series patterns laid the groundwork for what would later become one of the most successful British tableware patterns of all time: *The Botanic Garden*, created by Portmeirion Pottery in 1972. Portmeirion Village in Wales was founded in 1925 by Sir Clough Williams-Ellis as a fanciful modern utopia, and in 1960 his daughter Susan Williams-Ellis and her husband Euan Cooper-Willis created Portmeirion Pottery. The pattern they launched in 1972 was named after a poem written in 1818 by Erasmus Darwin, who was not only a poet but also an inventor, botanist, and grandfather of the famous Charles Darwin. The pattern featured thirty-five botanical illustrations taken from books published in 1818 and 1835, as well as other illustrations by William Clarke.[19] By 2009, Portmeirion Pottery was large enough to acquire the historic pottery companies of Royal Worcester and Spode, and the parent company was renamed as the Portmeirion Group.

Continuing the Pictorial Tradition

While the 1950s were a period of some experimentation in terms of pattern design, Johnson Brothers never departed entirely from the pictorial scenes that had formed the core of its greatest success. This was probably due in part to the company's deep conservatism, in keeping to the marketing strategies that had been profitable in the past. It would not have been possible, however, without the company's exceptionally talented staff of engravers, in the department headed by Bill Norbury. As a man who considered himself first and foremost an artist, he expected the members of his team to uphold the same high standards. This was not true of the engravers of other companies, as he described with some disdain in speaking of the postwar period:

> Next thing to happen was an increased demand for engravings of a more artistic appeal, and easier attraction [...] but unfortunately the designers had for many years neglected to hone their skills, as far as engraving was concerned, and now they had been caught napping. [...] The plain and simple fact is they simply were not good artists in the complete sense of the word, they were simple designers who could reasonably be expected to be able to draw a flower in detail but unable to make it realistic in appearance, life-like in other words, using every innuendo of light and shade to add to the effect of realism. (p. 55)

In 1951, the Festival of Britain was held as a symbolic celebration of postwar recovery in industry, arts, and science. Not coincidentally, that year was the centennial of the Great Exhibition of London in 1851. For a five-month period, from May to September 1951, the festival's main site on the South Bank of London hosted more than eight million visitors.[20] One of the exhibits was sponsored by Johnson Brothers, and they sent Bill Norbury to demonstrate the engraving process. He recalls the experience as follows:

Peter Johnson asked me to come down to his office. Bill, he says, you are to present us (the factory) at the Festival of Britain in London. Arrange your availability for a few weeks, away from your family. […] Peter drove us down to London, Elsie Bloor, Print Transferers Manageress, the Paintresses Department Manageress, and myself to the Festival Park on the side of the Thames. […] I was printing on one of our best presses and the girls did their own thing as they would perform them in a works environment. I also demonstrated the art of engraving, also answering any questions that they might have, also general questions regarding pottery, a rather full time. […] I had two crates of 7″ plates, the object to print 7″ Britain Castles, between times doing some engraving on a copper cylinder. The subject was a Game Bird, a grouse sitting in the heather. I was part way to producing a series of Game Birds in the factory at Stoke-on-Trent. Tom Ekin was working on one of them at Hanley Pottery. I used the different styles of engravers to the best advantage.[21]

The *Game Birds* pattern launched in 1951, and it was unusual in consisting of an illustration very much in the manner of John James Audubon's 1838 work, *Birds of America*. Instead of a normal scene with a background and sky, a pair of male and female birds is shown in profile, framed by a small amount of vegetation suggesting their natural habitat (Plate 11C). The background is left undecorated; in Audubon's prints, it was the ivory-colored page, and in the plate, it is plain ivory or off-white ceramic. The plate was a very simple round or oval shape, with no molded edge or border decoration to distract from the image. Although the pattern did not use Audubon's bird paintings as direct inspiration for how the birds are depicted, it is evident that these plates are intended to be appreciated as works of art, not only in regard to the image on the front but also in regard to the backstamp (Figure 5.1).

Game Birds included six different images: "Partridge," "Quail," "Woodcock," "Ruffed Grouse," "Pheasant," and "Wild Turkey."[22] It was sufficiently popular to have remained in production for thirty years, until 1982. Its success inspired another pattern called *Fish*, introduced in 1955, which also remained in production until 1982 (Plate 11D). That was produced on oval shapes, and there were seven different images created (Figure 5.2). According to Finegan, the original sixth image was of an eel, and this proved to be relatively unpopular among American purchasers. Inclusion of the eel may have represented a misunderstanding on the part of the British designers, who may have assumed that jellied eels were as familiar a food item in America as they were in Britain. This was not the case, however, so the eel was replaced with another fish.[23]

Norbury recalled the creation of the *Fish* pattern in detail:
The fish pattern came into being by virtue of its being held by our roving representative Bill Hall, our head salesman at Macy's of New York, U.S.A. Having in his possession 6 or 7 studies of fish, just illustrations, not artistically created studies in the true sense of the word, he said to me, "Bill, the directors got these and wondered what you could produce from them?" So I set one up on an 8 inch

Figure 5.1 Game Birds backstamp, Johnson Brothers, c. 1951.

plate and got to work, adding two little ones to create movement by placing them in a covering pose, and some plant growth adjacent, but opposing the converging fish pose to create interest. It made the loosely composed scene really spring into life, almost three-dimensional, and a new pattern was born! I composed the other studies in a similar way, they all seemed to be in action. Designing the remaining units was easy, the fish illustrations dead or more correctly lifeless looking, were ultimately transformed, and lent to the illustrations the illusion of life and living things. Thriving, vigorous, well, were the descriptive words that were the orders of the day. The new look of the pattern augured well for its success, and within a few months, it was flooding the production lines, and within a very few weeks, it was spilling into the shop windows in response to the demand, which exceeded all of our wildest dreams. Not everyone was interested in fish, but it achieved success beyond our expectations, even the fronds weaving and waving about in the currents in the invisible movements inherent in the

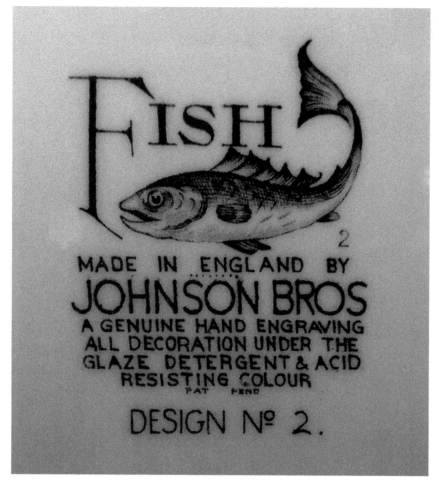

Figure 5.2 Fish backstamp, Johnson Brothers, *c.* 1955.

background which, looking at it from a practical point of view, was a simple solid block of ceramics. What we were trying to sell was an illusion of live active entities going about their daily business of searching for food. I was astonished when I realised that it really was no wonder that the fish theme had proved to be so popular. None of us had realised that "fishing" was the most popular sporting pastime, bar none. (p. 60)

The concept of creating an artistic scene filling the entire plate was carried out in other patterns as well, including two that were introduced in 1957: *Tally Ho* and *Olde English Countryside*. *Tally Ho* was, as the name suggests, based on scenes of foxhunting, complete with formally dressed riders on horseback, hounds, and a landscape background with trees which have lost most of their leaves, suggesting late autumn. Norbury recalled that the source images were a set of prints acquired by Shepard Johnson. The set included dinner plates, buffet-size plates, square salad plates, and cereal bowls, reproducing the following six images: "The Meet," "View Halloo," "The Jump," "Stirrup Cup," "Full Cry," and "The Kill."[24] The existence of large buffet-size plates and the relatively limited number of pieces suggest that it was intended for use in social gatherings, and perhaps the autumnal holiday of Thanksgiving. The pattern remained in production for thirteen years, until 1970, which seems perhaps surprising to the contemporary mentality of opposing hunting as a form of animal cruelty. At the time, even though English-style hunting was not part of American life, it was familiar through novels and movies, and represented a glimpse into a traditional, upper-class way of life.

Olde English Countryside was an even simpler pattern, with only one scene shown in minor variations throughout the entire service (Plate 12A). This design was a version of a work by Alfred Robert Quinton, a celebrated English watercolorist.[25] Quinton (1853–1934) specialized in scenes of country life, spending several months each year making sketches *en plein air* and then returning to his studio to create highly detailed versions. He produced around 2,000 works, which became famous after being published in several books and reproduced on postcards.[26] Quinton's views showed a highly idealized and sentimental version of rural life, with thatch-roofed, half-timbered cottages tucked behind lush vegetation with blooming flowers. The inhabitants were often shown in dress of the late nineteenth century, with women wearing long skirts and crisp white aprons.

The source image for *Olde English Countryside* was Quinton's painting of Wyre Village near Pershore in Worcestershire, which shows a man wearing a vest and white shirt sleeves herding cows down the lane that winds through the village.[27] That man and the cows have been deleted from the scene on the plate, although other details are faithfully reproduced, including not only the appearance of houses and foliage, but also a long-skirted woman and a little girl with black stockings standing to the left of the lane, and a stone monument in the background. To the left, above a row of treetops in the distant background, a hillside has been added, perhaps to balance out the composition with the roofs of the houses on the right. In the bottom foreground, perhaps in order to fill the now-empty space of the lane and to make a more pleasing composition, the artist added a hand-operated pump for water, a picket gate, and a collection of rocks and flowers.

This pattern was sufficiently popular to remain in production for twenty-six years, until 1983. In contrast to the upper-class elite society portrayed in *Tally Ho*, this was a depiction of "ordinary" people, to whom Americans could relate even if their way of life was completely different. Even more importantly, this romanticized version of English life was an overt appeal to tourism. By the late 1950s, even people in remote British villages owned cars, and nobody was herding cows down the middle of the street or wearing ankle-length skirts. But many of the thatched cottages did still exist, and could be visited. The pattern's name, with the antiquated spelling of "Olde," is a wink of acknowledgment of the fact that this idealized scene no longer existed in the present day, but Quinton's paintings were "proof" that they did once exist, and the plates preserved the image of that happy, innocent past.[28]

Among other Staffordshire companies producing patterns of similar inspiration was Myott, Son & Co. Ltd. Its pattern *England's Charm* was very similar to *Olde English Countryside*, featuring a quaint village scene with a few houses, a tavern, and a church high on the hill. A small stone bridge rises above a creek from which a man is allowing two horses to drink. It is not known when this pattern was introduced, but its backstamp wording of "all colours guaranteed permanent-detergent proof" places it within the era of the automatic dishwasher, that is, the early 1950s. The image may also have been inspired by an A. R. Quinton painting, or it may be a composite of elements from several paintings, since there are details resembling Quinton's views of "Coombe Bissett near Salisbury" and "Kersey Village, Suffolk."[29]

The Holiday Spirit

When Queen Elizabeth visited the Johnson Brothers showroom in Hanley in 1955, one of the patterns on display in the photograph described earlier was a holiday pattern for Americans: *Barnyard King*, introduced in 1950. This was among the first patterns aimed specifically at a holiday that only existed in the New World: Thanksgiving. It is celebrated both by Canadians and Americans, although each country has a different origin story; for Canada, it dates back to 1578 and the explorer Martin Frobisher, and for America, it dates back to 1620 and the Pilgrims. Nevertheless, the mode of celebration was similar in both countries, involving the consumption of turkey, sweet potatoes, and other foods indigenous to the New World.

A "Thanksgiving" plate already existed, as the buffet plate of *Historic America*. The advertisement for the pattern's launch in 1939 had included the description of the Currier & Ives scene "Home for Thanksgiving" on the "Turkey Platter" (see Chapter 3). A buffet plate had also been added, with another Currier & Ives scene relabeled as "Thanksgiving/Frozen Up." As mentioned earlier, that plate had received the addition of a live turkey in the foreground.

In the postwar effort to find new ways to whet the appetite of the American consumer, many companies fixed upon a "turkey" theme as a sure-fire way to sell more plates. Platters with turkey motifs had already been produced going back to the turn of the century by companies such as Copeland and Wedgwood, including examples of flow blue, and after the Second World War this was expanded to include sets of tableware by Spode, Enoch Wedgwood, Masons, Burslem, Doulton, Cauldon, Royal Staffordshire/Clarice Cliff, and others. Johnson Brothers made a significant contribution to the market of "turkey" ware; in addition to *Barnyard King*, they promoted three versions of *Wild Turkeys* (1951) and *His Majesty* (1959).

Barnyard King is, as its title suggests, a view of a domestically raised turkey in a fenced yard of a farm (Plate 12B). There are two structures in the background, a brick or stone house on the left and a barn on the right. Two tiny chickens and a rooster are in front of the barn, and through its open door one can just see the wheel and back end of a cart. There is also a border motif, including three repeated vignettes of a squirrel eating a nut. The backstamp features a smaller version of the turkey, and the plate has a plain round shape with a gadroon edge. The turkey is seen in profile, slightly off-center to the left, and the artist may have been somewhat confused about the appearance of a turkey, since the tail feathers are reminiscent of a giant nautilus shell. Also rather oddly, the turkey seems to be standing on cobblestones, which was not a common feature of American farmyards. These errors would appear to demonstrate that the British designers did not do a very thorough job of researching what American farms, or turkeys, really looked like. Consumers may not have given importance to these flaws, however, since the pattern was otherwise well engraved, with bright autumnal colors. It remained in production for twenty years, until 1970.

Wild Turkeys was a more artistically ambitious pattern, showing a turkey in a naturalistic woodland habitat. The turkey fills the center of the plate and is enhanced by hand-painted touches of red, green, and purple against the overall pattern color of dark brown. The plate has a molded shape with multiple scallops, which appears to have been designed uniquely for it, and only two other patterns are known to exist in this shape.[30] The border had an elaborate pattern of flowers and three vignettes of small game birds. The backstamp employed a unique handwritten script for the words "Wild Turkeys" and "Native American" appearing underneath. There is a smaller, different turkey depicted in the backstamp, and below that is the phrase "Windsor Ware" in the same script. Unlike earlier "WindsorWare" patterns, however, the two words are separate, and there is no shield with Windsor Castle. Barnyard King was not identified as a "WindsorWare" pattern, and 1950 may have been a time of transition in which some patterns used the phrase and others did not. The phrase itself may also have been considered a kind of Johnson Brothers trademark, no longer needing an overt reminder of its connection to the British royal family.

The variations of *Wild Turkeys* were with the words "Native American" on the backstamp, described above; plates with a backstamp title of *Woodland Wild Turkeys*; and a version entitled *Wild Turkeys "Native American"* showing a flying turkey on the dinner plate, an image used on some dinner plates of the first variation, but with a different border that has no vignettes. Instead, the border is the same one used for *Harvest Fruit*, a "WindsorWare" pattern with backstamp shield, issued in 1955,[31] so that variation was probably issued at around the same time. The existence of these multiple variations was probably a simple response to the pattern's success, hoping that the purchaser of one set would want to expand it with a variety of scenes and even border patterns.

The 1959 pattern *His Majesty* was even more successful, remaining in production for thirty-seven years, until 1996. It showed a large turkey in a nearly full-frontal view, in a somewhat odd setting: the turkey stands in front of a three-bar wooden fence, but it is surrounded by tall grass and is flanked by very thin, bare vertical stalks and a few bare branches tipped by what appear to be pine needles (Plate 12C). Perhaps to compensate for the sparseness of the foliage in the center image, the border shows a profusion of round apples, squash, and grapes, interspersed with flowers. Bill Norbury recalled this design with some dislike, since he thought the setting of a "thicket" was too busy and involved "too much labor without a return." By "return," he may have meant lack of artistic satisfaction, because the pattern was quite successful commercially. Most often, however, the engravers were not informed of the eventual reception of the patterns they created. They were not privy to sales figures, because profits were not shared with the workers. On many occasions in his memoirs, Norbury expressed frustration that the company directors reaped the benefits of the workers' skill and effort.

Another holiday that gave rise to tableware design was Christmas, which inspired hundreds of Staffordshire patterns over the course of many decades. The most successful Johnson Brothers Christmas pattern was *Merry Christmas*, issued in 1959 (Plate 12D). This design was one to which Louise Flather contributed, and it is an idealized view of a decorated Christmas tree, before which lies an inviting stack of wrapped presents. The tree stands to the right of a large open hearth with a roaring fire, although there is no fire screen, which makes the scene a bit uncomfortable for the safety-minded viewer. There are two red candles on the mantel, on either side of a pine wreath decorated with a red bow. The border motif is of holly and berries, and the plate is hand-painted with red and green accents on the border, with additional touches of red and yellow for the flames and yellow, green, blue, and red for the ornaments and presents. The pattern name of *Merry Christmas* is obviously aimed at Americans, since the corresponding phrase in England is "Happy Christmas."

This pattern was highly successful, remaining in production for thirty-five years, until 1994. The center image would be later be reused by another pattern, *The Friendly Village*, which will be discussed subsequently. In order to understand this pattern's appeal, it may be useful to compare it with another holiday pattern, Spode's *Christmas Tree*, introduced in 1938 and still highly popular today. The Spode pattern shows a tree decorated with ornaments, topped by a figure of Father Christmas holding a sack of toys, and with a pile of neatly wrapped presents at its foot, highlighted with pretty (but perhaps dangerous) sprigs of holly. A website of Spode history cites the pattern designer, Harold Holdway, as recalling that he was informed that in America, Christmas gifts were placed at the foot of the tree. He "accepted this with good grace," and changed his original design to add the gifts, which were not part of the British tradition. And in another indication that American consumers were the intended market, "factory legend suggests that Harold also had no idea what they [Americans] put at the top of the tree, which is why the Spode Christmas tree has a Santa instead of a fairy."[32]

In contrast, the Johnson Brothers image presents a narrative scene, showing the interior of a family home at a particular moment in time, the evening, when candles were lit and a fire warmed the room. It is possible for the viewer to imagine himself or herself in that room, feeling the warmth and comforted by the prosperity evident in the abundance of gifts and decorations. Both patterns evoke similar positive feelings about the Christmas holiday, but only the Johnson Brothers version takes a cinematic approach to creating a complete scene and mood.

It should be noted that the Johnson Brothers company continued to favor a "shotgun" approach to its patterns, having as many different choices for the consumer as possible, in the hope that one would strike its target. In the very same year that the individualized, creative patterns of *His Majesty* and *Merry Christmas* were introduced, 1959, there was another pattern called *Country Life* that was simply a copy of Currier & Ives's illustration "Frozen Up." That illustration had already been used in *Historic America* for the buffet plates, and perhaps unbeknownst to the British company directors, it had also inspired a 1950 pattern called *Currier & Ives*, made by the Royal China Company of Sebring, Ohio (see Chapter 3). Although the Johnson Brothers version was of better engraving quality and was attractively produced in brown multicolor, the American market for this scene was already well saturated. Norbury remembered it as a pattern that "didn't sell," and it was discontinued after only six years.

Nostalgia for a Past that Never Was

Perhaps the most creative category of narrative scene introduced in the 1950s was the nostalgic vision of places that never existed in reality. Gary Cross, writing about the opening of Disneyland in 1955, described Americans' "nostalgia for a romantic version of small towns":

> It was a secondhand nostalgia for those born too late to experience the real thing and who instead grew up in featureless suburbs. [...] Memory of a mediated past may have been more real than the one that they actually knew. Mobility and marriages across ethnic and neighborhood groups meant that "homesickness" (that is, nostalgia) might not be for a specific place but for a romantic idea.[33]

Johnson Brothers had already explored this notion in its idealized views of *Old Britain Castles* and *Historic America*, but those series were based on actual historic sites. In this case, tableware design offered an opportunity to create imaginary places, designed to evoke positive emotional responses. One very early example of this was the pattern *Castle on the Lake*, introduced in 1940 (design patent number 118580). This was a scene in which the foreground is composed of flowers and trees, and a "castle" is visible in the distant background on the left. That castle is not the familiar medieval structure of turrets and crenelated walls, but rather a squarish building with two towers, each one topped by a pointed dome. The overall effect is reminiscent of the Tower of London. The "lake" is suggested by simple horizontal lines, suggesting reflections in the water, and a few clouds float in the sky. The body is a simple round shape with a gadroon edge, and the backstamp is the name "Castle On The Lake" above the old-style angular crown. The pattern was made in pink, blue, mulberry, and brown multicolor, and it was in production for around thirty years, until 1970.[34]

The castle is dream-like, due to the intentional faintness with which it is stippled. The flowers in the foreground are engraved with higher contrast, and the profusion of full blooms suggests springtime. The viewer appears to be standing on the bank of the lake, looking across the still water. Overall, the pattern creates a soft, romantic mood.

It would not be until the 1950s, however, that the creation of patterns with imaginary scenes would truly take hold. In 1951, a pattern visually inspired by *Castle on the Lake* was launched, *The Old Mill*, also featuring elements positioned around a "lake" created by horizontal reflection lines (Plate 13A). A fanciful aspect of the illustration is the fact that the water mill seems to be built adjacent to the round stone tower of a small castle of which nothing else remains.

As described by Bill Norbury, the original drawing showed the title feature as a small, faraway image. He did not like that design and took it upon himself to change it:

> A very old pattern like its namesake, "The Old Mill," was not very impressive in any way. The half-size sprays [sections of transfer] left a lot of white space between elements that were not so important anyway. Only one of the three sprays had any interest: a water wheel in front of an ancient building, with a suggestion of water flowing by. So I took this spray, and by enlarging it to about three times the size, made a feature of it. It now became a healthy "Olde-Worlde Scene." (p. 63)

Norbury's lightly ironic spelling of "olde-worlde" indicates his awareness that this scene was an intentionally "quaint" idealization of the historic past. Unlike the rural scenes shown in the watercolor paintings of A. R. Quinton, this scene was not intended to represent any real place that could be visited by a tourist. Instead, it was a landscape of the imagination, which was appealing precisely because of its dream-like, timeless quality.

The concept of basing a pattern on a place that never existed led to the creation of *The Friendly Village*, a Johnson Brothers pattern that was in continuous production from its launch in 1953 to 2014, a period of sixty-one years. In 1948, Bill Norbury received a visit from a designer, "Mrs. Flather," from Macy's Department Store in New York.[35] This was Louise Flather, introduced earlier in this chapter. She presented to him sketches for a new pattern, and as he recalled, over the next several years he used twenty-eight men to engrave it. "Gordon [Worthington] was the first to start the pattern on its way. It was to be called 'Friendly Village,' based on American country life. Idyllic rural scenes, softened with a blanket of snow."[36]

The scenes depicted on pieces of *The Friendly Village* were executed with very high quality engraving, a characteristic that undoubtedly contributed to the pattern's success (Plate 13B). The images were crisp and clear, with some scenes attaining a near-photographic realism. The border was specially designed for the pattern, and it featured groupings of leaves with a few flowers, grasses, and a pine cone, creating an autumnal mood. A few of the scenes depicted snow, as Norbury mentioned, but others showed trees covered with leaves, corresponding to earlier seasons.

The pattern's name is an overt appeal to the emotions. It does not merely designate a hypothetical location, but it imbues that place with the personality trait of being "friendly." This anthropomorphic characterization allowed the purchaser to dispense with the idea of actual people, who could be problematic, and instead be reassured by the notion of the town itself being warm and welcoming. Many Americans might be surprised at the use of the word "village," which seems more English, instead of "town." Louise Flather, however, lived most of her life in New York, and New England is a region in the United States where small municipalities are still referred to as villages.

The names of the scenes, provided on each backstamp, are suggestive of a place that might have come out of Hollywood Central Casting for an "old-fashioned small town." The twelve scenes used for the buffet plates were "The Village Green"; "The Lily Pond"; "Willow by the Brook"; "The Covered Bridge"; "The Old Mill" (not the same image as in the pattern previously mentioned); "The Hayfield"; "The Village Street" (Plate 13B); "The Well"; "Autumn Mists" (showing a red barn and a tree-lined lane filled with morning fog, a difficult feat for the engraver to accomplish); "The Stone Wall"; "Sugar Maples"; and "The School House." Additional pieces featured "The Ice House" and "The Apple Orchard."

Finegan was able to obtain and reproduce an advertisement of this pattern, undated but probably from the 1970s. The advertisement states:

> "Friendly Village" is a nostalgic pattern depicting 16 different scenes in a small American country town. Soft, muted tones of brown, green, yellow, red and blue capture the natural colors of the seasons evoking pleasant memories of simple rural life. A genuine hand engraving finished under high glaze.[37]

The language of this description is highly manipulative. The pattern is "nostalgic," the colors are "natural," and the colors are capable of "evoking pleasant memories of simple rural life," even if those memories were of experiences never actually lived. The vast majority of purchasers visiting the housewares department of Macy's were not former inhabitants of small country towns. The advertising copy could nevertheless use the power of suggestion to persuade them that they knew what small-town life felt like. The copy further reassured them that "simple rural life" was pleasant. People who actually lived in small towns could have explained to them the ways in which that notion was fantasy, not reality, but that did not matter in the world of marketing and advertising.

The pattern featured a very distinctive backstamp as well (Figure 5.3). As previously noted, it was customary to have a backstamp image that was either a direct copy or a variation of a motif used in the actual design. *The Friendly Village*, however, used a motif of an old-fashioned rural mailbox on a wooden post, which is not found in any of the scenes depicted. The words "The Friendly Village" were inscribed on the side of the mailbox, where the family's name would usually be written. The mailbox "flag" was in the raised, upright position, indicating that mail had been delivered, which may have prompted another positive emotional response. As a visual symbol, this modest mailbox managed to capture the pattern's essential quality of homespun charm.

Figure 5.3 The Friendly Village backstamp, Johnson Brothers, *c.* 1953.

In 1954, Johnson Brothers introduced a whimsical pattern called *Apple Harvest*, which had a casual, almost cartoon-like quality (Plate 13C). It shows a farmer with rolled-up sleeves, wearing overalls and a straw hat, holding a pitchfork, and standing next to a highly stylized apple tree. Three bushel baskets full of apples are grouped around the tree trunk, along with a very small wheelbarrow. A red barn and a comical childishly drawn sheep appear in the background, and it shows Louise Flather's stylistic influence. The pattern had only the one image, reproduced in different proportions on the various pieces of the set, which would have made it relatively quick to develop and simple to manufacture. Its cartoonish character made it lighthearted and cheerful, but it was only in production for six years, from 1954 to 1960. It is possible that purchasers did not understand why a motif seemingly appropriate for children would be found on an adult table service. It was, however, a precursor to similar patterns that would be introduced a decade later, as will be discussed in Chapter 6.

A purely imaginary scene was the basis for another pattern, *Dream Town*, introduced in 1956 (Plate 13D). This unusual pattern had an intentionally blurry image of a river, with houses and trees rising on a hillside behind the far bank. The viewer's vantage point is on the near bank, and the scene is framed by trees. The plates were plain round in shape, and the image fills the plate all the way to the edge. This was also a pattern with only one image, reproduced on all the pieces of the set.

The *Dream Town* pattern may have been inspired by the popularity of the American musical theater production of *Brigadoon*, a romantic tale about a Scottish village that appeared only one day every 100 years. It opened in 1947 and was the first major success for collaborators Alan Jay Lerner and Frederick Loewe, who would later create *My Fair Lady* (1956) and *Camelot* (1960). *Brigadoon* enjoyed a long run both on Broadway and in the London West End, and in 1954 a film version was made starring Gene Kelly and Cyd Charisse.[38] The pattern launched about two years after the film and remained in production for eighteen years, until 1974.

It may have seemed a risk to create a pattern based on an ephemeral work of popular culture, but the reason for the success of the play and the film may be similar to the reason for the success of the ceramic pattern. The idea of being able to live happily forever in a magical place, protected from the reality of day-to-day existence, is a powerful fantasy. In the same way that most of the nostalgic patterns belonged to some unspecified time in history, the "good old days" of a simple rural life that was more fiction than fact, *Brigadoon* and *Dream Town* both dwelled, literally and visually, far back in the mists of time.

Norbury had a somewhat more prosaic recollection of how the *Dream Town* pattern evolved:

> The original sketch of Dream Town didn't look very encouraging. How to treat it, how to make it work. Then Mrs. Flather said to me, "Make it in a 'Renoir' style." Not really having an idea, I decided to have a go. Putting extra colour on by hand offered a great combination, but they never got it right. The engraving I styled was quite good. Some of the other pieces were not. (p. 49)

A final example of a pattern based upon an imaginary nostalgic scene was the evocatively titled *The Road Home*. It was also a single-motif pattern and was in production for about fifteen years. It depicts a winding lane, a small creek, and a town with several houses, a church, and two barns (Plate 14A). The foreground of the pattern is on the plate's lower rim, and it shows a section of a picket fence, with rosebushes growing on either side. The rosebushes show Flather's stylistic influence, with her characteristic stylized leaves and stems. In an imaginative touch, the viewer sees the horizontal plank to which the pickets are attached, which means that the viewer is actually standing on the inside of the fence. This provides a subtle psychological reassurance, because although the viewer may be looking at the road toward the town where others live, he or she is already safe at home, secure within his or her own little fence.

The backstamp of *The Road Home* is also an original composition, inspired by but not duplicating what is seen in the plate's main motif (Figure 5.4). It features

Figure 5.4 The Road Home backstamp, Johnson Brothers, *c.* 1954.

a picket fence, this time seen from the front side, and just behind it is a wooden post, with a cross-piece carved to point left, inscribed with the words "THE ROAD HOME." A small bird is perched on the sign, also facing left, and tendrils of a rosebush are winding around the sign in a gentle "embrace."

> The origin of *The Road Home* was described by Norbury:
> Gordon [Worthington] lived in Wolstanton, and […] I used to give him a lift home sometimes, if it fitted in with my programme. Near to where he lived was a cobbler's shop. In the shop window was a rear wall, and hanging in the space was a picture depicting a country lane travelling through a wood, with a country workman, on his way home. A very pleasant scene. Gordon managed to persuade the cobbler to let him have the picture as a favour. I am prepared here and now to admit, it really was for me! I had spotted something in the picture that touched a chord in my memory for some reason. With a little sweet talking I managed to call it my own!
>
> A couple of days later we sent it to New York, the good old U.S.A. And they [the staff at the Johnson Brothers New York office] in their turn showed it to Mrs. Flather, who was retained by Macy's of New York and was engaged by them to pick out and develop anything that she thought looked interesting, or had any potential that could be developed for U.S. interests. N.B.: for Developed substitute Exploit. Sure enough, she came through, within a short space of time it was a ceramic pattern. A short space of English time, although it seems to take longer here, it was in the shops. I had engaged Claude Whittingham to engrave it, he was the best possible alternative at the time and anyway I was too busy with other things, and it brought 1954 to a nice end. (p. 62)

Norbury's account displays some of his annoyance with the company directors and with the system in which the engravers responsible for the company's financial success were not given any share of it, or even acknowledged for their contributions. At the same time, however, his story confirms another link between an original work of art, that is, the picture on the cobbler's wall, and a tableware pattern that it inspired. The picture was undoubtedly an inexpensive print, not an original painting, but for Norbury, it nevertheless "touched a chord in my memory for some reason." It possessed the power to call forth an emotional response, and that power would be reflected in the tableware design, presenting a perfect combination of technical artistry and sentimental appeal.

Chapter 6

MODERN STYLE, NEW TRADITIONS

In the wake of the Second World War, British manufacturing experienced something of an identity crisis. As described by Graham M. McLaren:

> The debate subtly changed during the late 1940s from a clear divide between traditional design and a more contemporary idiom, to what type of design would provide the most effective and secure future for the industry in a changing world. The central crease of this blurred line became the question of what made British ceramic design peculiarly "British", in that the preservation of a national design identity in pottery was regarded as the best hope for the future.[1]

The responses were not uniform across the industry; at the same time when some pottery companies such as Johnson Brothers sought to recapture a sense of nostalgic tradition, as discussed in the previous chapter, other companies looked to the future with the creation of modernist designs.

Midwinter and Modernism

W. R. Midwinter Pottery in Burslem invested in highly stylized contemporary motifs, based on the designs of several artists, including Jessie Tait, Terence Conran, and Hugh Casson. Tait (1928–2010) was an artist who, like Bill Norbury many years earlier, had been recruited at a young age from an art school by Gordon Forsyth. She began working for Wood and Sons around 1945, at the age of seventeen, and then moved to Midwinter Pottery in 1946.[2]

In February 1953, Midwinter introduced a line called *Stylecraft*, including "40 new shapes and 36 contemporary patterns." Steven Jenkins commented that "the television screen-shaped plate was easy to stack and many of the dinnerware items boasted dual functions for extra economy."[3] The "television screen-shape" was a rounded oval, as found in the first televisions housed in wooden cabinets, and this visual link between tableware and the newly popular form of home entertainment would have been recognizable and appealing to the middle-class consumer of the time.

Two *Stylecraft* patterns by Tait were advertised in *The Pottery Gazette* in March 1956: "Primavera, a Jessie Tait design, is more strikingly contemporary; it is a hand-painted design under glaze in acid-proof colours. Homeweave is another genuine hand-painted design by Jessie Tait employing a simple modern treatment."[4] The dinner plate of *Primavera* had sixteen child-like shapes resembling leaves, flowers, fans, and spirals, described by Jenkins as follows: "using organic motifs against amoebic and abstract shapes surrounded by a 'texture' of dots, the whole mood of the 1950s seems to be evoked."[5] *Homeweave* was a simplified plaid pattern for which the lines were painted freehand. This method of production was a significant departure from the transfer method, the results of which had slight variations but were generally very consistent. Painting by hand meant that every piece was individual, and the intentionally shaky result of painting "straight" lines highlighted that individuality.

Midwinter also advertised a pattern called *Salad Ware*, designed by Terence Conran, which had cartoon-like sketches of different fruits and vegetables. The pieces were designed by Roy Midwinter in the "Fashion" shape, and these included a triangular "Boomerang dish."[6] Other Midwinter patterns of the mid-1950s through the early 1960s included stripes, starbursts, snowflakes, and a myriad of abstract shapes, often having a hand-drawn or painted style and featuring strong primary colors.[7] The Midwinter company was clearly seeking to fill a niche market of buyers seeking a trendy, youthful style, rejecting the tradition-based associations upon which a company like Johnson Brothers depended.

Designer Hugh Casson created two patterns for Midwinter that were pictorial, but taking a completely different approach from that of Johnson Brothers. Instead of meticulously copying a detailed painting or print, Casson made sketches of the two French tourist destinations, *Riviera* (1954) and *Cannes* (1960).[8] These were serial patterns, featuring a different sketch on each piece, but the style was very casual, using only minimal lines and a few splashes of color against a plain white background. The impression created is similar to the types of sketches that could be purchased from an artist on a beach or promenade, showing cafés with striped awnings and ocean views. This was the romantic French Riviera of Alfred Hitchcock's movie *To Catch a Thief* (1955), starring Cary Grant and Grace Kelly.

One common characteristic of these modernist designs was their intentional transience. They were not generally intended to be used for traditional holiday celebrations or to be treasured as future heirlooms, and they did not seek to suggest the owners' upper-class status. Instead, the patterns appeared fresh and bold, often even startling, characteristics that did not have much longevity. Customers were likely to get tired of these designs more quickly, and this would of course lead to more frequent purchases, working to the manufacturers' advantage. Such a marketing strategy relied upon the consumers' economic prosperity, that is, having enough income to own multiple sets of tableware and to replace them often. It also created a multitiered approach to tableware within a single household, separating heavier, casual patterns with catchy designs from more formal patterns reserved for special occasions.

Guardians of Tradition

As pottery design moved into the 1960s, Midwinter was consistently producing patterns with bold geometric motifs and contrasting colors. In contrast, the new decade of the 1960s brought little discernible change to Johnson Brothers pattern design. The company carefully maintained its brand with floral designs such as *Wiltshire* (1960) and *Devon Sprays* (1962), using English names, and *Rose Bouquet* (1963), all of which could easily have been produced during the 1950s.

Narrative pictorial patterns were also part of the company's traditional identity. *Mill Stream*, introduced in 1960, was a pictorial single-scene motif of a small village by the side of a winding stream, featuring a waterfall created by a mill. In an advertisement of 1961, it was featured along with *The Old Mill* (1952) and *Olde English Countryside* (1957), and the following text: "Mill Stream, a romantic, charming pattern reproduced from an Early 19th Century painting and handsomely framed by a bower of flowers. Hand painted, of course, and underglaze."[9] The pattern would remain in production for twenty-five years, until 1985, which indicates that regardless of the trends of "mod" style throughout the sixties and seventies, such traditional scenes never lost their appeal.

Another pictorial pattern was *Tulip Time*, introduced in 1962 (design patent number 192969). This was a single-scene motif of a Dutch village with a windmill and large round church, on the bank of a winding stream. Trails of smoke can be seen rising from several small houses, placing the scene in a nostalgic past, and there are two sailboats and a pair of swans. The foreground is composed of four little girls holding hands, wearing traditional flared headdresses and wooden shoes, standing in a clearing of a field of tulips. The border features six sprays of stylized flowers, some of which resemble tulips. This pattern was quite unusual in featuring a non-English scene, but it was very reminiscent of what was produced in Holland on "Delft" tiles and other ceramic souvenirs, which might give it a sense of quaint familiarity in the eyes of its American purchasers.

The most successful of the 1960s narrative designs, however, was *Coaching Scenes*. Introduced in 1963, it had a remarkable thirty-six-year run, being produced until 1999.[10] This pattern had all of the Johnson Brothers "bells and whistles": a British historical concept and pattern name; a decorative border with rococo scrolls and floral sprays; different scenes depicted on pieces of various shapes; and offered in a variety of colors to suit the taste of the individual customer (blue, pink, green, and brown multicolor). In order to simplify the production, some scenes were repeated on several pieces. The vignettes include "Coaching Scenes," which depicts a passenger coach drawn by four horses pulling away from a tavern in a country village, and "Coach Office" (Plate 14B) shows a coach full of passengers standing in front of the "White Horse Tavern & Family Hotel," with a cobblestone street indicating the location as a city. In "Hunting Country," the coach is ambling along a country road, apparently passing through a hunt in progress, since two dogs are racing past the coach in the foreground and the background has four riders on horseback galloping across the fields. "Gate Keeper" shows the coach paused in front of a wooden gate, and a coachman is blowing his long horn to summon the gatekeeper from his cottage, seen on the right.

Coaching Scenes was not the only pattern produced in the 1960s that returned to the theme of British history. A closely similar pattern featuring a nineteenth-century mail coach was *Royal Mail* by Myott,[11] and Ridgway produced a pattern called *The Original Coaching Days & Coaching Ways*. Other British-inspired patterns included *Royal Homes of Britain*, by Enoch Wedgwood. The resurgence in popularity of British historical themes may have been at least partly a result of the media celebrity of the British royal family, on both sides of the Atlantic. Queen Elizabeth's two youngest children, Andrew and Edward, were born in 1960 and 1964, adding to the popular demand for publicity, and the queen and her family were often seen in televised news footage. In 1966, a documentary on "Royal Palaces of Britain" was produced jointly by the British networks BBC and ITV, and it had a highly successful airing on Christmas Day.[12]

The ever-popular *Old Britain Castles* also received updates in the form of newly designed pieces. Norbury created the image for a 12-inch round "chop" plate of Haddon Hall, with a different view from the one engraved by Fennell on the small plate of the original series. This view is quite different in concept from the series' typical castle views, showing an interior courtyard, with a stone stair railing highlighted in the foreground. Norbury's daughter Kathleen recalled seeing him work at home on this engraving, which would place the time frame in the late 1960s or early 1970s.[13] The source image is "Haddon Hall from the Terrace," published in an 1876 book of views of *Picturesque Europe, Volume 1: The British Isles*.[14] The scene is of an inner courtyard of the house, and the viewpoint is from the top of the terrace. An example is also known of an *Old Britain Castles* "Haddon Hall" 11-inch "grill plate" with three wells, showing the same image on the chop plate as well as smaller views of a staircase and of the house as seen from the river. All three images are faithfully reproduced from illustrations in *Picturesque Europe*.[15] Some historical license was obviously taken, since the chop plate image of 1876 is identified at the lower right as "Haddon Hall in 1792." This was undoubtedly done to make it consistent with other images in the *Old Britain Castles* series.

American Folklife

In 1965, Johnson Brothers launched a new production line that hearkened back to the past, but also followed the trend of "contemporary casual." This series was called "Old Granite," and the name was an allusion to the "graniteware" that had launched the company's first commercial success in the late nineteenth century. The name also suggested the rock-like durability of "ironstone," which was a term used by many companies. The signature body of this series was light brown in color, with "speckles" that suggested the appearance of actual granite (Figure 6.1).

The patterns of "Old Granite" are linked to American folk life, and even though 1965 was somewhat in advance of the 1960s "hippie" culture, there was already a resurgence of interest in preserving traditions that were fast disappearing in

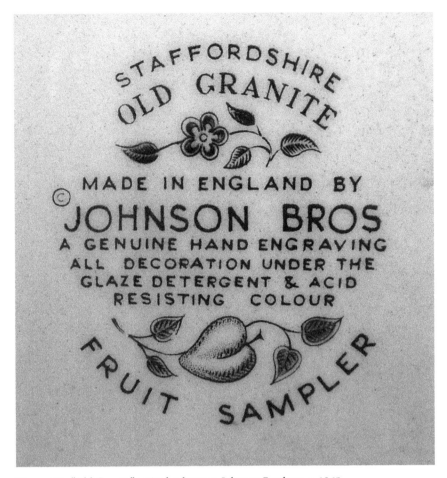

Figure 6.1 "Old Granite" series backstamp, Johnson Brothers, *c*. 1965.

the modern, urbanized, and industrialized world. The town of Newport, Rhode Island, already enjoying success with the annual Newport Jazz Festival since 1954, sponsored the Newport Folk Festival in 1959. That event was cofounded by folk singer Pete Seeger, and in future years the Festival helped launch the careers of singers who achieved international fame, such as Joan Baez and Bob Dylan. The Smithsonian Institution in Washington, DC, considered by most Americans to be their "national" museum, hired a former organizer of the Newport Folk Festival, Ralph Rinzler, and entrusted him with launching a "Festival of American Folklife" in 1967. This was a two-week summer event conceived as a "research-based presentation of contemporary living cultural traditions," which brought "musicians, artists, performers, craftspeople, workers, cooks, storytellers, and others to the National Mall to demonstrate the skills, knowledge, and aesthetics that embody the creative vitality of community-based traditions."[16]

The folk-inspired patterns of tableware by Johnson Brothers began with names from American history: *Jamestown*, after the first permanent English colony established in Virginia, in 1607; and *Salem*, after the Massachusetts town founded in 1626 (and most famous for the witch trials of 1692). *Jamestown* features a cartoonish, highly stylized two-handled vase with a pedestal base, from which are sprouting sprays of flowers composed of patchwork snippets of striped and plaid fabric (Plate 14C). It appears to be a Louise Flather design, with her characteristic pointed ovoid leaves. In contrast, *Salem* is a realistic, detailed rendering of a woven, handled basket overflowing with fruits still attached to the vine, including strawberries and grapes. It may also be a Flather design, but has a more elegant and artistic feel than the playful *Jamestown*.

Another source of inspiration for the "Old Granite" pattern motifs seems to have been the American "Pennsylvania Dutch" culture, found within rural communities established by German (Deutsch) immigrants in the nineteenth century. There were still living descendants of Amish and Mennonite settlers, who decorated functional objects such as furniture and quilts with traditional motifs, often selling them to "English" (non-Amish) tourists. Typical designs included rosettes, stars, circles, hearts, and "tree of life" patterns with mirror-image symmetry. Some of these designs were made for "hex signs," presumably hung on barns or houses to ward off evil spirits (since "hex" is the German word for "witch"). The hex signs, however, were not part of Amish tradition and were deliberately introduced in the mid-1930s to encourage tourism.[17]

In Johnson Brothers' "Old Granite" series, *Lancaster* is a pattern named for a town in western Pennsylvania, in the heart of Amish country, and it has a border pattern of stylized fruits and flowers that resemble cut-out stencil patterns. *Gretchen* features a typical German girl's name, for a border pattern of stylized flowers very similar to those shown in *Jamestown*. *Sun Up* features a center motif of a rooster, surrounded by stylized flowers, in a clear allusion to the fact that a day on the farm would usually begin with a rooster crowing at daybreak.

Other patterns seem to have been inspired directly by traditional crafts. *Fruit Sampler* is a multi-motif pattern that features a different fruit on each shape (Plate 14D). What makes this pattern distinctive, however, is the fact that the image looks embroidered, with small visible stitches. The border pattern is also composed of repeated stitch motifs, making it evident that "sampler" does not refer to the assortment of fruit. Instead, it refers to an embroidery "sampler," traditionally created by young girls who were practicing and perfecting their skills with different types of embroidery stitches. *Cherry Thieves* is an asymmetrical variation of an old quilt pattern, featuring two birds in the act of "stealing" ripe cherries. The highly stylized flowers have "stitchery" decoration that is suggestive of crewel embroidery.

The "Old Granite" patterns appear to have sold well enough to inspire another pattern, *Hearts and Flowers*, issued in 1967. This was a single-motif pattern, with a center design of a young couple in traditional German-style dress, including a large hat, knee breeches, and shoe buckles for the boy, and a bonnet and embroidered apron for the girl. They are holding hands, and are framed by very stylized flowers and two "hearts" along a central vertical axis. Bill Norbury recalled this pattern as one that was imposed, not allowing the engraver to interpret it, and he dismissed it as "a wooden design, junk." It was nevertheless the most popular of all the "Old Granite" patterns, remaining in production for twenty-four years, until 1991. This demonstrated that although the pattern did not meet Norbury's artistic standards, American purchasers recognized it as emblematic of Pennsylvania Dutch tradition and therefore embraced its "country-style" quaintness.

Another "Old Granite" addition was much more short-lived. *Sugar and Spice* was introduced in 1971 as an exclusive for Sears Roebuck and Co., but it only lasted for five years. This pattern had multiple motifs, but all of them were frankly cartoonish in nature, including a dinner plate featuring three plump gentlemen in "colonial" dress, awkwardly dancing and playing instruments at the base of a tree with patchwork fabric leaves. This was another design likely created by Flather, but in this case, the association with authentic historical tradition is absent. The title of *Sugar and Spice* is also incomprehensible, since the phrase is part of the nursery rhyme about "sugar and spice, and everything nice, that's what little girls are made of." The completing verses are "snips and snails, and puppy dog tails, that's what little boys are made of." The images bear no relation to the rhyme, other than suggesting the awkward drawings of young children, and although the design is lively, it could be seen either as whimsical exaggeration or as mocking caricature. It must be said in fairness, however, that the patterns *Sun Up*, with its evocative name and rooster motif, and *Salem*, with high artistic values, were also short-lived, each one being produced for only five years (1965–70).

The Wedgwood Acquisitions of 1968

In 1963, Wedgwood hired a new managing director, Arthur Bryan, a former bank clerk and a bomb aimer during the Second World War, who had risen through the ranks of the company from management trainee to president of the company's US operations from 1960–63.[18] According to Bryan's obituary in the London *Financial Times*:

> Bryan then led a period of expansion unparalleled in Wedgwood's history, taking over companies such as William Adams, Susie Cooper and Royal Tuscan. After Wedgwood was floated on the London Stock Exchange in 1967, Bryan became chairman the following year. Acquisitions continued of famous names such as Johnson Brothers, Coalport, Midwinter, J&G Meakin, Mason's Ironstone and Precision Studios.[19]

In 1968, Johnson Brothers was operating five factories, and this merger alone doubled the size of the Wedgwood company.[20] David Johnson, part of the fourth generation of Johnsons involved in running the company at the time, recalled that the proposed merger with Wedgwood split the family, and many of the younger generation Johnsons were opposed, but the decision was made by the "older generation," that is, David's father Shepard and his uncles James and Christopher.[21] Despite that opposition, one outcome of the acquisition was clearly the opportunity to benefit professionally and financially, as David subsequently left the company and became managing director of Midwinter, and his cousin Christopher went to work for Wedgwood in Barlaston, eventually rising to the position of manufacturing and technical director.[22] In 1983, David was able to purchase the hotelware division of Royal Doulton, and he formed a new company, Steelite International plc, serving as its chairman. In 2002, he sold Steelite to its management for a sum approximated at £35 million, according to the *Sunday Times*.[23]

There was one company that held out against acquisition, and that was Enoch Wedgwood Ltd. of Tunstall. The original Enoch Wedgwood was a distant cousin of the more famous Josiah, and he was a cofounder of Podmore, Walker & Co. in 1835. That firm did business until 1860, when it was renamed as Wedgwood and Co.[24] In 1965, the firm renamed itself as Enoch Wedgwood & Co. Anecdotal history in the area is that the larger Wedgwood company had sued its rival for trademark infringement, but was unsuccessful, because the descendants of Enoch had just as much of a right to use their family name as did the descendants of Josiah.[25] In 1980, however, the larger company got its wish, when it bought out Enoch Wedgwood and promptly rechristened it Unicorn Pottery, after the name of that company's manufacturing plant.

These multiple mergers had a direct consequence upon the production of the formerly independent small companies. Some of the operations were consolidated, and Bill Norbury was assigned responsibility for engraving:

> One of the Johnson Brothers Directors informed me directly (an unusual event in its own right) that "Wedgwood's" had taken over control of "Johnson Brothers" and they had also taken over control of "Meakins", "Midwinters", "Adams" and "Masons". It was further to be recognised that I was to be in charge of all engravers and engraving policies at work in all factories within the group. I visited "Adams" engraving department for the purpose of meeting Roy [Kirkham]. He wasn't too pleased, until I told him that I hadn't arranged it on a basis of personal profit and that in fact it was the responsibility of the companies involved and their Directors. That in fact I was so surprised as he that I had been chosen and had become the El Supremo of all Engravers. (p. 69)[26]

Norbury believed that he was able to bring about an elevation of the quality of wares being produced in the companies placed under his supervision. This consolidation, however, also worked against the small companies' ability to retain an individual brand identity. In addition, the directors of Wedgwood had ultimate power over the quality and quantity of what could be produced under each name, and over time, this would lead to the elimination of competing brands that generated less revenue. It would also allow Wedgwood to reserve the products of highest quality and price, for sale under its own "luxury" brand.

Wedgwood's chairman Arthur Bryan was knighted in 1976 for his services to export, and by 1977, the Wedgwood Group (as it was then called) operated twenty factories, "accounting for 20 percent of the British ceramic industry's output and 25 percent of its exports."[27]

Corporate Identity Crisis in the 1970s

Popular culture in the early 1970s embraced a number of conflicting trends. On one hand, the "hippie" or "counterculture" movement in America rejected conventional authority and modern industrialization, valuing individual freedom and advocating a "simple" life. On the other hand, however, a strong sense of conservatism remained, defending the values of "the establishment." This created a real dilemma for British companies attempting to understand the American market. Some companies, like Midwinter, focused on simplified "modern" designs, but Johnson Brothers' solution was to try to provide something for all tastes. As a result, the stylistic coherence that had given Johnson Brothers a recognizable "look" in the 1950s was fast disappearing.

Paisley was a pattern of 1970 that attempted to reflect the "hippie" movement, reproducing an Indian-inspired textile motif. The designer undoubtedly hoped that it would look "mod," and perhaps even psychedelic, but Bill Norbury missed the point, commenting that he disliked the motif because it "had no point to it."[28] The only thing he did like was the word "Paisley" in the backstamp, for which he invented a new style of lettering (Figure 6.2). Had he lived in a later generation, he would perhaps have developed this into an alphabet that we might know today as a "Norbury" font. The pattern itself did not catch on, however, and ended after only four years.

Another textile-like pattern was *Country Cupboard*, which lacked the familiar backstamp identifier of "a genuine hand engraving," and in fact the printing looks mechanical and imprecise. With its motif of flat, two-dimensional white flowers and leaves against a dark blue background, it does have a "back to nature" feel, but it could have been made by any pottery company, including one in the United States or Japan. The pattern was also short-lived, being produced for only four years, from 1973 through 1977.

At the same time, however, there was an attempt to continue the Johnson Brothers tradition of well-executed narrative scenes. *Alice in Wonderland* was a pattern produced in 1974, for the specialized market of children's tableware (Plate 15A).[29] The plate had a center design of Alice having tea with the White Rabbit, Dormouse, and Mad Hatter, and eight small vignettes around the border show other scenes from the famous book by Lewis Carroll (Charles Dodgson), with illustrations by John Tenniel. It is very likely because the source was a book published in 1865 that the engravings on the plate have a traditional feel, closely resembling the style of the original printed illustrations.

Another example of a narrative pattern was *Neighbors*, a multi-motif design introduced in 1974. That was the year in which *Historic America* was finally

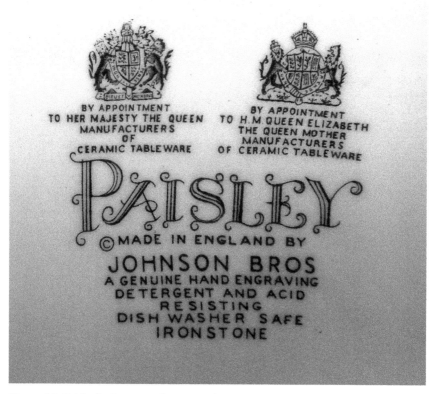

Figure 6.2 Paisley backstamp, Johnson Brothers, *c.* 1970.

discontinued, and a decision was made to copy its border of oak leaves and acorns on the new pattern. This may have proven to be an unfortunate miscalculation, since the border was never the most appealing aspect of the older design, and these oak leaves look even more oddly misshapen than the originals, which Norbury had compared to cabbage leaves. The scenes selected for *Neighbors* attempt to show life in small-town America, at some point in the past when women still wore long skirts and bonnets. The dinner plate is named "Band Concert" (Plate 15B) and shows a Victorian gazebo with uniformed musicians playing, while young couples dance, children play with kites and balloons, and other bystanders watch. The bread and butter plate shows a "Clambake" on a beach, presumably in New England, with sailing ships and a lighthouse in the background. A cup and saucer depicted a "Barn Raising," and a cereal bowl depicted a "Barn Dance." Despite the best efforts of the artist and engraver, however, the pattern only lasted for three years.

The commercial failure of *Neighbors* may have been a matter of poor timing. By the mid-1970s, American culture was being redefined by public protests against the Vietnam War and against discrimination based on race, gender, and social class. The old-fashioned rural scenes depicted by *Neighbors* may have reflected the traditional values of conservative white America, but they no longer resembled either a sentimental recollection or a social ideal for many potential consumers.

Some commercial success was achieved, however, by patterns that were commissioned as exclusives for large, successful retailers. *Petite Fleur* was a pattern produced in 1976 for Laura Ashley, originally a textile and wallpaper company named for its founder, but which expanded to include many types of decorative household goods. This pattern had an overall motif of small sprigs of flowers, with stylized snippets of ribbon and a rope pattern around the border (Plate 15C). It was undoubtedly the creation of a Laura Ashley designer, since their table patterns were intended to coordinate with other items such as linens and wallpaper. The backstamp (Figure 6.3) features the Laura Ashley brand mark, and also credits

Figure 6.3 Petite Fleur backstamp, by Johnson Brothers for Laura Ashley, *c.* 1976.

the Paris Bibliothèque des Arts Décoratifs (Library of Decorative Arts) before mentioning Johnson Brothers.

This would seem quite a comedown for Johnson Brothers, having to take third place behind the Laura Ashley company and the French library holding rights to the motif that inspired the design. On the positive side, however, the pattern used the "Old Granite" body that had been created in 1965, and this may have been a way of using up old unused stock. *Petite Fleur* was more successful than many other patterns of the time, surviving for fourteen years.

Heritage Hall

Another pattern of 1977 that had a respectable longevity was *Heritage Hall*, produced for the American retailer Sears Roebuck & Company for twelve years. The pattern had its own backstamp (Figure 6.4), with the name "Heritage Hall" arched over a five-pointed crown and stylized letters "S" and "R" flanked by lions rampant. A banner below states "Made in Staffordshire England," followed by the name Johnson Brothers, although in some examples the name of Johnson Brothers does not appear.

Figure 6.4 Heritage Hall backstamp, Johnson Brothers for Sears Roebuck & Co., *c.* 1977.

The pattern had an intricate border of scrolls, stylized flowers and a textile-like geometric pattern, similar but not identical to the border created for *Coaching Scenes* fourteen years earlier. For this pattern, the designers returned to the company's most tried-and-true concept: a multi-motif pattern that depicted authentic historical scenes and created high-quality visual art on tableware. In this case, the various subjects were styles of architecture associated with different time periods and geographical areas within the United States, and each backstamp bore the name of an architectural style and a short phrase describing its characteristics.

The dinner plate of *Heritage Hall* (Plate 15D) was "Georgian Town House, a popular town house design found in many eastern cities towards the end of the 18th century." The salad plate was "French Provincial, a typical home of the 'Vieux Carre' district of New Orleans," and the bread and butter plate was "Spanish American Hacienda, tiled roof adobe – stucco construction typical in the Spanish colonies and south western United States." Other pieces featured "Pennsylvania Fieldstone, a ruggedly designed home found throughout the Pennsylvania countryside," "Colonial Overhang, 17th century typical New England home," and "Southern Plantation, a typical Greek Revival period during the early 19th century." These six motifs were each used on two or more pieces, as for example the "Georgian Town House" appeared on the dinner plate, coffee mug, and covered tureen. All of the images show a house rendered in precise detail, but it is set within a pleasing landscape and is enlivened by people and animals that contribute to an appropriate and sometimes amusing narrative. In the "Spanish Hacienda" view, for example (Plate 16A), there is a bench in the foreground, upon which is seated a lady wearing a mantilla and carrying a fan, accompanied by a man playing a guitar. In the middle ground, a donkey is tethered to what looks like an orange tree. In the "Pennsylvania Fieldstone" image, there is a horse-drawn buggy and numerous human and animal figures, including a dog that is having a face-off confrontation with a duck.

The year 1977 was the year when Bill Norbury retired from Johnson Brothers, after a fifty-year career. Although he does not mention *Heritage Hall* in his memoirs, he would probably have had some involvement in the pattern's development, a presumption supported by the high quality of the pattern's execution, and by the fact that it was the last multi-motif narrative pattern that was entirely original and not a reissue of an older pattern, as would occur later on. The illustrations were also designed in the labor-intensive traditional way, with modifications to make the image fit the form of each piece by adding, subtracting, or repositioning various elements. *Heritage Hall* could quite easily have been produced in the 1950s rather than the late 1970s, but that was not detrimental to its success, and it was not discontinued until 1989.

Eternal Beau

A pattern of a very different nature was introduced in 1981, *Eternal Beau*. This was the creation of a New York designer, Sarina Mascheroni, and it became a great success in terms of longevity, remaining in production for thirty-three years, until 2014. It featured a relatively simple border pattern of sprays of small pink flowers on green stems, loosely intertwined with a satin-like tan ribbon (Plate 16B). A line of green rimmed each piece, providing contrast against the white body color, and on larger pieces such as plates, the ribbon included a bow. This pattern had a number of advantages in addition to its understated, pleasing design. The body shape was unusual compared to other patterns, in that it had an octagonal shape, not only for the edges of plates and bowls, but also used in the body of the cups and teapots. The plate edges and underside of the cups' octagonal body were also given texture by a row of raised dots inside of two delicate raised lines. The octagonal shape was not new for the Johnson Brothers company, having been used for at least eighteen patterns produced before 1940,[30] and the octagon with raised dots was introduced in the all-white *Heritage* pattern, created in 1963. That shape was used on at least twenty-one additional patterns, including *Eternal Beau*. The original backstamp also had a ribbon design, one of the last occurrences of a backstamp with a design that was complementary to the image on the front, and it credited the designer with the words "A Sarina Mascheroni Design."

The timing was right for the introduction of a romantic, traditional pattern, because July 29, 1981, was the date of the wedding of Prince Charles and Lady Diana Spencer. The royal wedding had dominated the worldwide media since the couple announced their engagement on February 24 of that year. *Eternal Beau* was also among the first British-made patterns to advertise in its backstamp that it was "dishwasher and microwave safe." Even though most ceramics without metallic decoration could be safely used in a microwave oven, this declaration was reassuring to potential customers. Although home microwaves had been introduced in the late 1960s, they were not widely used until the early 1980s, when they became more affordable.

Eternal Beau would go on to become one of the company's all-time biggest sellers, not only in America but also at home in Britain, but ironically its success may have contributed to the eventual weakening of the Johnson Brothers company. Many of the patterns subsequently produced had delicate contemporary designs, which could have been produced by Wedgwood itself, and this would prove to be threatening to the parent company.

Summerfields is an example of a high-quality contemporary design, introduced in 1985, that had the same plain round body shape and weight as "fine china" selling at much higher prices (Plate 16C). It featured a border of only three pink poppy-like blossoms, with pink and gray buds on gray "stems" reduced to simple lines. Further graphic contrast is provided by a black line just inside the plate's border, and by black stamens in the center of each flower. The backstamp (Figure 6.5) echoed the refined pattern on the front, printed in the same colors of black, gray, and pink.

Summer Chintz, also introduced in 1985, had a border pattern of stylized pink, blue, and yellow flowers and green leaves, on a fluted body shape rimmed by a line of pink. While this design was more traditional than *Summerfields*, it was also a good seller, remaining in production for twenty-three years.

Figure 6.5 Summerfields backstamp, Johnson Brothers, *c.* 1985.

Summer Chintz also used a new backstamp design (Figure 6.6), with the arched letters "JOHNSON BRO^S/SINCE 1883/®." Below this is the following self-promotional statement: "Johnson Brothers has been making fine tableware for over 100 years, establishing a proud reputation for craftsmanship and quality of design." The pattern name "Summer Chintz" is next, with a stylized flower bud in place of the dot over the letter I, then "Designed by Julie Holland."

The significant elements of this backstamp are to praise the company as a producer of "fine tableware" and to name the designer, as had been done with *Eternal Beau*. This was not customary in products of mid-range quality, but was done for higher-end wares, especially when the designer was a recognized name from the fashion industry. This attempt to elevate the product's perceived status may have been a tactical error, because now Johnson Brothers was appearing to compete for the same customers as the Wedgwood brand.

Figure 6.6 Summer Chintz backstamp, Johnson Brothers, *c.* 1985.

Wedgwood Mergers and Acquisitions

By 1986, Wedgwood had sales of 152 million pounds a year. This made it an attractive target of a takeover bid, perhaps with some poetic justice, considering its own earlier actions toward the smaller Staffordshire companies. According to the *Financial Times*, Wedgwood's chairman Sir Arthur Bryan "bitterly opposed a hostile bid by London International Group, which owned Royal Worcester and Spode fine china." This bid was resisted successfully, but in order to protect the company from future attempts, Bryan was forced to take a dramatic step:

> [He] agreed in 1986 to a pound(s) 250m "white knight" takeover by Waterford, the Irish crystal manufacturer […] Relations soon soured and Bryan accused the

new management, headed by an ex-Ford executive, of trying to run it like a car company. Bryan became president of Waterford Wedgwood in 1987 but retired a year later.[31]

Michael Perry recounts what happened next:

> In the late-1980s the new conglomerate faced increasing production costs combined with recession in its key North American markets and in 1988 private investors led by Irish businessman J.F. O'Reilly offered a company buyout. Although initially refused, O'Reilly and his co-investors acquired 15% of Waterford Wedgwood in 1990 and under a new management team the company returned to profitability in 1992.[32]

During this turbulent period, Wedgwood retrenched, discontinuing several of the formerly independent brands within the group. Midwinter stopped production in 1987, and Adams followed in 1992, ending a company that by some accounts could trace its lineage back to 1657. The individual labels of Johnson Brothers, Mason's, and Meakin survived, although with more limited ranges of production, and for a period of time, the smaller companies' wares were marketed under the name of "Creative Tableware," with the logo of a black bull seen in profile, with a "charging" posture of head down and tail waving (Figure 6.7). This logo formerly belonged to J. & G. Meakin, introduced around 1965 with the phrase "Bull in a China Shop." When Meakin was acquired by Wedgwood in 1970, two years after the Johnson Brothers acquisition,[33] Wedgwood acquired the rights to its logos as well as its designs.

On October 16, 1991, the Stoke *Evening Sentinel* published an advertising supplement devoted to Johnson Brothers, entitled "New name for quality tableware."[34] This supplement appears to promote a corporate decision to allow the reintroduction of the company name of Johnson Brothers. One of the many paid advertisements states: "We are proud of our association with Johnson Brothers and the fact that we have supplied to their factories a wide range of forming, processing and decorating equipment. We trust that the return to their famous brand name will bring them even greater success in the future."[35] *The Sentinel* reporter describes the company's recent history as follows:

> As a group within a group—the parent Wedgwood organisation—Johnson's embrace past tradition with former prowess absorbing the household names of J. and G. Meakin, Unicorn, Midwinter and Franciscan, but retaining the best for the last as a slim-Jim contender within the new market arena. Ten years of cossetting boardroom surgery, another name for rationalisation, has eliminated overlap, pared down excess and whittled a product range of 300-plus to 60. [...] Gone is the flab, former name and its china shop image—and although the bull remains, its outline is leaner. Under its proud new banner Johnson Brothers today employs some 1,500 workers, produced more than 800,000 pieces weekly in three close-knit factory units and flys a banner proclaiming two Royal

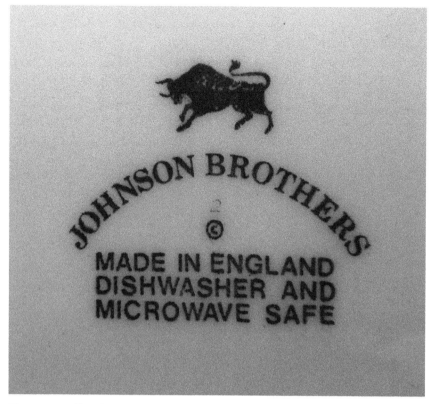

Figure 6.7 Bull Backstamp, Johnson Brothers, 1970s–1990s.

Warrants in support of its traditional and continuing boast to produce nothing less than English tableware at its finest.[36]

The new logo included two Royal Warrants (Figure 6.8), from Her Majesty the Queen and from H. M. Queen Elizabeth the Queen Mother, as manufacturers of ceramic tableware, which according to the supplement, were granted in 1978. (A company brochure printed in 1999 gives the date as 1970.) The supplement also highlights a quote from the Wedgwood Group chief executive, Kneale Ashwell:

> The new Johnson Brothers corporate identity marks the completion of an extensive rationalisation programme which began in the early 1980's, during which the famous names of Midwinter, Franciscan, J & G Meakin and Unicorn Tableware were brought together with Johnson Brothers into a cohesive group. Recognised as a leading supplier of well designed, affordable, all occasion tableware, Johnson Brothers is now set to face the exciting future.[37]

JOHNSON BROTHERS

Fine English Tableware

Manufactured to the highest standards of Fine English Tableware since 1883

Johnson Brothers — a name synonymous with Value for Money and Quality

MEMBER OF THE WEDGWOOD GROUP

Fresh Fruit — another winner from the Johnson Brothers stable

JOHNSON BROTHERS · P.O. BOX 10 STOKE-ON-TRENT ST1 3LN · Telephone (0782) 202123

Figure 6.8 Advertisement from *The Sentinel*, October 16, 1991.

Ashwell's statement includes a key phrase: "affordable, all occasion tableware." This reveals that although the company's name, factories, and workers survived the "rationalisation," or downsizing, their assigned role would be to fill the niche for low-end goods in the corporate organization. High-end goods would henceforth be reserved for the Wedgwood name.

The specific patterns mentioned in the supplement are relatively few. The reporter quotes Tom Bloor, the company marketing director:

> "We are a nation of gardeners and there's a Englishness about our products that's warm, friendly—and especially appealing to the foreigner." Hence he states, the runaway success of co-ordinate ranges such as "Eternal Beau"—perhaps the best-selling collection in the field—"Summer Chintz", "Summerfields", and "Fresh Fruit", the latest to take the market by storm.[38]

Fresh Fruit used the same octagonal body shape as *Eternal Beau*, and it also featured a dark green highlight around the rim. The single motif was an attractive spray of apples, a pear, grapes, and blackberries, offset by another spray of grapes, berries, and currants. Botanical accuracy was evidently not a goal, as the apples and pear are improbably attached to the same stem. *Fresh Fruit* remained in production until 2014, the same year in which *Eternal Beau* was discontinued.

Another pattern featured in the supplement, however, is *His Majesty*, the turkey pattern dating from 1959. That pattern is on the supplement's first page, in a photograph showing "a highly-skilled painter decorating a plate" (actually the full-size turkey platter). It is also mentioned in an article describing the patterns displayed in the Johnson Brothers showroom, and so is *Willow*, the Johnson Brothers version of the ubiquitous "blue willow" pattern, which the company had produced since the 1920s. Given that the vast production of at least six former companies of the Wedgwood Group had been reduced down to only sixty patterns, the survival of these two reflects the continued reliance upon wares that had had long-term success in the American market.

Recycling the Past

The uncertainty caused by the ongoing corporate mergers and subsequent shutdowns of acquired companies was undoubtedly an important factor in Johnson Brothers' increasing conservatism in regard to design. The company maintained production of a handful of patterns with consistent sales, such as *His Majesty, Willow*, and *Eternal Beau* mentioned above, and the 1963 pattern *Coaching Scenes*. This was not enough, however, so the company design staff looked to the past, to find patterns to copy and reissue in updated form.

One of those patterns was *Christmas Tree*, the Spode pattern that had remained popular since its introduction in 1938. Other similar patterns had been successful in the American market, such as *Happy Holidays* (1986–2014) and *Christmastime* (1991–2014) by the Japanese maker Nikko.[39] Johnson Brothers therefore decided to enter the competition with *Victorian Christmas*, launched in 1994. Unfortunately, however, there was nothing to distinguish this design from its rivals. Nikko's *Christmastime* had already appropriated the octagon shape that otherwise might have made it recognizable as a Johnson Brothers pattern, and Spode's version was not only much better known but also much more artistic, making *Victorian Christmas* seem flat and uninspired. It was nevertheless produced for eight years. In 2001, the decision was made to take the tree from that pattern and print it in pink or green, on a blank plate with an *Old Britain Castles* pink border. That pattern, labeled on the backstamp as "Christmas/Old Britain Castles," lasted from 2002 to 2014.

Another case in which a pattern was copied from an earlier version was *Fruit Sampler*, originally part of the "Old Granite" series of 1965, which was reissued in 1996. This was the multi-motif design with a different type of fruit on different pieces. There was a critical element missing, however; apparently the later designer did not understand that "sampler" was a reference to sewing, and did not recognize that the center motif and border were intended to suggest embroidery stitches. The new *Fruit Sampler* had center fruit motifs that seem to be photographed from a pastel drawing, and the border was simplified, from eight bands clearly representing different types of stitches, to three lines of stylized leaves and flowers made of lines and dashes. The design retained the general appearance but not the clever meaning of the original.

In the meantime, the cycle of corporate mergers was continuing. Once again on a quest to acquire rival companies, Waterford Wedgwood acquired a British crystal manufacturer, Stuart & Sons Ltd., in 1995; the German china and crystal company Rosenthal in 1998; the US cookware company All-Clad in 1999; and the German porcelain company Hutschenreuther in 2000.[40]

Williams-Sonoma and the "Wedgwood Archives"

There was also a partnership that was not a merger, but rather a collaboration, in which the American cookware company Williams-Sonoma marketed a series of designs produced by Wedgwood. On October 3, 2000, the Stoke *Sentinel* published a story entitled "140 New Jobs at Wedgwood":

> Wedgwood said the deal, worth 1.25 million [pounds] in its first year and 3 million the following year, was the result of collaboration with a Williams-Sonoma design team led by style guru Peri Wolfman. Chief executive Brian Patterson said: "Although the new patterns are based on the heritage, elegance and romance of Wedgwood's long history, they also manage to be vibrant and modern, fitting in with the contemporary demands of the American consumer". [...] Wedgwood confirmed the four new designs were inspired by the historic Highgrove, Mayfair, Kent, and Plymouth patterns preserved in its archive.[41]

Figure 6.9 Plymouth backstamp, Williams-Sonoma, *c.* 2000.

It was accurate to say that these names corresponded to ones previously used by Wedgwood; *Mayfair* had been used for at least four separate patterns, and *Highgrove*, the name of a house famously used by Prince Charles and Princess Diana, had been in production from 1991 to 1998. (The name was no longer as appealing after the royals divorced in 1996, and the princess' death in 1997.) The motifs, however, all differed from the ones in the original patterns. The Williams-Sonoma *Catalogue for Cooks, Christmas 2000* shows *Plymouth* with a beige body and no motif in the center, and the border was exactly the same as the oak leaf and acorn border of *Historic America*. A salad plate repeated the oak leaf and acorn pattern, but without the mesh-like background and scalloped edge. The body of the teacup repeated the full *Historic America* border with scallops and mesh, and the saucer and rimmed soup bowl used the border of *The Friendly Village*. The catalogue copy includes this description on p. 51:

> Perfect for autumn meals, our transferware is made by Josiah Wedgwood & Sons, the renowned English company founded in 1759. The motif of acorns and wildflowers is based on one from the Wedgwood archives. The designs vary within each place setting. Microwave and dishwasher safe.

On the same page, the catalogue describes a "Transferware Turkey Platter":

> A family heirloom if ever there were one, this earthenware platter is made exclusively for Williams-Sonoma by Josiah Wedgwood & Son. The pattern, called "His Majesty," replicates an original from the company's archives and is applied using a 19th-century technique: It's first hand engraved on a copper roller, then printed on tissue paper and transferred onto the platter—hence the term "transferware." The platter will show off your holiday bird in grand style and also makes a beautiful display piece. Microwave and dishwasher safe. (p. 51)

The platter's central motif is exactly the same *His Majesty* as the one Bill Norbury had engraved and Johnson Brothers had produced from 1959 through 1996. Only three years later, it appeared again under the name of Wedgwood, as the Williams-Sonoma exclusive pattern. The platter's body shape was also the same one used by Johnson Brothers, but the border design was actually copied from the one used in *The Friendly Village*. It was technically correct to state that the "original" was "from the company's archives," in the sense that Wedgwood was the corporate owner of all wares manufactured by Johnson Brothers, even those designs introduced before the merger in 1968. It was, however, intentionally misleading to the customer, who would assume that it was an historical Wedgwood pattern. The name of Wedgwood carried much more name-recognition and prestige than Johnson Brothers in the eyes of the Williams-Sonoma company and their American customers, justifying the platter's price of ninety-eight dollars.

In its 2001 Holiday catalogue, distributed before Thanksgiving, Williams-Sonoma advertised an expanded line of "Wedgwood" patterns that included a *Royal Game* large platter in green, with the same body shape as the platter of *His*

Majesty, but a different border. The central motif was a pair of pheasants featured in Johnson Brothers' 1951 pattern *Game Birds*, another Norbury engraving. The pattern *Mayfair* had a set of Christmas-themed salad plates called *Christmas Eve*, using the exact same image as Johnson Brothers' *Merry Christmas* of 1959.

Not all of the Williams-Sonoma Wedgwood patterns were borrowed from Johnson Brothers, and one of them was newly created for the collaboration, a *Mayfair* cake plate of "Olde St. Nick." That design shows Santa Claus and a reindeer facing the viewer, next to a pillar helpfully labeled on top as "North Pole." There is also a building behind the two figures, with a sign reading "U.S. Post Office North Pole." The concept behind this design is somewhat confusing, since Santa Claus famously delivers gifts by traveling to homes in his sleigh, not by carrying them to a branch of the post office. Santa also has an unusual facial expression and gesture, with his lips pursed into a small "o" and the index figure of his left hand pointed upward. The explanation for what Santa is trying to tell us remains a mystery, at least to this author.

The Williams-Sonoma Wedgwood collaboration was not a commercial success. According to Replacements.com, *Plymouth* and *Mayfair* were both discontinued in 2004, and they do not appear in the company's Thanksgiving 2004 catalogue. Instead, they were replaced by a new collection "based on originals from Spode archives," blending "new elements with historic Spode designs dating from the early 1880s."

Historic America II

In 2002, Johnson Brothers launched a reimagined version of its famous pattern, called *Historic America II* (Plate 16D). The pattern consisted of a mixture of some images that had been used in the original series, and new images that were chosen specifically for this series. The border was also completely different, which made sense at the time, because Williams-Sonoma was marketing the original one in the *Plymouth* pattern, under the Wedgwood name. The new border had branchlets of small oak leaves and very large acorns, alternating with small sprays of ivy. The background of the original border was formed of small circles, resembling netting, and the new background was a series of crossed diagonal lines, resembling fishnet stockings. The edge of the original border was a pattern that suggests to this author the crimped edge of a pie crust, and the new version had a series of irregularly formed tiny five-point stars. A banner was also added on the lower center edge of the image, identifying the scene. The backstamp reproduces the original eagle and two banners, but instead of giving the "title" of the scene on the banners, the upper one says "Johnson Bros." and the lower one says "Made in England." In the center, between the upper and lower banners, are the words HISTORIC AMERICA II, and below the lower banner it states "Dishwasher and Microwave Safe." The visual quality of the series overall was not as high as in the original pattern, but as in the case of Royal's *Memory Lane*, a buyer who was not able to compare one piece against another may not have been aware of that contrast.

Historic America II had an extensive product list, and scenes that were duplicated from the earlier pattern were put on different pieces. St. Louis, previously on a soup bowl, was on a square salad plate; the Capitol in Washington, DC, previously on a square salad plate, was on a dinner plate; Wall Street, previously on a medium plate, was on the inside of a vegetable bowl. Boston, Massachusetts, which was previously the image of the dinner plate, was on a salad plate. The St. Louis image resembles the one used in the original series, but the images of the Capitol, Wall Street, and Boston were inexplicably reversed, as mirror images of the originals. There were also multiple scenes for some pieces of the same size, undoubtedly to encourage a "collecting" impulse on the part of the buyer, with nine images for dinner plates (10¾ inches in diameter) and nine images for square salad plates (7¾ inches).[42]

The most significant departure from the original *Historic America*, however, was in the choice of the new scenes that were added. Of the nine scenes used for dinner plates, only two were repeats from the first series (the Capitol in Washington, the Flying Cloud clipper ship), and some of the new scenes were clearly based upon modern photographs: the Empire State Building, the Brooklyn Bridge, the Statue of Liberty, a view of "Central Park—Bethesda Fountain," and "100 Years of Flight," featuring a biplane with a man (presumably Orville or Wilbur Wright) standing nearby. The new square salad plates included the Statue of Liberty (in a different view from the dinner plate) and no fewer than four images of Texas. Of those four, one was from the earlier series, a view of the Alamo previously used on a coffee cup (and again, reversed in the new version), but the other scenes were of a "Cattle Drive," "West Pecos," and most jarringly, "The Texas Oil Boom," with an image of a derrick gushing forth oil. The salad plates also include hand-drawn images of a flag, entitled "Stars and Stripes," and "American Bald Eagle," and in both cases there are lines added to suggest the rays of the sun. Another new image appeared on a 10-inch serving bowl, of "Pt. Marshal," which this author had to look up in order to identify. It is actually a minor landmark in Maine, known as the Marshall Point Lighthouse, the current building of which dates from 1857. It is not known why this item was included among other locations that were much more famous.

Some of the changes made were somewhat puzzling, such as placing a decorative image in the bottom center inside a bowl, where it would remain invisible when used. This is the case with the "Natural Bridge in Virginia," placed inside a 5½-inch bowl. When this was done in the original series, the entire interior surface was decorated, and the border of each piece was uniquely designed to fill the entirety of the concavely curved portion. In *Historic America II*, the border was unchanged, often leaving a large white space between the border and the image. Some of the most detailed scenes were treated in this manner, including "Wall Street" inside a round vegetable bowl (8 inches), and a "soup/cereal" bowl (6¾ inches) with a tiny scene of the "New York Crystal Palace." The Crystal Palace image was previously on a large cake plate, where every detail of the illustration was visible. Such a plate would also be used only on rare occasions, and therefore its primary purpose would be for display.

According to Replacements.com, *Historic America II* was only in production for two years, from 2002 through 2003. Its designers had failed to take into account the reasons behind the widespread popularity and longevity of the original series, and foremost among these reasons was the absolute imperative that the images be of true artistic quality. This was not observed, as can be seen from visible pixelation resulting from a low-quality digital scan of the original plates or the photographs from which the new scenes were created. No one looking at a plate of *Historic America II* was likely to confuse it with a nineteenth-century engraving hanging in a museum.

Second, the subjects chosen often lacked artistic appeal. The biplane or the oil derrick may have had a significant role in the economic development of a region, or even a nation, but they are not inherently charming subjects that call forth the spirit of the pioneers or the grandeur of natural landscapes. Images such as "West Pecos," showing a cowboy on horseback in front of a saloon-like building, did not recognize the fact that Americans were saturated with such stereotyped images, from decades of Western movies and television series. In the case of the poorly drawn flag and eagle haloed by "rays of glory," the images lost any connection to "high art" or to the authenticity of the historical views, the two key components of this tableware's original identity.

From Staffordshire to Han Dan

On June 5, 2003, the *New York Times* ran the following item in its "World Business Briefing":

> The maker of crystal and tableware Waterford Wedgwood said it would cut more than 10 percent of its British work force and move production of earthenware out of Britain to cut costs. Manufacturing of Johnson Brothers, a line of moderately priced tableware, is being relocated to Asia. Johnson, founded in 1883, was bought by Wedgwood in 1968. The move will eliminate 1,058 jobs and close two factories in England. Overall profit for the year ended March 31 was up 14 percent, to 64.2 million euros ($75.3 million), but profit in the unit that includes Johnson Brothers was down 69 percent, to 3 million euros.[43]

On June 11, *The Guardian* in London ran another story, which gave further details; the two factories were the Eagle and Alexandra potteries, and the 1,000 lost jobs represented "a third of Wedgwood's workers. The Johnson range can be made 70 percent more cheaply in the Far East."[44] This turn of events was not without precedent, as many British companies were joining the ranks of companies worldwide, seeking to reduce costs by outsourcing to Asia.[45] Johnson Brothers production was relocated to Han Dan, China,[46] near the historical porcelain capital of Jingdezhen. The Johnson Brothers backstamp dropped the phrase "Made in England," and instead carried the words "England 1883" (Figure 6.10). There was no indication of the true location of manufacture, except on the temporary sticker containing the product bar code, which had the words "Made in China."

Figure 6.10 Johnson Brothers England 1883 backstamp, c. 2007.

At first, the impact on Johnson Brothers design was not dramatic; strong sellers like *The Friendly Village* and *Eternal Beau* carried on as usual, and some new designs were introduced, although these tended to follow closely upon what had come before. One critical difference, however, was that the quality of decoration was lower in comparison to the earlier patterns. There was also a marked conservatism, even timidity, in the types of patterns introduced. In 2004, a new turkey pattern was launched, entitled *Autumn Monarch*. The following description is from an advertising brochure, and it acknowledges that the pattern is in fact a compilation of elements from previous designs.

> Johnson Brothers' Friendly Village was introduced in the USA in 1953. It depicts rural American village and farm scenes in autumn colorations. The pattern features a leaf motif around each individual country scene and is produced in a dark brown color with simple blue, green and yellow color highlights. His Majesty followed shortly in 1959, a traditional holiday pattern depicting a turkey scene. His Majesty includes beautiful pumpkin and harvest time fruit motifs in the border. The American themes propelled these patterns to become the most collectible Johnson Brothers patterns in the USA. Both continue to be produced and remain best sellers today. For the first time, Autumn Monarch, pulls together several of these archival elements from the popular Johnson Brothers patterns to

create a brand new pattern. The princely turkey is seen in a farm setting, in rich hues of brown, pink, green, and gold. The border design features both seasonal fruit and intricately detailed leaves. Every item is produced in durable stoneware ideal for today's casual everyday use and is dishwasher and microwave safe. This unique dinnerware is perfect for setting your table and is surely destined to become an American classic.

The description above is correct, in that the border was essentially the same as the one used for *The Friendly Village*, but with the addition of the squash-and-fruit motifs used in *His Majesty*. The turkey portrayed, however, was not the same one in *His Majesty*. That turkey, as mentioned above, had been appropriated by Williams-Sonoma. It did not in fact correspond to a turkey in any known Johnson Brothers pattern, although it was somewhat similar to a turkey in an unnamed Enoch Wedgwood pattern probably dating from the mid-1960s. The background setting, with a barn and chickens, was actually copied from *Barnyard King*, the Johnson Brothers pattern of 1950.

One attempt at originality was a pattern called *Girls Born to Shop*, stating on the backstamp "© 2005 H&H Ltd, Produced under license by johnson brothers® England 1883." This was an unusual pattern to say the least, with cartoon images of exaggeratedly thin young women in comical scenes, based on irreverent sayings mostly having to do with being overweight or avoiding housework. It was not a complete set, but included at least six motifs for dessert/pie plates, one bowl, and twenty-four motifs for coffee mugs. Some of the sayings are self-affirming, such as "The best man for the job is a woman," and some are humorous takes on modern life, such as "I eat all the main food groups, microwave, fast and frozen." A few of them, however, are somewhat mean-spirited: "Lord if you won't make me skinny, please make my friends fat," and "Fridge pickers wear bigger knickers."[47] The term "knickers" suggests that at least some of the designers involved were British, since this term is not used in American English, and their attempts at "feminist" humor sometimes veered uncomfortably close to misogyny.

In contrast, other patterns created after the company production moved to China reflect extreme caution, resulting in blandness and lack of visual interest. *Sienna* had a simple banded border and might have appeared contemporary if it had been produced in 1966, instead of 2006; it lasted only three years. *Basket Weave*, introduced in 2007, was on a grayish-tan body, and its decoration looks like a very faint photograph of a woven basket, in pale green ink. It is not surprising that the pattern was discontinued only a year later, in 2008.

The Fate of Wedgwood

In 2003, at virtually the same time that Johnson Brothers production was outsourced to China, the parent company increased its existing 14.9 percent share of Royal Doulton to 21 percent. According to Michael Perry:

In April 2005 Waterford Wedgwood acquired the remaining 79% of Royal Doulton's share capital, thus acquiring the rights to the key Doulton, Mintons, and Royal Albert brands. Far from stabilizing the financial position of Waterford Wedgwood, the 2005 purchase of Royal Doulton for £90 million exacerbated its financial difficulties and by September 2008 the Group's net debt had reaching an unsustainable £377 million. A share issue in September 2008 to raise £122 million to pay down debt raised only half the required funds, and on 2nd December 2008 the company announced that it had breached loan covenants with its banks. Three extensions to the deadline for payment were negotiated, but on 5th January 2009 Waterford Wedgwood plc was placed in the hands of administrators.[48]

Sir Arthur Bryan, the retired company chairman, was quoted as saying at the time, "the board made a botch of it."[49]

Not long afterward, on February 28, 2009, the *Wall Street Journal* reported that Waterford Wedgwood had found a buyer: KPS Capital Partners, a New York private equity group.[50] On March 26, a new company was formed, WWRD Holding Ltd, the letters of which were an acronym for Waterford Wedgwood Royal Doulton. As reported by *The Telegraph*:

> Shortly after the takeover, KPS parachuted in an entirely new management team and overhauled the company to put its Waterford, Wedgwood, Royal Doulton and Royal Albert brands under one umbrella business. This new management team focused on a "new business strategy and results-driven corporate culture" KPS said. Michael Psaros, managing partner of KPS, said that the original business "was thoroughly shattered, every part of it needed to be fixed. The business failed for a number of reasons, but not because of the recession, that's a false narrative," he said before explaining that under the original management the company's brands had separate manufacturing, supply and marketing facilities which eroded profits. "Businesses don't end up in trouble, they are managed into the ditch," Mr Psaros added.[51]

Six years later, in May 2015, KPS sold Waterford Wedgwood to the Fiskars company, headquartered in Helsinki, Finland, and best known in America for its line of scissors. According to the company's own stock exchange release on May 11, "Fiskars continues executing its growth strategy and becomes a leading global branded consumer goods company in the luxury and premium home and lifestyle products market."[52] At the time, Fiskars also owned the Danish porcelain company Royal Copenhagen, acquired in 2012, the Slovenian crystal company Rogaška, and product lines under the names of fashion designers Vera Wang and Jasper Conran, celebrity chef Gordon Ramsay, and the Australian model Miranda Kerr.

Fiskars's "luxury and premium" identity did not allow for the inclusion of a brand such as Johnson Brothers, which Wedgwood had already relegated to the role of "everyday, all-occasion" tableware. Replacements.com lists the date of 2014 for the discontinuation of the patterns *Old Britain Castles* and *Eternal Beau*, and it appears that by the time KPS was acquired by Fiskars in 2015, Johnson Brothers had officially ceased to exist. The one-time "Great American firm," which found its greatest success in creating scenes from British and American history, had itself become a relic of the past.

Conclusion:
ENDINGS AND BEGINNINGS

Toward the end of Bill Norbury's memoir, in a passage probably written around 1999, he made the following rueful comment:

> The other day I happened to pass by the Hanley and Imperial Potteries, in both cases a sad scene of utter desolation. Dozens of printers and print transferrers had been working there on the patterns I had produced. I noticed that there were vandals inside, not the elder Johnsons Family this time but unemployed youths. (p. 174)

Norbury died in July of that year, and did not live to see the systematic eradication of Johnson Brothers' physical presence, which would take place in the next several years. The first factory, Pankhurst's Charles Street Works acquired by Frederick and Alfred Johnson in 1882 or 1883, had been closed during the depression of the 1930s, and although its exact date of demolition is unknown, by 2010 it had become the site of a shopping arcade and a center for the charitable organization Women's Royal Volunteer Services (WRVS).[1]

There were four company factories on Eastwood Road in Hanley, alongside the Caldon Canal. The first was built originally by J. & G. Meakin in 1883, and was called the Eastwood Pottery. That building had been sold to Johnson Brothers around 1958, when Meakin relocated to the Eagle Pottery, and by 1996, it was sold again, to the firm of Emma Bridgewater, a designer of pottery hand-decorated with cheerful motifs such as polka dots and chickens.[2] The Eagle Pottery, to which Meakin had relocated in 1958, was acquired by Johnson Brothers when Meakin production was ended in 2000. When Johnson Brothers production was moved to China in 2003, the pottery was closed, and it was demolished in 2005.

The Hanley Pottery, the second factory on Eastwood Road, was originally built in 1859, but it was part of the Johnson Brothers holdings by 1897. It was closed in 1993, and was demolished in 2005 for the construction of a housing development. The third factory, the Trent Sanitary Works, was erected in 1896, and was demolished in 2004. The Imperial Pottery, on Eastwood Road between Franklyn Street and the Caldon Canal, was operating by 1900, but was closed around 2004 and demolished in 2005. The Waterside Primary School now stands on the site.[3]

The company's fifth factory, the Alexandra Pottery, was built by Johnson Brothers in 1886 on Scotia Road in Tunstall, the only pottery located outside of Hanley. The factory was closed in October 2003, and was demolished for the construction of a retail park built in 2005.

Although the physical record was destroyed, that did not mean that the community lost all interest in the potteries that had provided the livelihood of generations of families. On February 26, 2007, the *Birmingham Post* reported that the former site of the Johnson Brothers Hanley Pottery was being excavated:

> Students are helping archaeologists in a race against time to save part of Stoke-on-Trent's pottery heritage on a plot of land due for a new housing estate. A team of experts have uncovered the foundations of a 19th century bottle kiln oven in Hanley, said to be the best preserved example ever. However, bulldozers are soon to move on to the land, known as Hanley Works, to make way for 71 new homes. They will tear up the ground where the former pottery firm Johnson Brothers' factory once stood on Bottleslow Street on which the kiln and other artefacts from the past have been found. The Stoke-on-Trent Archaeology Service has now drafted in forensic science students from Staffordshire University to help record the historic findings before they are lost. Dr. John Casella, senior lecturer in forensics at the university, said: "It is very rare to find sites in such good condition as this. […] It is fantastic that we can also help the archaeology service to record Stoke-on-Trent's rich past and preserve these findings for future generations to learn from when the real evidence has been destroyed."[4]

In addition to the gathering of archaeological data, there has also been an effort to record the collective memory of surviving individuals who worked in the pottery trade. Emma Bridgewater, owner of the former Eastwood Pottery operated by Johnson Brothers, sponsored the "Eastwood Works Community Project" in 2014, inviting local residents to attend a series of coffee mornings to reminisce. She was quoted by the Stoke *Sentinel* as saying:

> When speaking to local people there are so many wonderful stories about the factory and its surrounding area that it would be lovely to capture those that we can before they are forgotten, and to display them in an archive here at the factory for all to enjoy. We were looking to do something simple to celebrate 30 years, and what better way than to celebrate nearly 130 years of the factory itself.[5]

There was no hope of ever recapturing the industry's glory days. In an article of 2011, *The Telegraph* acknowledged the decline of the pottery industry in Stoke-on-Trent:

> In the late 19th century the region was the epicentre of the world's ceramic production, home to more than 2,000 kilns firing millions of products a year. But within 100 years a sharp decline in British manufacturing, which led to the closure of mines, steelworks and factories, brought Stoke, and the industry that

was integral to its identity, to its knees. As recently as the 1970s there were 200 factories still operating in the area; today there are about 30. Between 1998 and 2008 the Potteries lost more than 20,000 jobs.[6]

The article continues in a more hopeful vein, however, describing a "new breed of manufacturers who are picking up the pieces and putting its china back on the map." Foremost among these was Emma Bridgewater, described as "the most high-profile member of Stoke-on-Trent's new guard." Her company's website states that as of 2017, it was producing 1.3 million pieces of pottery each year.

Another success story discussed in the article was the Portmeirion pottery, founded in 1960 by Susan Williams-Ellis, which in 2009 had acquired Spode, Royal Worcester, and Pimpernel, a manufacturer of placemats and coasters, forming the Portmeirion Group. As the article states, the company "took the bold step of reversing the region's manufacturing trend—it actually returned some of Spode's production from China and Malaysia to Stoke [...] the reinstatement of the Made in England stamp on the bottom of a Blue Italian tea cup will bring back some of the cachet that had been lost." An earlier Spode pattern from 1986, *Woodland*, was also described as being planned for reintroduction. The article noted that the Denby pottery firm of Derbyshire owned and operated the historic Burleigh Pottery, and mentioned four young designers whose works were being produced in Stoke: Andrew Tanner, Reiko Kaneko, Kaoru Parry, and Katy Potts.

The year 2011 was also notable as the founding date of a new company in Stoke: 1882 Ltd., the codirectors of which were Christopher Johnson and his daughter Emily. The company's mission statement was as follows:

> In 1882 the Johnson Brothers began producing ceramics in the heart of the Stoke-on-Trent potteries. 134 years later 1882 Ltd. continues the Johnson legacy with the company name evoking the deep routes [sic] of the family heritage. 1882 Ltd. was formed in 2011 by fifth generation Emily Johnson and her father, Christopher, who has worked in the industry since 1958. 1882 Ltd.'s mission is to champion inventively designed ceramic products from lighting to domestic ware to works of art whilst employing the manufacturing heritage of Stoke on Trent and promoting the British ceramic industry. In collaborating with exceptionally talented designers to realise their interpretation of a very traditional material and craft, 1882 Ltd. will bring innovative ceramics to a wider audience while supporting a valuable UK resource.[7]

As noted in Chapter 1, the actual earliest date recorded for a firm doing business as "Johnson Brothers" was 1872, and although the company's self-proclaimed founding date was 1883, the record is unclear as to exactly when the Johnsons took over the Pankhurst factory, which went bankrupt in 1882. Wedgwood owned the trademark of "Johnson Brothers/Since 1883," but there was nothing to prevent a new company from moving that date back by one year, especially because the partners of 1882 Ltd. were both members of the Johnson family and could claim whatever date they wished.

1882 Ltd. received favorable press, including an article in the London *Daily Telegraph* of August 13, 2016, which describes the company's origins as follows:

> Emily's objective was to bring ceramics production under the family name back to Britain. The idea for 1882 started when Emily, who was selling advertising in Los Angeles at the time, went to Christopher with some designs she had created for ceramic lighting. "Dad had retired as head of manufacturing at Waterford Wedgwood, and he wasn't taking to it very well," she says. "He looked at my designs, said, 'They're impossible to do,' and jumped at the challenge." Five years on, Emily and Christopher continue to embrace challenges, and have made a name for themselves by collaborating with cutting-edge designers on design-led industrial ceramics, sold from their website and at retailers such as Selfridges, The Conran Shop and SCP.[8] One of their main criteria when approaching a designer is that they have never worked with ceramics before. [...] She is passionate about keeping the ceramics industry, and the skills involved in factory production, alive.[9]

In analyzing this present-day Staffordshire pottery, one can see echoes of the factors that contributed to the wares' success in previous generations. Although they appear to be at opposite ends of the design spectrum, Emma Bridgewater and 1882 Ltd. have much in common. Both companies take pride in the Staffordshire heritage, and believe in the superior quality of ceramics made locally, as well as in the prestige of objects that are "Made in England." Both potteries also insist upon honoring the creativity of an individual designer, whether it be Emma Bridgewater herself or a contemporary artist who normally works in another medium. And both companies view their productions as works of art, whether it be a cheerful motif on a mug as in the case of Bridgewater, or highly conceptual, avant-garde shapes that push the boundaries of technique as in the case of 1882 Ltd.

In this sense, the next generation of Staffordshire potters has much in common with their predecessors. The understanding that tableware is a form of art is an idea that has not been significantly altered, even though its physical manifestations have changed to reflect the aesthetic values of their times. Bill Norbury, who spent a lifetime creating designs for "ordinary" tableware, never ceased to consider himself an artist first and foremost. In describing his design for *Camellia*, he wrote:

> I was really inspired to have taken this one, the dust-like stipple, one dot at a time and placed freely to really look free. It seemed to go on just as in a dream, no glaringly obvious pattern, just as if part of the basic shadows within the flower petals. Gentle as a butterfly's wing, then the graver lines following, just as gentle, like gossamer, together to the shades. It was truly beautiful, like the flower itself, gentle and delicate in the extreme. I was so pleased by what I had achieved, a sort of divine inspiration. I hope people don't take offence at this statement, but if that is what you feel then you should say it. (p. 72)

Norbury's artistic legacy is in no way diminished by the fact that it was mass-produced on thousands of pieces. On the contrary, this meant that there were vast numbers of people who saw, in his own words, "my efforts such as they were, spread worldwide on pottery" (p. 178). His story continues to be told, as do the stories of other artists like him, thanks to the medium of tableware.

NOTES

Introduction

1. An image of this bowl is shown in Plate 7B.
2. An image of this plate is shown in Plate 7A.
3. These statements were made by residents of Stoke-on-Trent in the course of interviews conducted by the author in July 1998.
4. A useful compendium of pottery firms that produced competing patterns of tableware is Paul Atterbury, Ellen Paul Denker and Maureen Batkin, *Miller's Twentieth-Century Ceramics, A Collector's Guide to British and North American Factory-Produced Ceramics*, revised edition (London: Miller's [Octopus Publishing Group Ltd.], 2005). See also the comprehensively researched and beautifully illustrated work by Charles L. Venable, Ellen P. Denker, Katherine C. Grier and Stephen G. Harrison, *China and Glass in America 1880–1980, From Tabletop to TV Tray*, exhibition catalogue (Dallas, TX: Dallas Museum of Art; New York: Distributed by Harry N. Abrams, 2000).
5. G.W. Rhead and F.A. Rhead, *Staffordshire Pots and Potters* (London: Hutchinson and Co., 1906), pp. 313–14.
6. *The Pottery Gazette*, March 2, 1908, p. 325.
7. Ibid., p. 326.
8. *The Pottery Gazette*, April 1, 1909, p. 446.
9. Mary J. Finegan, *Johnson Brothers Dinnerware, Pattern Directory & Price Guide* (Statesville, NC: Signature Press, 1993; second edition, Boone, NC: Minor's Printing Company, 2003). Dates of pattern production will be taken from Finegan's second edition, unless stated otherwise.
10. William H. VanBuskirk, *The Johnson Bros., A Dynasty in Clay* (Big Rock, IL: s.n., 1998).
11. Ibid., p. 16. VanBuskirk established the dating based on backstamp marks for Johnson Brothers published by Geoffrey A. Godden, *Encyclopaedia of British Pottery and Porcelain Marks* (London: Herbert Jenkins, 1964).
12. Bob Page and Dale Frederiksen, *Johnson Brothers Classic English Dinnerware* (Greensboro, NC: Page/Frederiksen Publications, 2003).
13. Joe Keller and Mark Gibbs, *English Transferware, Popular 20th Century Patterns* (Atglen, PA: Schiffer Publishing Ltd., 2005), pp. 29–31, 39–51, 72–81, 119–24, 134–46.
14. Details of Norbury's experiences were related by him in a personal interview with the author on July 7, 1998.
15. William Norbury, *Designs on a Career as a Decorator* (unpublished manuscript, 1999), 178 pages; quoted by permission of the author. Quotations are edited to correct minor errors, but Norbury's personal voice and writing style will not be altered.

Chapter 1

1. For a detailed discussion of the export records of Staffordshire manufacturers from 1775 to 1880, see Neil Ewins, "'Supplying the Present Wants of Our Yankee Cousins': Staffordshire Ceramics and the American Market 1775–1880," *Journal of Ceramic History* 15, 1997, pp. 1–154.
2. Griselda Lewis, *A Collector's History of British Pottery* (New York: Viking Press, 1969), p. 95.
3. A history of the Spode pottery company describes the technique as being adopted by the Spode Factory around 1784; see Royal Academy of Arts, *200 Years of Spode* [catalogue of exhibition 8 August–4 October 1970] (London: Royal Academy of Arts, 1970), p. 7.
4. Edwin Atlee Barber, *Anglo-American Pottery: Old English China with American Views* (Philadelphia, PA: Patterson & White Co., 1901), p. 159.
5. Frank Stefano, Jr., *Pictorial Souvenirs and Commemoratives of North America* (New York: E.P. Dutton & Co., 1976), p. 5.
6. Ellouise Baker Larsen, *American Historical Views on Staffordshire China* (first edition 1939, reprinted New York: Dover Publications, 1975), p. 126. The Harvard College plate is also reproduced in Jeanne Morgan Zarucchi, "Visions of America: Johnson Brothers Pottery in the US Market, 1872–2002," *The Journal of Popular Culture* 38:1, 2004, p. 188, courtesy of The Winterthur Library, Printed Book and Periodical Collection.
7. The match between Ralph Stevenson & Williams' oak leaf and acorn border and the border of Johnson Brothers' *Historic America* was previously recognized by Stefano, pp. 66–7.
8. Sam Laidacker, *The Standard Catalogue of Anglo-American China from 1810 to 1850* (Scranton, PA: Sam Laidacker, 1938), p. 45. Bartlett's illustrations were published in Nathaniel P. Willis, *American Scenery: Or Land, Lake, and River Illustrations of Transatlantic Nature*, 2 vols. (London: George Virtue, 1840).
9. Geoffrey A. Godden, *Jewitt's Ceramic Art of Great Britain, 1800–1900* (London: Barrie & Jenkins, 1972), p. 503.
10. Ewins, "Supplying the Present Wants," p. 12.
11. "The Johnson Family Tree," an unpublished genealogy chart dated 1997, provided to the author by David Johnson. Some additional information about the Johnson family history is taken from an unpublished typescript, "The Story of Johnson Brothers," a photocopy of which was provided to the author by Christopher Johnson. The date and author of this document are unknown.
12. The marriage date of September 9, 1851, is confirmed by "The Johnson Family Tree," but the birth of Henry is inaccurately listed as 1851, not 1852. Further detail is provided, however, by the genealogy website http://www.meakinatelmstead.me.uk/MeakinJenkinsFamilyTree2016/ps01/ps01_149.htm, accessed July 30, 2017. That site provides the dates of birth, marriage, and death when known, for Robert, Sarah, and their progeny, and in addition to confirming the marriage date, it states the following: "Scandal has it that she 'ran off with the coachman' […] Harry born within 6 months of marriage." Robert was listed in the 1881 census as a "retired farmer."
13. According to http://www.thepotteries.org/allpotters/607.htm, Pankhurst went bankrupt in 1882. "The Story of Johnson Brothers," p. 1, states that Frederick and Alfred Johnson began operating the Charles Street Works in 1883.

14 The earliest record of a firm doing business as "Johnson Brothers" is from 1872, the date printed twice on the cover of an "Earthenware Foreign Price List" published by the Allbut and Daniel Printing Works in Percy Street, Hanley. A photocopy of the cover page of this document was provided to the author by David Johnson in 1998. The price list names the Hanley Pottery, which began operations in 1889, and the Trent Pottery, which began operating in 1896, so if "1872" was a typographical error, it is difficult to guess what the correct year may have been. This contradiction cannot be resolved by the present author.
15 "The Story of Johnson Brothers," p. 1.
16 Godden, *Jewitt's Ceramic Art*, pp. 13 and 552.
17 Http://www.thepotteries.org/mark/g/grindley.htm, accessed October 30, 2016.
18 Godden, *Jewitt's Ceramic Art*, p. 738.
19 "The Story of Johnson Brothers," p. 1.
20 Godden, *Jewitt's Ceramic Art*, p. 355.
21 Ralph M. Kovel and Terry H. Kovel, *Dictionary of Marks: Pottery and Porcelain* (New York: Crown Publishers, 1953, 22nd printing 1973), pp. 104–7.
22 Godden, *Jewitt's Ceramic Art*, p. 339.
23 Kovel, *Dictionary of Marks*, pp. 106–7.
24 Http://www.thepotteries.org/mark/m/meakin_alfred.html, accessed November 7, 2016.
25 Godden, *Jewitt's Ceramic Art*, p. 110.
26 The "BB" mark was used by Minton, a Stoke firm, between 1820 and 1860; http://www.thepotteries.org/mark/b/, accessed November 7, 2016.
27 Http://www.etymonline.com/index.php?term=Columbia, accessed October 29, 2016.
28 Robert Copeland, "The Marketing of Blue and White Wares," in Gaye Blake Roberts, ed., *True Blue, Transfer Printed Earthenware* (East Hagbourne: The Friends of Blue, 1998), p. 17.
29 British design registration number 323031.
30 The author thanks Dr. Peter F. Stevens, Missouri Botanical Garden, St. Louis, Missouri, for making this identification.
31 Http://www.waldorfnewyork.com/about-the-waldorf/hotel-history.html, accessed October 29, 2016.
32 "The Story of Johnson Brothers," p. 3.
33 Http://www.collectorsweekly.com/china-and-dinnerware/flow-blue, accessed October 10, 2016. The technique was developed in order to imitate Chinese blue-and-white porcelain wares, exported to England.
34 Christopher J.S. Johnson, "Foreword," in Jeanne Morgan Zarucchi, ed., *Johnson Brothers in America: A Century of Design, Catalogue of a Special Exhibition for the Wedgwood International Seminar* (St. Louis: Gallery 210, University of Missouri-St. Louis, 2000), pp. vii–viii.
35 VanBuskirk, *The Johnson Bros*.
36 Ibid., pp. 43–4.
37 Ibid., p. 51.
38 Ibid., p. 40.
39 Ibid., p. 6 and Figure 49. The three patterns, *Claremont, Brooklyn*, and *Florida*, are listed in Page and Frederiksen as "JB-18 Shape (Scalloped)," p. 45.
40 Ibid., p. 17.
41 Ibid., p. 18.
42 Ibid., pp. 43–4.

43 Http://ww.ci.claremont.ca.us/about-us/city-profile/history-of-claremont, accessed December 2, 2016.
44 Http://ww.straushistoricalsociety.org/lazarus–sara-straus, accessed October 26, 2016.
45 "The Story of Johnson Brothers," p. 2.
46 VanBuskirk, *The Johnson Bros.*, pp. 4–12.
47 *The Pottery Gazette*, April 1, 1909, p. 446.
48 Jon R. Moen and Ellis W. Tallman, "The Panic of 1907," December 4, 2015. http://www.federalreservehistory.org/Events/DetailView/97, accessed October 31, 2016.
49 *The Pottery Gazette*, April 1, 1909, p. 446.
50 Frank J. Sheridan, *The Pottery Industry* (Washington, DC: Government Printing Office, 1915), pp. 50–1. Additional statistics provided are cited on pp. 51, 423, 424, and 429.
51 Ibid., p. 394.

Chapter 2

1 "The Story of Johnson Brothers," pp. 3–4.
2 "World War I: Lest We Forget the 13,000 Who Died for Staffordshire and Stoke-on-Trent," *The Sentinel*, November 11, 2013.
3 Regina Lee Blaszczyk, *Imagining Consumers, Design and Innovation from Wedgwood to Corning* (Baltimore, MD: The Johns Hopkins University Press, 2000), pp. 118–19.
4 Mary Miley Theobald, "The Colonial Revival: The Past That Never Dies," *Colonial Williamsburg, The Journal of the Colonial Williamsburg Foundation* 24:2, Summer 2002, p. 81. See also Elizabeth McKellar, "Representing the Georgian: Constructing Interiors in Early Twentieth-Century Publications, 1890–1930," *Journal of Design History* 20:4, 2007, pp. 325–44.
5 Ibid., p. 81.
6 Tere Hagan, *Silverplated Flatware*, fourth edition (Paducah, KY: Collector Books, 1990), p. 197.
7 Ibid., p. 355.
8 Finegan, *Johnson Brothers Dinnerware*, p. 27.
9 The author thanks Dr. Anuradha Vedagiri, University of Missouri-St. Louis, for this linguistic information.
10 *The World Book Dictionary*, vol. II (Chicago: World Book Inc, 1990), p. 1515.
11 *Belleek Living, Belleek Pottery's Official Website*, Company Profile, www.belleek.ie, accessed September 23, 2009.
12 All six plates are illustrated in Page and Frederiksen, p. 155.
13 Https://www.lenox.com/about-us, accessed February 26, 2017.
14 "Lenox Workers Still Produce U.S.-Made China," *Raleigh News and Observer*, August 3, 2013.
15 Natalie Shearer, "The Making of a Love Triangle: Stravinsky's Ballet Petrushka," *The Classical Music Pages Quarterly*, 1996, Library of Congress archived record, http://webarchive.loc.gov/all/20090614095743/http:/w3.rz-berlin.mpg.de/cmp/stravinsky_shearer.html, accessed August 2, 2017.
16 Http://www.modernismgallery.com/1925+paris+exposition+art+deco+chinaware+les+fontaines+for+johnson+brothers/, accessed February 12, 2017.
17 Https://www.lenox.com/about-us, accessed February 26, 2017.

18. Page and Frederiksen, p. 108, as JB14, classified under "JB-28 Shape (Scalloped)," which is actually not scalloped but octagonal, with a flat rim. All octagonal patterns are featured on pp. 108–11.
19. Page and Frederiksen, "JB-27 (Scalloped)," lists 17 such patterns, pp. 112–13.
20. Blaszczyk, *Imagining Consumers*, pp. 140 and 146.
21. An advertisement from the archives of the Wedgwood Museum, consulted by the author in July 1998, describes "Greydawn Hotel Ware" and states that it was introduced in 1929.
22. Page and Frederiksen, "JB-8 Shape (Scalloped)," pp. 19–25. The "Dawn" series is reproduced on p. 19.
23. Regina Lee Blaszczyk, *The Color Revolution* (Cambridge, MA: The MIT Press, 2012), p. 86. The illustration described is on p. 87.
24. *Greydawn* advertisement.
25. *Rosedawn* advertisement from the Wedgwood Museum, viewed July 1998.
26. According to Finegan, *Rosedawn* was discontinued in 1970, *Goldendawn* and *Greendawn* were discontinued in 1977, and *Greydawn* was produced until 1987 (pp. 128 and 141).
27. Ibid., pp. 26–7, 124–5, and 132.
28. Ibid., pp. 120–2, 124, 132, 136, and 140.
29. Replacements Ltd. pattern code WWLACCP, "Lavender on Cream Color (Plain)," produced *c.* 1930–83.
30. Finegan lists two patterns as "Old Staffordshire": *Dubarry* and *Malvern*, pp. 124 and 132, and Page and Frederiksen list "Old Staffordshire" as a body shape, not a backstamp, pp. 69–72, with thirty patterns, of which several are more recent than the period when the "Old Staffordshire" stamp was in use. The author has seen examples of *Rouen* and *Ningpo*, confirming that they had the backstamp.
31. A copy of the letter was provided to Mary Finegan on a visit to Stoke-on-Trent in 1988, and she sent a copy of its first page to the author. The name of the company representative is unknown.
32. The title page also states: "Printed for John Walker Engraver, Rosomans Street, Clerkenwell, 1799." Gale Document CW3303989236, *Eighteenth Century Collections Online*, accessed October 6, 2009, at Washington University in St. Louis. The original source of the scanned volume was the British Library.
33. Dorothy Summers, *The Great Ouse: The History of a River Navigation* (Newton Abbott: David & Charles, 1973), p. 90. This source was noted by Finegan, *Johnson Brothers Dinnerware*, p. 44.
34. "Stafford Castle," drawn by Frederick Calvert, engraved by T. Radclyffe, in William West, *Picturesque Views and Descriptions of Cities, Towns, Castles, Mansions and Other Objects of Interesting Features in Staffordshire and Shropshire* (Birmingham: William Emans, Bromsgrove Street, 1830), image copyright William Salt Library. There is a librarian's notation that this is the "South east view showing the twin towers as rebuilt in 1815." Https://www.search.staffspasttrack.org.uk/Details.aspx?&ResourceID=8600&PageIndex=2&SearchType=2&ThemeID=150 and www.abebooks.co.uk, accessed May 17, 2017.
35. The print bears the legend of "Dugdale's England and Wales Delineated," referring to the series of partworks by Thomas Dugdale, *England and Wales Delineated*, also published as *Curiosities of Great Britain, England & Wales Delineated*, printed in multiple volumes by the London publishing family of John Tallis, his widow Lucinda, his sons John and Frederick Tallis, or his daughter Lucinda, between 1838 and 1860.

No specific volume can be cited, since artworks were reprinted in various subsections and the dates of individual parts are often not printed. The author thanks Laurence Worms of Ash Rare Books, London, for this information.
36   Finegan, *Johnson Brothers Dinnerware*, pp. 44–6.
37   Page and Frederiksen, pp. 86–7. *Old Britain Castles* is under their classification of "Sovereign Shape (Scalloped)."
38   Http://ww.thepotteries.org/potters/ridgway.htm, accessed February 13, 2017.
39   United States Patent and Trademark Office, "TAF [Technology Assessment and Forecast] Report, Issue Dates and Patent Numbers Since 1836," April 2002, https://www.uspto.gov/web/offices/ac/ido/oeip/taf/issudate.pdf, accessed February 15, 2017. Subsequent references to US design patent numbers and dates will refer to this source.
40   The pattern is pictured in Finegan, *Johnson Brothers Dinnerware*, p. 99, and the backstamp inscription was confirmed by an online photograph, http://www.replaceyourchina.com/johnson-bros-brothers-old-english-queens-bouquet-tea-plates-3879-p.asp, accessed February 26, 2017.
41   Page and Frederiksen, "Old English Shape," pp. 55–65, describing the gadroon edge as "scalloped."
42   Page and Frederiksen, "Old Chelsea," pp. 91–6.

Chapter 3

1   Stefano, *Pictorial Souvenirs*, p. 73.
2   *The Inter-Nation: A Journal of Economic Affairs* 1:11, June 1907, s.p. [93].
3   *The Federation Bulletin, A Magazine for the Woman of To-Day*, National Official Organ of the General Federation of Women's Clubs, 6:1, October 1908, Boston, MA, p. 32. Punctuation has been modified for clarity.
4   "The North Face in 1892," http://www.whitehousemuseum.org/residence-history.htm, accessed March 3, 2017.
5   Thompson Westcott, *The Historic Mansions and Buildings of Philadelphia* (Philadelphia, PA: Porter & Coates, 1877), p. 237.
6   Rev. S.F. Hotchkin, *Ancient and Modern Germantown, Mount Airy and Chestnut Hill* (Philadelphia, PA: P.W. Ziegler & Co., 1889). The illustration is plate 40, inserted after p. 192.
7   Silas Weir Mitchell, *Hugh Wynne, Free Quaker, Sometime Brevet Lieutenant-Colonel on the Staff of His Excellency George Washington* (London: T. Fisher Unwin, 1897).
8   *Hugh Wynne, Free Quaker* was reissued in two editions in 2016, by Leopold Classic Library and CreateSpace Independent Publishing Platform.
9   An image of the bookplate may be seen at https://en.wikipedia.org/wiki/Coat_of_arms_of_the_Washington_family#/media/File:George_Washington%E2%80%99s_bookplate._Sotheby%27s.jpg. It was also featured in the website of the Sons of Liberty Chapter of the Sons of the American Revolution, http://www.revolutionarywararchives.org/washandgen.html, accessed July 20, 2017.
10 Stefano, *Pictorial Souvenirs*, illustration 61, p. 50. Some of the scenes in the series were identified in web searches on sites such as www.ebay.com.
11 Norbury states: "1936, 1937, 1938, These years were hectic for me, I had been promoted to Manager of the Engraving Department at Hanley Pottery (49)."
12 Http://www.green-wood.com/2012/printmakers-currier-and-ives/, accessed March 5, 2017.

13 Bernard F. Reilly, Jr., "Introduction," in Gale Research Company, *Currier & Ives, A Catalogue Raisonné*, 2 vols. (Detroit: Gale Research Company, 1984), I, p. xxxv.
14 See Chapter 1, note 8.
15 William Cullen Bryant, ed., *Picturesque America; or, The Land We Live In. A Delineation of the Mountains, Rivers, Lakes, Forests, Waterfalls, Shores, Cañons, Valleys, Cities and Other Picturesque Features of Our Country* (New York: D. Appleton and Company, 1872-74).
16 Henry Lewis, "View of Saint Louis," printed in Aachen, Germany by C.H. Müller, and published in Dusseldorf by Arnz & Co. in 1854-57, in John W. Reps, *Saint Louis Illustrated: Nineteenth-Century Engravings and Lithographs of a Mississippi River Metropolis* (Columbia, MO: University of Missouri Press, 1989), p. 60.
17 Aaron Stein, "California & Oregon Stage Company. Carries Wells, Fargo & Co^s Express and the U.S. Mail. View of Mount Shasta 14,442 f^t above the sea—on C&O stage route." Honeyman Collection of Early Californian and Western Pictorial Material via the California Digital Library. The original illustration is believed to have been created by William Keith in 1853, and was reproduced with modifications by an unknown artist in a broadside distributed around 1860 by the firm of Britton and Rey. Stein is credited with the version published in 1872, based on a signature, "A. Stein." Born in 1853, he would have been too young to produce the version from 1860. The above information is from the website http://www.siskiyous.edu/shasta/art/ill.htm, accessed March 8, 2017.
18 Personal communication to the author, July 7, 1998.
19 Larsen, *American Historical Views*.
20 Finegan, *Johnson Brothers Dinnerware*, pp. 48-54.
21 Http://www.pdxhistory.com/html/frederick_nelson.html, accessed March 6, 2017.
22 References to Currier & Ives prints will include the catalogue number found in Gale Research Company, *Currier & Ives, A Catalogue Raisonné*.
23 George Henry Durrie, artist, and John Schutler, engraver, "Home to Thanksgiving" (New York: Currier & Ives, 1867), Gale 3115. It should be noted that the original print title was "Home to Thanksgiving," and this was changed on the plate to "Home for Thanksgiving," to make the phrase more natural for a contemporary American speaker.
24 George Cooke, artist, and William James Bennett, engraver, "Richmond, from the Hill above the Waterworks" (New York: Lewis P. Clover, *c.* 1834), Library of Congress control number 96510852.
25 Henry Firks, "San Francisco 1849" (San Francisco: Schmidt Label & Lithographic Company, *c.* 1886), Library of Congress control number 95511004. The image from the source illustration was significantly reduced in order to fit the dimensions of the teacup.
26 The place name "Colma" is a spelling error, for "Coloma." That town was the nearest one to Sutter's Creek, where the gold discovery was made.
27 William Henry Bartlett, "Railroad Scene, Little Falls (Valley of the Mohawk)," in Willis, *American Scenery*.
28 "Robert Fulton's 'Clermont' on the Hudson," artist unknown, 1813. I.N. Phelps Stokes Collection, The New York Public Library.
29 "Low Water in the Mississippi," Frances F. Palmer (New York: Currier & Ives, 1867), Gale 4149.
30 Augustus Köllner, artist, and Laurent Deroy, lithographer, "Wall Street, N.Y. 1847," Library of Congress, control number 93504426.

31 Augustus Köllner, artist, and Laurent Deroy, lithographer, "Broad-Way," c. 1855 (New York and Paris: Goupil & Co., 1855), http://visualizingnyc.org/wp-content/uploads/2014/07/NY-114.jpg, accessed March 24, 2017.
32 "The Grand Drive, Central Park, N.Y.," artist unknown (New York: Currier & Ives, c. 1869), Gale 2693. This image is seen on a large handled cup, 4 ½ inches in diameter at the rim, not a "mug" with vertical sides, as it is defined by most Americans. Replacements Ltd. describes it as a "joke cup," sold with a saucer featuring "Stage and Mail Coach / View of Mount Shasta." If there was an American-style mug produced for the series, it is unknown to this author.
33 William Henry Bartlett, "The Ferry at Brooklyn New York," in Willis, *American Scenery*. The backstamp states "Ferry Boat / Brooklyn, New York."
34 Frances F. Palmer, "New York Crystal Palace / for the exhibition of the industry of all nations," 1853 (New York: Currier & Ives, 1853), Gale 4827.
35 Frances F. Palmer, "The Rocky Mountains: Emigrants Crossing the Plains" (New York: Currier & Ives, 1866), Gale 5633.
36 See note 17 above.
37 Robert Havell, Jr., "View of Niagara Falls," c. 1845, colored by firm of Havell & Spearing, Library of Congress, control number 2004667266.
38 "The President's House," artist "Wade," engraver "CHB," 1854, from *Gleason's Pictorial Drawing-Room Companion*, vol. 6:153, Library of Congress, control number 94503445. The advertisement refers to "The White House," but the actual backstamp of the demitasse saucer accurately states "The President's House."
39 William Henry Bartlett, "View of the Capitol at Washington," in Willis, *American Scenery*.
40 Alexander Robertson, artist, and Francis Jukes, engraver, "Mount Vernon in Virginia" (London: F. Jukes, 1800), Library of Congress, control number 98501460.
41 "Monticello, The Home of Thomas Jefferson," artist unknown, printed "1 January 1819." Http://www.gettyimages.com/license/504027264, accessed March 30, 2017.
42 J. Davis, "Hancock House, Boston," in John Howard Hinton, ed., *The History and Topography of the United States of North America* (London and New York: J. Tallis and Co., 1850), II, p. 474.
43 "Independence Hall, Philadelphia 1776," artist unknown (New York: Currier & Ives, undated), Gale 3287. Modifications have been made to the scene, changing or deleting carriages and pedestrians, adding trees at far left and far right, and adding a woman and child in the foreground for human interest.
44 Robert Havell, "View of the City of Boston from Dorchester Heights" (New York: Robert Havell, 1841), Library of Congress, control number 2004672548.
45 There are two possible sources for this image, which are virtually identical to each other: Charles Parsons, "Sacramento City, Cᵃ from the foot of J Steet, showing I., J., & K. Sts. With the Sierra Nevada in the distance," 1849 (New York: Stringer & Townsend, c. 1850), Library of Congress, control number 93511486; and "Sacramento City in Californien," c. 1850, in Herrmann J. Meyer, *Meyer's Universum, or Views of the Most Remarkable Places and Objects of All Countries* (New York: H.J. Meyer, 1852–53), Missouri History Museum identifier N45770. Meyer is sometimes credited as the artist of the prints in this volume, but the Museum of Fine Arts in Boston identifies him as the publisher, and lists numerous artists and engravers (http://www.mfa.org/collections/object/meyers-universum-or-views-of-the-most-remarkable-places-and-objects-of-all-countries-265499, accessed March 11, 2017). Meyer probably printed an engraving based on Parsons' original drawing.

46 "Am Kai (Levée) in New Orleans," artist unknown, c. 1850, in Meyer, *Meyer's Universum*.
47 "Old Fort Dearborn, with Surroundings in 1856," artist unknown (Chicago: Rufus Blanchard, c. 1894), Library of Congress control number 2012645255. The image was heavily edited, to remove several buildings adjacent to the old fort and adding the figures of a man and a boy, but the source is recognizable, thanks to a tree in the foreground and a picket fence with an open gate.
48 Henry Fenn, "West Point and the Highlands," c. 1869, in Bryant, *Picturesque America*.
49 "Kansas," artist unknown, in Charles A. Dana, ed., *The United States Illustrated*, vol. 2, The West (New York: Herrmann J. Meyer, s.d. [1853–55]). John Mason Peck Collection of the St. Louis Mercantile Library at the University of Missouri-St. Louis, accession number 121829. The engraving is found between pages 132 and 133. Additional copies of the same engraving have appeared in online antique gallery listings, printed on the front with the name of a German publisher, Bibliographisches Institut. That press was located in Hildburghausen between 1828 and 1874, and was founded by Joseph Meyer, the father of Herrmann J. Meyer. This indicates that the same engravings of American scenes were sold by the Meyers, father and son, on both sides of the Atlantic.
50 John William Hill, "View on the Erie Canal," c. 1829, watercolor on paper. I.N. Phelps Stokes Collection, New York Public Library. The image was edited, removing an amusing vignette in the foreground, of a man herding a large pig with several piglets.
51 Edward P. Alexander, Mary Alexander, and Juilee Decker, *Museums in Motion, An Introduction to the History and Function of Museums*, third edition (Lanham, MD: Rowman & Littlefield, 2017), p. 67.
52 Ada Walker Camehl, *The Blue-China Book: Early American Scenes and History Pictured in the Pottery of the Time* (New York: E.P. Dutton & Co., 1916, reprinted New York: Dover Publications, Inc., 1977), p. 59.
53 "Wall Street New York," c. 1850, in Meyer, *Meyer's Universum*, p. 273.
54 G. Cooke, artist, and William James Bennett, engraver, "City of Washington from Beyond the Navy Yard," c. 1833 (New York: Lewis P. Clover, c. 1834), Library of Congress Collection of Popular Graphic Arts, control number 92520609.
55 Jacob C. Ward, "View of the Natural Bridge, Virginia" (New York: Lewis P. Clover, c. 1835), New York Public Library I.N. Stokes Collection, Stokes C.1835-F-29.
56 A photocopy of this undated advertisement was provided to the author by Leonora Vance Stulz of Long Island, New York, June 3, 2008.
57 "Frozen-Up," artist unknown (New York: Currier & Ives, 1872), Gale 2335.
58 Https://www.themagnificentmile.com/neighborhood/history/, accessed March 6, 2017.
59 Http://www.history.org/Almanack/places/hb/hbcap.cfm, accessed May 29, 2017.
60 A photocopy of this advertisement was provided to the author by Leonora Vance Stulz, June 3, 2008.
61 Http://www.worthpoint.com/worthopedia/set-12-macy-wedgwood-york-1792769646, accessed March 28, 2017.
62 Mark Gonzalez, *An Overview of Homer Laughlin Dinnerware* (Gas City, IN: L-W Book Sales, 2002), pp. 119–22.
63 Website of the Historical Society of Pennsylvania, http://www2.hsp.org/collections/manuscripts/b/Beale2007.html, accessed March 29, 2017.
64 Https://www.kovels.com/collectors-concerns/adams-currier-a-ives-plate/print.html, accessed March 29, 2017.

Notes

65 Frances F. Palmer, "A Midnight Race on the Mississippi," (New York: Currier & Ives, 1890), Gale 4478.
66 Https://www.terapeak.com/worth/vintage-1950-s-adams-plate-currier-ives-10-5-husking-multi-colored/151989072232/, accessed March 29, 2017.
67 Laurie Cigan, "Collecting Royal China Currier and Ives Dinnerware," http://www.ebay.com/gds/Collecting-Royal-China-Currier-Ives-Dinnerware-/10000000000846166/g.html, accessed March 29, 2017; quoted by permission. Replacements Ltd. (www.replacements.com) gives the date of discontinuation as 1970.
68 Http://www.thedepartmentstoremuseum.org/2010/05/b-altman-co-new-york-city.html, accessed March 29, 2017.
69 Http://collectingwedgwood.com/identification-and-dating, accessed March 29, 2017.
70 Https://www.rubylane.com/item/161143-A6271/Wedgwood-x22Philadelphia-Bowlx22-Estate-General-Alex78ander, accessed March 29, 2017.
71 Https://www.wedgwood.co.uk/tableware/by-collection/edme, accessed March 29, 2017.
72 Debbie Coe and Randy Coe, *Liberty Blue Dinnerware* (Atglen, PA: Schiffer Publishing, 2006), p. 15.
73 Http://www.robbinsnest.com/china/liberty-blue/, accessed March 29, 2017.
74 Http://www.robbinsnest.com/images/lb/liberty-blue-union-ad.jpg, accessed March 29, 2017.

Chapter 4

1 There are numerous books published for collectors of souvenir plates; two well-illustrated examples are Arene Burgess, *A Collector's Guide to Souvenir Plates* (Atglen, PA: Schiffer Publishing, 1996), and Monica Lynn Clements and Patricia Rosser Clements, *Popular Souvenir Plates* (Atglen, PA: Schiffer Publishing, 1998).
2 Stefano, *Pictorial Souvenirs*, pp. 99–100.
3 Ibid., p. 101.
4 Ibid., figure 119, p. 102.
5 Kathleen Moenster, "1904 World's Fair Souvenirs," posted August 10, 2015, National Park Service, Jefferson National Expansion Memorial (St. Louis), https://www.nps.gov/jeff/blogs/1904-world-s-fair-souvenirs.htm, accessed March 31, 2017.
6 Finegan, *Johnson Brothers Dinnerware*, p. 122, and https://www.replacements.com/webquote/jb_cep.htm, accessed March 31, 2017.
7 Stefano, *Pictorial Souvenirs*, p. 66. The plate is illustrated in figure 86, p. 67.
8 Ibid., p. 57.
9 Http://library.duke.edu/rubenstein/findingaids/uaplates/, accessed April 3, 2017.
10 A photocopy of the brochure was provided to the author by Leonora Vance Stulz.
11 "Chadwell" is not listed in Finegan, but is featured in Page and Frederiksen, 61. Three other patterns of identical design, but featuring different floral centers and in one case maroon-colored accent bands instead of blue, are listed as "JB 439," "JB 662," and "JB 425," pp. 61–2.
12 Page and Frederiksen list 96 patterns of what they categorize as the "(Scalloped) Old English Shape," pp. 55–65.

13 Finegan gives a date of 1951 for this plate, but the presence of what appears to be a jet airliner in the sky would date it from no earlier than 1958, when Pan American Airlines introduced the Boeing 707 plane for intercontinental travel. It is possible that the plane could have been added to the design after it was first issued.
14 Http://www.history.org/history/teaching/enewsletter/volume4/july06/restoration.cfm, accessed April 26, 2017. www.history.org is the official website of the Colonial Williamsburg Foundation.
15 Http://www.referenceforbusiness.com/history2/19/Colonial-Williamsburg-Foundation.html, accessed April 26, 2017.
16 Http://www.pem.org/library/blog/?p=2124 and http://www.nytimes.com/1975/01/11/archives/samuel-chamberlain-dies-at-79-author-photographer-etcher.html, accessed April 26, 2017.
17 Https://commons.wikimedia.org/wiki/File:VirginiaColonyArmsRetouch.png, accessed April 26, 2017.
18 Stefano, *Pictorial Souvenirs*, pp. 54–6.
19 Gonzalez, *An Overview of Homer Laughlin*, pp. 254–5.
20 Http://www.pgfso.com, accessed April 26, 2017.
21 Finegan, *Johnson Brothers Dinnerware*, p. 149.
22 Https://uwaterloo.ca/mennonite-archives-ontario/photograph-and-slide-collections/david-hunsberger-collection, accessed April 26, 2017. Scenes on the plate have been verified as having been inspired by Hunsberger photographs, including "CA MAO Hist.Mss. 10.28-DH-599, Doon tower in Doon, Ontario. June 1950" and "CA MAO Hist.Mss. 10.28-DH-846, Balls Mill above Vineland, Ontario. September 1953."
23 The dates of the American commemoratives in the following section are from Finegan, *Johnson Brothers Dinnerware*, pp. 148–9.
24 Http://www.pdxhistory.com/html/meier_-_frank.html, accessed April 30, 2017.
25 Henry James Warre, "Oregon City," *c.* 1845, from *Sketches in North America and the Oregon Territory* (London: Dickinson & Co., 1848). Published courtesy of the Library of Congress, in Carlos A. Schwantes, *Long Day's Journey—The Steamboat & Stagecoach Era in the Northern West* (Seattle, WA: University of Washington Press, 1999), p. 10.
26 Https://www.nps.gov/parkhistory/online_books/harrison/harrison5.htm, accessed April 30, 2017.
27 Https://www.thetrain.com/lodging/the-grand-canyon-railway-hotel/hotel-history/, accessed April 30, 2017.
28 Http://harvey-house.info/arizona, accessed April 30, 2017.
29 Personal communication, July 7, 1998.
30 Http://www.thecanadianencyclopedia.ca/en/article/hudsons-bay-company/, accessed May 6, 2017.

Chapter 5

1 *Board of Trade Journal* (London: His Majesty's Stationery Office, 1952), 162, p. 1091.
2 Patrick J. Maguire, "Patriotism, Politics and Production," in Patrick J. Maguire and Jonathan M. Woodham, eds., *Design and Cultural Politics in Post-war Britain: The "Britain Can Make It" Exhibition of 1946* (London and Washington, DC: Leicester University Press, 1997), p. 39.

3   Page and Frederiksen, "Old Chelsea Shape (Scalloped)," pp. 91–6. Forty-nine patterns in this shape are listed, ranging in date from *Sheraton* in 1944 to *Susanna*, produced in 1978 for the Laura Ashley company. The majority of patterns in this shape were produced from 1950 to 1960.
4   Page and Frederiksen, "Sovereign Shape (Scalloped)," pp. 82–90.
5   Charles Major, *Dorothy Vernon of Haddon Hall* (New York: The Macmillan Company, 1902), Library of Congress OCLC number 1160473; "Dorothy Vernon of Haddon Hall" (play, December 1903–January 1904, Lyric Theater, New York), https://www.ibdb.com/broadway-production/dorothy-vernon-of-haddon-hall-5800; "Dorothy Vernon of Haddon Hall" (movie, 1924), http://www.imbdb.com/title/tt0014854; sites accessed May 19, 2017.
6   Photograph taken by Reg Speller, Getty Images Archive, http://media.gettyimages.com/photos/queen-elizabeth-ii-visits-the-showroom-of-the-johnson-brothers-china-picture-id80395570?s=612x612, accessed May 17, 2017.
7   The queen's selection of the *Hampton* pattern was noted in company records retained in the Wedgwood Museum, Barlaston, and consulted by the author in July 1998.
8   Page and Frederiksen, "Georgian Shape (Scalloped)," pp. 79–81; only about a dozen patterns were produced in this shape.
9   "Mount Vernon (Rear View) in 1796," artist George Isham Parkyns, engraver James Duthie, *c.* 1855. Mount Vernon Prints and Drawings Collection, object number EV-3090. The view appears to have been inspired by an earlier print with very similar figures in the foreground, dated *c.* 1816, and drawn by Giulio Ferrario (object number EV 3840/RP-459).
10 Gonzalez, *An Overview of Homer Laughlin*, pp. 58–9.
11 Advertisement in *Prestige and Progress—A Survey of Industrial North Staffordshire*, publication of the North Staffordshire Chamber of Commerce, 1955; http://www.thepotteries.org/advert_wk/004.htm, accessed February 13, 2017.
12 Bob Page, Dale Frederiksen, Dean Six, and Jaime Robinson, *Franciscan, An American Dinnerware Tradition* (Greensboro, NC: Page/Frederiksen Publishing Company, 1999).
13 Http://www.wedgwoodmuseum.org.uk/collections/other-collections, accessed May 18, 2017.
14 "Louise W. Flather," obituary in the *Poughkeepsie Journal* (Poughkeepsie, New York), May 23, 1990, 2B. Additional information about Flather's work was obtained from a selection of Flather's personal papers and from personal communication with Leonora Vance Stulz, Flather's granddaughter, June 3–4, 2008.
15 Family lore is that all of the designs included in the portfolio were created by Flather, but this is not substantiated. Some of them, like *Margaret Rose* (1939) and *Devonshire* (1940), appear to predate her association with Johnson Brothers. The portfolio may have included not only samples of her own work, but also designs that she used for inspiration, designs that represented the company's "brand," or simply designs that she liked.
16 The detailed leaf in this pattern bears a strong resemblance to Japanese hops (*Humulus japonicus*), which has leaves of 5–7 lobes. This Asian species was introduced to the United States as an ornamental, and is not known to grow wild anywhere except in certain areas of Illinois. http://www.forestventure.com/speciesdetail.cshtml?id=161975, accessed May 20, 2017.
17 Http://www.thepotteries.org/allpotters/261.htm, accessed May 22, 2017.
18 Photocopy provided to the author by William Norbury, July 1998.

19 Http://www.portmeirion.com/about/botanic-garden, accessed May 22, 2017.
20 Http://www.historic-uk.com/HistoryUK/HistoryofBritain/The-Festival-of-Britain-1951/, accessed May 20, 2017.
21 Norbury, *Designs on a Career*, p. 80. He evidently did not recall the name of the Paintresses manager at the time of writing the memoir.
22 Finegan, *Johnson Brothers Dinnerware*, p. 128.
23 All seven images of the *Fish* pattern are shown in Page and Frederiksen, p. 193.
24 Finegan, *Johnson Brothers Dinnerware*, p. 144.
25 This was previously noted by Finegan, p. 137, with credit to Ginny Oswald for having provided the information.
26 Http://www.suffolkpainters.co.uk/index.cgi?choice=painter&pid=932, accessed May 21, 2017.
27 This illustration was featured on the cover jacket and on p. 99 of Alan C. Jenkins, *A. R. Quinton's England, A Portrait of Rural Life at the Turn of the Century* (Exeter: Webb & Bower, 1987). It was also published on a postcard printed by J. Salmon Ltd., series no. 1357 (Jenkins, p. 128).
28 For a thoughtful analysis of how the British past was idealized, see David Lowenthal, *The Past Is a Foreign Country* (Cambridge: Cambridge University Press, 1985).
29 Jenkins, *A. R. Quinton's England*, pp. 90 and 115.
30 Page and Frederiksen, "JB-2 Shape (Scalloped)," p. 13. In addition to the three versions of *Wild Turkeys*, it was used for *Winter Holiday* and *Harvest* (named by Finegan as *Harvest Fruit*).
31 Finegan states that this pattern was introduced in 1960, but the design patent number of 175738 corresponds to 1955.
32 Http://spodehistory.blogspot.co.uk/2010/12/spodes-christmas-tree-pattern.html, accessed June 15, 2017.
33 Gary Cross, *Consumed Nostalgia: Memory in the Age of Fast Capitalism* (New York: Columbia University Press, 2015), p. 209. See also Eric Hobsbawn and Terence Ranger, eds., *The Invention of Tradition* (Cambridge: Cambridge University Press, 1983).
34 Finegan, *Johnson Brothers Dinnerware*, p. 121. She states the date of the pattern's launch as 1939, but that is earlier than the date of issuance of the patent design number. It is possible that the design was in fact launched earlier, with the printed phrase "patent pending," as was the case with many designs.
35 On p. 19, he gives the date as 1946, but later, on p. 88, he gives it as 1948. The latter date is more logical, since it would have meant the pattern was in development for about four years, not six.
36 Norbury, *Designs on a Career*, pp. 85 and 88.
37 Finegan, *Johnson Brothers Dinnerware*, p. 66.
38 Http://www.theatrehistory.com/american/musical007.html, accessed May 24, 2017.

Chapter 6

1 Graham M. McLaren, "Moving Forwards but Looking Backwards: The Dynamics of Design Change in the Early Post-war Pottery Industry," in Maguire and Woodham, *Design and Cultural Politics in Post-war Britain*, p. 93.

2   Steven Jenkins, *Midwinter Pottery, A Revolution in British Tableware*, edited by Paul Atterbury (Somerset: Richard Dennis, 1997, second edition 2003), pp. 7–8. See also "Dorothy Jessie Tait," obituary by Charlotte Higgins, *The Guardian*, February 12, 2010.
3   Jenkins, *Midwinter Pottery*, p. 14.
4   *The Pottery Gazette and Glass Trade Review*, March 1956, p. 397, illustrated in Jenkins, *Midwinter Pottery*, p. 17.
5   Jenkins, *Midwinter Pottery*, p. 18.
6   Ibid., p. 17.
7   Ibid., pp. 41–84.
8   Ibid., p. 46.
9   Photocopy of advertisement from Louise Flather papers, provided to the author by Leonora Vance Stultz; the publication in which the advertisement was printed is unknown. Norbury engraved the front decoration and designed the backstamp of this pattern (personal communication, July 7, 1998).
10 These production dates are as stated on www.replacements.com, accessed June 10, 2017. Finegan gives the production dates as 1963–97.
11 Keller and Gibbs, *English Transferware*, p. 159.
12 Michael Paterson, *A Brief History of the Private Life of Elizabeth II* (Philadelphia, PA: Running Press, 2011), pp. 111–13.
13 Personal communication, September 29, 2000.
14 William Henry James Boot, "Haddon Hall from the Terrace," in Bayard Taylor, ed., *Picturesque Europe, Volume 1: The British Isles* (New York: D. Appleton and Co., 1876).
15 Old Britain Castles "Haddon Hall" grill plate, seen at https://www.blueandwhite.com/products.asp?p=JOHN22835, accessed May 16, 2017. All three images are from *Picturesque Europe*, on pp. 1, 3, and 6.
16 Http://festival.si.edu/about-us/mission-and-history/smithsonian, accessed June 22, 2017. The event would later be renamed as the Smithsonian Folklife Festival, dropping the word "American" in recognition of the fact that it included global arts and artists, not just those from the United States.
17 "The Story of the Hex Sign," http://www.amishnews.com/featurearticles/Storyofhexsigns.htm, accessed June 2, 2017.
18 Brian Groom, "Sir Arthur Bryan, UK Industrialist, 1923–2011," *Financial Times*, March 5, 2011, p. 8.
19 Ibid., p. 8.
20 Michael Perry, *A Handbook of British Pottery Manufacturers: 1900–2010* (Joondalup, Western Australia: Ocean Publishing, 2010), p. 99. Online version at www.potteryhistories.com.
21 Personal communication, July 1998.
22 *Waterford Wedgwood Review of 1998* ("Produced by NLA/Intershare, Printed in England by First Impression," 1998), p. 99.
23 "David Johnson," *The Sunday Times*, April 26, 2009.
24 Http://www.thepotteries.org/mark/w/wedgwood_enoch.html, accessed June 12, 2017.
25 Personal communication with Anne Williams, Barlaston, July 1998.
26 According to Replacements.com, Masons was not acquired by Wedgwood until 1973; Http://www.replacements.com/mfghist/masons.htm, accessed June 12, 2017.
27 "Sir Arthur Bryan," *The Times*, February 24, 2011, p. 48. A detailed chronology of the Staffordshire "Mergers, Sellouts and Takeovers" may be found in Kathy Niblett,

Dynamic Design: The British Pottery Industry 1940–1990 (Stoke-on-Trent: City Museum & Art Gallery, 1990), pp. 37–87.
28 Personal communication, July 7, 1998.
29 Although this pattern is not listed in Finegan, a reference to the production date of this pattern was found in a list of patterns and price lists consulted by the author at the Wedgwood Museum, July 1998.
30 Page and Fredericksen, pp. 107–11. The dating is by this author.
31 Groom, "Sir Arthur Bryan," p. 8.
32 Perry, *A Handbook of British Pottery Manufacturers*, p. 99.
33 Http://www.thepotteries.org/allpotters/725.htm, accessed June 20, 2017.
34 *The Sentinel*, Wednesday October 16, 1991, pp. 19–34.
35 Advertisement for Service (Engineers) PLC, Cobridge; *The Sentinel*, p. 20.
36 *The Sentinel*, p. 19.
37 Ibid., p. 22.
38 Ibid., p. 21.
39 Http://drdinnerware.blogspot.com/2014/07/nikko-christmastime-and-happy-holidays.html, accessed June 17, 2017.
40 Perry, *A Handbook of British Pottery Manufacturers*, p. 99.
41 Steven Houghton, "140 New Jobs at Wedgwood," *The Sentinel*, October 3, 2000. http://www.thisisstaffordshire.com, accessed October 3, 2000.
42 Http://www.replacements.com/webquote/jb_hiabr.htm, accessed March 30, 2017. The backstamp information was obtained from images of plates advertised for sale on internet sites such as eBay.
43 Heather Timmons, "Britain: Cuts at China Maker," *The New York Times*, June 5, 2003.
44 Charlotte Higgins, "China Crisis," *The Guardian* (London), June 11, 2003.
45 For a full discussion of the relocation of Staffordshire pottery production to Asia, see Neil Ewins, *Ceramics and Globalization: Staffordshire Ceramics, Made in China* (London: Bloomsbury Academic, 2017).
46 Ibid., p. 118.
47 Http://www.replacements.com/webquote/jb_gibs.htm, accessed June 19, 2017.
48 Perry, *A Handbook of British Pottery Manufacturers*, p. 99.
49 Groom, "Sir Arthur Bryan," p. 8.
50 Aaron O. Patrick, "Waterford Assets in U.K., Ireland Acquired by KPS," *The Wall Street Journal*, February 28, 2009.
51 Ashley Armstrong, "Waterford Wedgwood Sold to Finnish Heritage Brand," *The Telegraph*, May 11, 2015.
52 Https://www.fiskarsgroup.com/media/press-releases/fiskars-corporation-acquires-the-renowned-wwrd-and-extends-its-portfolio-with-iconic-luxury-home-and-lifestyle-brands, accessed June 20, 2017.

Conclusion

1 Dates of the potteries' operation and demolition are taken from http://www.thepotteries.org, accessed June 21, 2017.
2 http://emmabridgewaterfactory.co.uk/pages/about-the-factory/, accessed June 21, 2017.

3 https://www.google.com/maps/place/Hanley,+Stoke-on-Trent,+UK/@53.0200479,-2.1736505,17z/data=!4m5!3m4!1s0x487a42820633fb27:0x2266c33ce771db9d!8m2!3d53.023414!4d-2.1723921, accessed July 24, 2017.
4 "Students Drafted in to Record Rare Find," *Birmingham Post*, Monday February 26, 2007, 4.
5 "Project Will Uncover History of Emma Bridgewater Factory," *The Sentinel*, August 28, 2014.
6 David Nicholls, "All Fired Up: The Future of Pottery," *The Telegraph*, January 26, 2011.
7 http://1882ltd.com/about/, accessed June 21, 2017.
8 SCP is a home furnishings retailer in London. See https://www.scp.co.uk/collections/1882-ltd-collection. Tableware by 1882 Ltd. is also sold by Barneys New York, a luxury retailer.
9 Jessica Doyle, "Kith and Kiln; A Renewed Appetite for British-made Ceramics and Fresh Ideas from a Young Generation of Potters Has Led to a Revival of Independent, Family-run Companies," *The Daily Telegraph* (London), *Telegraph Magazine*, August 13, 2016, pp. 52–7.

BIBLIOGRAPHY

Alexander, Edward P., Alexander, Mary and Decker, Juilee, *Museums in Motion, An Introduction to the History and Function of Museums*, third edition, Lanham, MD: Rowman & Littlefield, 2017.

Armstrong, Ashley, "Waterford Wedgwood Sold to Finnish Heritage Brand," *The Telegraph*, May 11, 2015.

Atterbury, Paul, Denker, Ellen Paul and Batkin, Maureen, *Miller's Twentieth-Century Ceramics, A Collector's Guide to British and North American Factory-Produced Ceramics*, revised edition, London: Miller's (Octopus Publishing Group Ltd.), 2005.

Barber, Edwin Atlee, *Anglo-American Pottery: Old English China with American Views*, Philadelphia, PA: Patterson & White Co., 1901.

Blaszczyk, Regina Lee, *Imagining Consumers, Design and Innovation from Wedgwood to Corning*, Baltimore, MD: The Johns Hopkins University Press, 2000.

Blaszczyk, Regina Lee, *The Color Revolution*, Cambridge, MA: The MIT Press, 2012.

Board of Trade Journal, London: His Majesty's Stationery Office, 1952.

Bryant, William Cullen (ed.), *Picturesque America; Or, The Land We Live In. A Delineation of the Mountains, Rivers, Lakes, Forests, Waterfalls, Shores, Cañons, Valleys, Cities and Other Picturesque Features of Our Country*, New York: D. Appleton and Co., 1872–4.

Burgess, Arene, *A Collector's Guide to Souvenir Plates*, Atglen, PA: Schiffer Publishing, 1996.

Camehl, Ada Walker, *The Blue-China Book: Early American Scenes and History Pictured in the Pottery of the Time*, New York: E. P. Dutton & Co., 1916; reprinted New York: Dover Publications, 1977.

Clements, Monica Lynn and Clements, Patricia Rosser, *Popular Souvenir Plates*, Atglen, PA: Schiffer Publishing, 1998.

Coe, Debbie and Coe, Randy, *Liberty Blue Dinnerware*, Atglen, PA: Schiffer Publishing, 2006.

Copeland, Robert, "The Marketing of Blue and White Wares," in Gaye Blake Roberts (ed.), *True Blue, Transfer Printed Earthenware*, East Hagbourne: The Friends of Blue, 1998.

Cross, Gary, *Consumed Nostalgia: Memory in the Age of Fast Capitalism*, New York: Columbia University Press, 2015.

Dana, Charles A. (ed.), *The United States Illustrated*, vol. 2, "The West," New York: Herrmann J. Meyer, s.d. [1853–5].

"David Johnson," *The Sunday Times*, April 26, 2009.

Doyle, Jessica, "Kith and Kiln; A Renewed Appetite for British-made Ceramics and Fresh Ideas from a Young Generation of Potters Has Led to a Revival of Independent, Family-run Companies," *The Daily Telegraph* (London), *Telegraph Magazine*, August 13, 2016, pp. 52–7.

Dugdale, Thomas, *England and Wales Delineated* (also published as *Curiosities of Great Britain, England and Wales Delineated*), multiple volumes, London: John or L. [Lucinda] Tallis, 1838–60.

Ewins, Neil, *Ceramics and Globalization: Staffordshire Ceramics, Made in China*, London: Bloomsbury Academic, 2017.

Ewins, Neil, "'Supplying the Present Wants of Our Yankee Cousins': Staffordshire Ceramics and the American Market 1775-1880," *Journal of Ceramic History*, 15 (1997), pp. 1-154.

Finegan, Mary J., *Johnson Brothers Dinnerware, Pattern Directory & Price Guide*, second edition, Boone, NC: Minor's Printing Co., 2003.

Gale Research Company, *Currier & Ives, A Catalogue Raisonné*, 2 vols., Detroit: Gale Research Company, 1984.

Godden, Geoffrey A., *Encyclopaedia of British Pottery and Porcelain Marks*, London: Herbert Jenkins, 1964.

Godden, Geoffrey A., *Jewitt's Ceramic Art of Great Britain, 1800-1900*, London: Barrie & Jenkins, 1972.

Gonzalez, Mark, *An Overview of Homer Laughlin Dinnerware*, Gas City, IN: L-W Book Sales, 2002.

Groom, Brian, "Sir Arthur Bryan, UK Industrialist, 1923-2011," obituary, *Financial Times*, March 5, 2011, p. 8.

Hagan, Tere, *Silverplated Flatware*, fourth edition, Paducah, KY: Collector Books, 1990.

Higgins, Charlotte, "China Crisis," *The Guardian* (London), June 11, 2003.

Higgins, Charlotte, "Dorothy Jessie Tait," obituary, *The Guardian*, February 12, 2010.

Hinton, John Howard, *The History and Topography of the United States of North America*, vol. 2, Boston, MA: Samuel Walker, 1855.

Hobsbawn, Eric and Ranger, Terence (eds.), *The Invention of Tradition*, Cambridge: Cambridge University Press, 1983.

Hotchkin, Reverend S. F., *Ancient and Modern Germantown, Mount Airy and Chestnut Hill*, Philadelphia, PA: P. W. Ziegler & Co., 1889.

Houghton, Steven, "140 New Jobs at Wedgwood," *The Sentinel*, October 3, 2000.

Jenkins, Alan C., *A. R. Quinton's England, A Portrait of Rural Life at the Turn of the Century*, Exeter: Webb & Bower, 1987.

Jenkins, Steven, *Midwinter Pottery, A Revolution in British Tableware*, Paul Atterbury (ed.), second edition, Somerset: Richard Dennis, 2003.

Keller, Joe and Gibbs, Mark, *English Transferware, Popular 20th Century Patterns*, Atglen, PA: Schiffer Publishing, 2005.

Kovel, Ralph M. and Kovel, Terry H., *Dictionary of Marks: Pottery and Porcelain*, New York: Crown Publishers, 22nd printing, 1973.

Laidacker, Sam, *The Standard Catalogue of Anglo-American China from 1810 to 1850*, Scranton, PA: Sam Laidacker, 1938.

Larsen, Ellouise Baker, *American Historical Views on Staffordshire China*, New York: Doubleday, Doran & Co., 1939, reprinted New York: Dover Publications, 1975.

"Lenox Workers Still Produce U.S.-Made China," *Raleigh News and Observer* (Raleigh, NC), August 3, 2013.

Lewis, Griselda, *A Collector's History of British Pottery*, New York: Viking Press, 1969.

"Louise W. Flather," obituary, *Poughkeepsie Journal* (Poughkeepsie, NY), May 23, 1990, p. 2B.

Lowenthal, David, *The Past Is a Foreign Country*, Cambridge: Cambridge University Press, 1985.

Maguire, Patrick J., "Patriotism, Politics and Production," in Patrick J. Maguire and Jonathan M. Woodham (eds.), *Design and Cultural Politics in Post-war Britain: The "Britain Can Make It" Exhibition of 1946*, London and Washington: Leicester University Press, 1997.

Maguire, Patrick J. and Woodham, Jonathan M. (eds.), *Design and Cultural Politics in Post-war Britain: The "Britain Can Make It" Exhibition of 1946*, London and Washington: Leicester University Press, 1997.

Major, Charles, *Dorothy Vernon of Haddon Hall*, New York: The Macmillan Co., 1902.

McKellar, Elizabeth, "Representing the Georgian: Constructing Interiors in Early Twentieth-Century Publications, 1890–1930," *Journal of Design History*, 20:4 (2007), pp. 325–44.

McLaren, Graham M., "Moving Forwards but Looking Backwards: The Dynamics of Design Change in the Early Post-war Pottery Industry," in Patrick J. Maguire and Jonathan M. Woodham (eds.), *Design and Cultural Politics in Post-war Britain, The Britain Can Make It Exhibition of 1946*, London and Washington: Leicester University Press, 1997.

Meyer, Herrmann J., *Meyer's Universum, or Views of the Most Remarkable Places and Objects of All Countries*, New York: H. J. Meyer, 1852–3.

Mitchell, Silas Weir, *Hugh Wynne, Free Quaker, Sometime Brevet Lieutenant-Colonel on the Staff of His Excellency George Washington*, London: T. Fisher Unwin, 1897.

"New Name for Quality Tableware," *The Sentinel*, Wednesday October 16, 1991, pp. 19–34.

Niblett, Kathy, *Dynamic Design: The British Pottery Industry 1940–1990*, Stoke-on-Trent: City Museum & Art Gallery, 1990.

Nicholls, David, "All Fired Up: The Future of Pottery," *The Telegraph*, January 26, 2011.

NLA/Intershare, *Waterford Wedgwood Review of 1998*, S.n. [England]: First Impression, 1998.

Norbury, William, *Designs on a Career as a Decorator*, unpublished manuscript, 1999.

Page, Bob and Frederiksen, Dale, *Johnson Brothers Classic English Dinnerware*, Greensboro, NC: Page/Frederiksen Publications, 2003.

Page, Bob, Frederiksen, Dale, Six, Dean and Robinson, Jaime, *Franciscan, An American Dinnerware Tradition*, Greensboro, NC: Page/Frederiksen Publishing Co., 1999.

Paterson, Michael, *A Brief History of the Private Life of Elizabeth II*, Philadelphia, PA: Running Press, 2011.

Patrick, Aaron O., "Waterford Assets in U.K., Ireland Acquired by KPS," *The Wall Street Journal*, February 28, 2009.

Perry, Michael, *A Handbook of British Pottery Manufacturers: 1900–2010*, Joondalup: Ocean Publishing, 2010. Online version at www.potteryhistories.com.

"Project will Uncover History of Emma Bridgewater Factory," *The Sentinel*, August 28, 2014.

Reps, John W., *Saint Louis Illustrated: Nineteenth-Century Engravings and Lithographs of a Mississippi River Metropolis*, Columbia, MO: University of Missouri Press, 1989.

Rhead, G. W. and Rhead, F. A., *Staffordshire Pots and Potters*, London: Hutchinson and Co., 1906.

Royal Academy of Arts, *200 Years of Spode*, catalogue of exhibition 8 August–4 October 1970, London: Royal Academy of Arts, 1970.

Schwantes, Carlos A., *Long Day's Journey—The Steamboat & Stagecoach Era in the Northern West*, Seattle: University of Washington Press, 1999.

Shearer, Natalie, "The Making of a Love Triangle: Stravinsky's Ballet Petrushka," *The Classical Music Pages*, 1996, Library of Congress archived record http://webarchive.loc.gov/all/20090614095743/http:/w3.rz-berlin.mpg.de/cmp/stravinsky_shearer.html, accessed August 2, 2017.

Sheridan, Frank J., *The Pottery Industry*, Washington, DC: Government Printing Office, 1915.

"Sir Arthur Bryan," obituary, *The Times*, February 24, 2011.

Stefano Jr., Frank, *Pictorial Souvenirs and Commemoratives of North America*, New York: E. P. Dutton & Co., 1976.

"Students Drafted In to Record Rare Find," *Birmingham Post*, Monday February 26, 2007, p. 4.

Summers, Dorothy, *The Great Ouse: The History of a River Navigation*, Newton Abbott: David & Charles, 1973.

Taylor, Bayard (ed.), *Picturesque Europe, Volume 1: The British Isles*, New York: D. Appleton and Co., 1876; London: Cassell, Petter & Galpin, *c.* 1876–8.

The Federation Bulletin, A Magazine for the Woman of To-Day, National Official Organ of the General Federation of Women's Clubs, 6:1 (Boston, MA), October 1908.

The Inter-Nation: A Journal of Economic Affairs, June 1907, s.p. [93].

The Pottery Gazette and Glass Trade Review (London), March 2, 1908, p. 325 and April 1, 1909, p. 446.

"The Story of Johnson Brothers," unpublished typescript, s.d.

Theobald, Mary Miley, "The Colonial Revival, The Past That Never Dies," *Colonial Williamsburg, The Journal of the Colonial Williamsburg Foundation*, 24:2 (Summer 2002), pp. 81–5.

Timmons, Heather, "Britain: Cuts at China Maker," *The New York Times*, June 5, 2003.

United States Patent and Trademark Office, "TAF [Technology Assessment and Forecast] Report, Issue Dates and Patent Numbers Since 1836," April 2002.

VanBuskirk, William H., *The Johnson Bros., A Dynasty in Clay*, Big Rock, IL: s.n., 1998.

Venable, Charles L., Denker, Ellen P., Grier, Katherine C. and Harrison, Stephen G., *China and Glass in America 1880–1990, From Tabletop to TV Tray*, exhibition catalogue, Dallas, TX: Dallas Museum of Art; New York: Distributed by Harry N. Abrams, 2000.

Walker, John, *The Itinerant: A Select Collection of Interesting and Picturesque Views in Great Britain and Ireland, Engraved from Original Paintings & Drawings by Eminent Artists*, Clerkenwell (London): John Walker, 1799.

Warre, Henry James, *Sketches in North America and the Oregon Territory*, London: Dickinson & Co., 1848.

West, William, *Picturesque Views and Descriptions of Cities, Towns, Castles, Mansions and Other Objects of Interesting Features in Staffordshire and Shropshire*, Birmingham: William Emans, 1830.

Westcott, Thompson, *The Historic Mansions and Buildings of Philadelphia*, Philadelphia, PA: Porter & Coates, 1877.

Willis, Nathaniel P., *American Scenery: Or Land, Lake, and River Illustrations of Transatlantic Nature*, 2 vols., London: George Virtue, 1840.

"World War I: Lest We Forget the 13,000 Who Died for Staffordshire and Stoke-on-Trent," *The Sentinel*, Stoke-on-Trent, November 11, 2013.

Zarucchi, Jeanne Morgan, *Johnson Brothers in America: A Century of Design, Catalogue of a Special Exhibition for the Wedgwood International Seminar*, St. Louis, MO: Gallery 210, University of Missouri-St. Louis, 2000.

Zarucchi, Jeanne Morgan, "Visions of America: Johnson Brothers Pottery in the US Market, 1872–2002," *The Journal of Popular Culture*, 38 (2004), pp. 186–206.

INDEX OF TABLEWARE PATTERNS

All companies are Staffordshire unless noted otherwise

Adams, William & Sons
   Blue Willow 30
   Currier & Ives 74
Adderley, W. A. & Co.
   Alton 13
Allerton's
   Blue Willow 30
Anchor Hocking (US)
   Currier & Ives 74
Aynsley
   Indian Tree 30

Booth, T. G. & F.
   America 13
   Blue Willow 30
Brownfield, William & Sons
   Wisconsin 13
Burgess & Leigh
   Blue Willow 30

Cauldon
   unnamed botanical pattern 107
Churchill
   Blue Willow 30
   Indian Tree 30
Coalport
   Blue Willow 30
   Indian Tree 30

Enco National Inc. (US importer)
   New York City souvenir 87–8

Furnivals
   Queen Elizabeth II coronation
      souvenir 83
F. W. G. (full name unknown)
   unnamed pattern 13

Gimson, Wallis & Co.
   University of Toronto and Prince of
      Wales' visit souvenir 80

Gladding McBean & Co. (US)
   Desert Rose 105
   Franciscan Apple 105
Grimwades Ltd.
   Nancy 17
Grindley, W. H. & Co.
   Malta 13

Homer Laughlin China Company (US)
   Blue Willow 30
   Fiesta 104–5
   Historical America 74

Johnson Brothers
   Albany 21
   Alberta, Canada souvenir 97–9
   Alice in Wonderland 133
   Andorra 20
   Apple Harvest 120–1
   Argyle 20
   The Arizona Plate 94–5
   Astoria 20
   Aubrey 20
   Autumn Monarch 150–1
   Autumn's Delight 106
   Azalea 108
   Barnyard King 103, 114–15, 151
   Basket Weave 150–1
   Begonia 20
   Belvedere (Old English series) 40
   Bermuda 34
   Bird of Paradise 102–3
   The Blue Danube 20
   Brittany 20
   Brooklyn 21
   Camellia 108, 158
   Carnival 105
   Castle on the Lake 117–18
   A Century of Progress 1833–1933 79–80
   Chadwell 82
   Charlton 34

Index of Tableware Patterns

Cherry Thieves (Old Granite series) 130
Chicago 84
Chintz (Old English series) 40
Claremont 21
Clarissa 20
Clayton 20
Clematis 20
Coaching Scenes 127–8, 137, 144
Columbia 14–15, 21
Columbus 34
Constance 20
Coral 20
Country Cupboard 133
Country Life 117
Cornwall 20
Dartmouth 16
Davenport 32
A Day in June 106–7
Devonshire 49, 102
Devon Sprays 127
Dorchester 102
Dorothy 20
Dream Town 121
Dresden 20
Dubarry (Old Staffordshire series) 40
Edgvale 23
Empire State Building 85–7
English Bouquet 46–8
English Chippendale 46–8
English Countryside 46–8
English Garden 20
English Oak (series) 40
Eternal Beau 137–9, 143–4, 150, 153
Exeter 20
Fish 110–12
Floating Leaves 106
Florida 18, 20–1
Fortuna 20
Franklin 26
Fresh Fruit 143
The Friendly Village 116, 118–20, 146, 150–1
Fruit Sampler (Old Granite series) 130, 144
Fulton 20
Game Birds 110–11, 147
Garden Bouquet (WindsorWare series) 52
Garfield 34
Georgia 19, 21
Girls Born to Shop 151

Goldendawn 39
The Great State of California 95–6
Greendawn 39
Gretchen (Old Granite series) 130
Greydawn 38–40
Guernsey 34
Haddon Hall 103
Hague 20
Hampton 103
Harvest Fruit 103, 115
Harvest Time 102–3, 106
Hearts and Flowers (Old Granite series) 130–1
Heritage 138
Heritage Hall 136–7
His Majesty 114–17, 144, 146–7, 151
Historic America 1, 4, 58–78, 94, 104, 108, 114, 117, 133, 146, 148
Historic America II 147–9
Holland 20
Hop 12
Hudson's Bay Company (*see* Alberta and Vancouver)
Indian Tree 30–1, 34
Jamestown (Old Granite series) 130
Japan 20
Jefferson 34
Jewel 20
Kenworth 20
Lace 106
Lancaster (Old Granite series) 130
Les Fontaines 35–6
Lily 20–1
Lincoln 34
Madison 34
The Madras 25
Manhattan 18–19, 21
Margaret Rose 48
Marlborough 34
The Marquis (WindsorWare series) 52
Mayflower 34
Mentone 20
Merry Christmas 116–17, 147
Mill Stream 127
Mongolia 20–1
Montana 21
Mount Rushmore 96–7
Mount Vernon 104
Neapolitan 20
Neighbors 133–4

Ningpo (Old Staffordshire series) 40
Normandy 20
Old Britain Castles 4, 41–6, 58–9, 103–4, 117, 128, 144, 153
Old Chelsea (series) 40
Old English (series) 40, 44, 48
Old English Clover (Old English series) 40
Old English Trellis (Victorian series) 40
Old Flower Prints 107–8
Old Granite (series) 128–31, 136, 144
The Old Mill 118, 127
Old Staffordshire (series) 40
Olde English Countryside 112–14, 127
Oregon 18–19
The Oregon Plate 93–5
Oriental 20
Oxford 20–1
Paisley 133–4
Paris 16–17, 19–20
Peach Blossom 20
Peachbloom 105
Pekin 20
Pennsylvania German Folklore Society 92–3
Persian 20
Petite Fleur 135–6
Petroushka 35
Petunia 14
Pomona (WindsorWare series) 51–2, 102
Poppy 20
Princeton 21
Queen Elizabeth II coronation souvenir 82–3
Queens Bouquet (Old English series) 48
Raleigh 21
Regent 20
Regis 16
Richmond 20–1
The Road Home 121–3
The Rococo 34
Rolland 16
Rose Bouquet 127
Rose Chintz 102, 106
Rosedawn 39–40
Rouen (Old Staffordshire series) 40
Royston 20
St. Louis 19, 21

Salem 130–1
Salisbury 20
Savannah 18, 21
Savoy 20
Sheraton (WindsorWare series) 50–2, 102
Sienna 151
Springtime 34
Stanley 20
Sterling 20–1
Sugar and Spice 131
Summer Chintz 138–40, 143
Summerfields 138–9, 143
Sun Up 130–1
Tally Ho 112–13
Tokio 20
Trieste 20
Tulip 20
Tulip Time 127
Turin 20
Valencia Lace 26
Vancouver, Canada souvenir 97–9
Venice 20
Victoria 34
Victorian (series) 44
Victorian Christmas 144
Vienna 16–17, 19
Waldorf 18
Warwick 20
Waverly 20
Wild Turkeys 114–15
Wild Turkeys "Native American" 115
Willow 30, 103, 143
Wiltshire 127
Winchester 102
WindsorWare (series) 49–52, 104, 115
Woodland Wild Turkeys 115

Lenox China Company (US)
   Autumn 34
   Fountain 35–6

Maddock
   Indian Tree 30
Meakin, Alfred
   unnamed pattern, registration number 391493, 25
Midwinter, W. R.
   Cannes 126

Homeweave (Stylecraft series) 126
Primavera (Stylecraft series) 126
Riviera 126
Salad Ware 126
Stylecraft (series) 125
Minton
    unnamed pattern 13
Monarch China Company (US)
    Currier & Ives 74
Myott
    England's Charm 114
    Indian Tree 30
    Royal Mail 128

Nikko (Japan)
    Christmastime 144
    Happy Holidays 144

Oneida Ltd. (US manufacturer of silverplated flatware)
    Adam (silver plate pattern) 33
    Bird of Paradise (silver plate pattern) 33
    Grosvenor (silver plate pattern) 32–3
    Hampton Court (silver plate pattern) 33
    Patrician (silver plate pattern) 33
    Paul Revere (silver plate pattern) 33

Portmeirion
    The Botanic Garden 109

Ridgway
    Blue Willow 30
    Historic Castles 44
    The Original Coaching Days & Coaching Ways 128
Ridgway, William
    "American Views" 8
Rowland & Marcellus (US importer, maker unknown)
    St. Louis, Missouri souvenir 78
    World's Fair, St. Louis souvenir 78
Royal China Company (US)
    Currier & Ives 74, 117
    Indian Tree 30
    Memory Lane 75, 147
Royal Doulton
    Blue Willow 30

Spode
    Blue Willow 30
    Christmas Tree 116, 144
    Indian Tree 30
    Rosebud Chintz 102
    Woodland 157
Straus, L. & Sons (US importer, maker unknown)
    Watteau 22
Syracuse (US)
    Indian Tree 30

Taylor Smith Taylor (US)
    Currier & Ives 74
Turner, G. W. & Sons
    Brazil 13

Villeroy & Boch (Luxembourg)
    The Delicious Apple 105

Wedgwood, Enoch
    Liberty Blue 76
    Royal Homes of Britain 128
Wedgwood, Josiah
    Duke University 81–2
    "Edme" shape 75–6, 90
    Harvard College Tercentenary 81
    Old Blue Historical 53–8, 60, 72–3, 80, 88
    Old New York 72–3, 75
    St. John the Divine (New York City) 91–2
    Scenes of Old New York 75
    Views of Rome (by G. B. Piranesi) 90–1
    Williamsburg Restoration 88, 104
Wilkinson, A. J.
    Queen Elizabeth II coronation souvenir 83
Williams-Sonoma (US)
    Highgrove 145–6
    His Majesty 146
    Kent 145
    Mayfair 145–7
    Plymouth 145–7
    Royal Game 146
Wood
    Blue Willow 30
    Queen Elizabeth II coronation souvenir 83

INDEX

Individual pattern names are listed separately in the **Index of Tableware Patterns**

"100 Years of Flight" 148
1882 Ltd. 157-8, 175
Adam, Robert 32
Adams, President John 56, 58
Adams pottery 2, 11, 74, 131-2, 141
Adderley, W. A. & Co. 13
aesthetic movement 12-14, 21, 80
The Alamo, Texas 68, 148
Alberta, Canada 97-9
Alden, Priscilla and John 54
Alexander, Edward P. 168
Alexander, Mary 168
Alexandra Pottery (factory) 22, 156
American bald eagle 148
American Revolution Bicentennial 76
"American views" on Staffordshire pottery 8, 41, 53, 61
Am Kai (levee), New Orleans 70
Anchor Hocking Company 74
A&P Grocery Stores 74
Arlington House, Virginia 54
art deco 35-6
Art Institute of Chicago 79, 84
art nouveau 17-18, 25
Ashwell, Kneale 142-3
Astor House, New York City 66
asymmetrical pottery shape 12, 30
Atterbury, Paul 160

backstamps 10-12, 15-18, 23-5, 30-1, 44, 62-3, 74, 84-7, 90, 102-3, 108, 135-6, 139-40, 142, 145, 150
Bailey, Banks & Biddle department store 75
B. Altman & Co. department store 75
Barber, Edwin Atlee 8, 161
Barnum, P. T. 66, 69
Barnum's Museum, New York City 63, 66, 69
Barr & Co. department store 78

Bartlett, William Henry 8, 60, 166-7
Basilica of St. Mary Major, Rome 91
Bates, Eli 79
Batkin, Mary 160
Battle of Lexington 54
Beale, Joseph Boggs 74
Belleek 33, 163
Benjamin Franklin Federal Savings and Loan Association 76
Bennett, William James 168
The Best Friend of Charleston (steam engine) 65
The Bible: In the Beginning (film) 88
Birks, Steve 45
Blarney Castle 43, 46
Blaszczyk, Regina Lee 36, 38, 163-4
Bloor, Tom 143
Bond, Henry Winsor 43
Boot, William Henry James 173
Booth, T. G. & F. 13
Boston, Massachusetts 1, 67, 70, 148
Boston Tea Party 55
botanical illustration 107-9
Bridgewater, Emma 156-7, 175
Broadway, New York City 63, 66, 69, 73
Brooklyn Bridge 148
Brooklyn Ferry, New York 66, 69
Brown University 80
Brownfield, William & Sons 13
Bryan, Sir Arthur 131, 133, 140-1, 152, 173-4
Bryant, William Cullen 60, 166, 168
Buffalo, New York 78
Bunker Hill Monument, Boston 53-5
Burgess, Arene 169
Burleigh pottery 157
Burslem pottery 114

Calvert, Frederick 43, 164
Cambridge 43

Camehl, Ada Walker 168
Canterbury 43
The Capitol, Washington 1, 53, 55, 67, 96, 148
The Capitol, Williamsburg 65, 71–2
Carpenter's Hall, Philadelphia 54
Casson, Hugh, designer 125–6
Castle Garden, New York City 73
cattle drive 148
Cauldon pottery 107, 114
Central Park, New York City 66, 69–70, 73, 148
Chamberlain, Samuel 89, 104
Charles Street Works 8, 9, 155, 161
Chew House, Philadelphia 54, 57
Chicago 61, 68, 71, 78–9, 84–5
Chicago Court House 79
Chippendale, Thomas 47
Christmas 70, 116, 128, 146
City Hall, New York City 73
Clarice Cliff pottery 36, 114
Clements, Monica Lynn and Patricia Rosser 169
Clementson Brothers Ltd. pottery 11
The Clermont (steamboat) 66, 74
Cleveland, President Grover 55–6
Coalport pottery 131
Coe, Debbie and Randy 169
colonial revival 31–3, 40, 47
Conran, Jasper, designer 152
Conran, Terence, designer 125–6
Constitution (US Frigate) 54
Conway Castle 42, 44
Cooke, George 166
Cooper, Peter 65
Copeland pottery 58, 114
Copeland, Robert 14, 162
Cornell University 80
Cornwallis, General 58
covered wagons 1, 63, 67, 69
"Creative Tableware" 141
Cross, Gary 117, 172
Crown Ducal Ware 58
Currier & Ives 60, 65, 70–1, 74–5, 114, 117
Currier, Nathaniel 60
Cushing, Archbishop Richard J. 91

Dana, Charles A. 168
Decker, Juilee 168

Declaration of Independence 54
Denby pottery 157
Denison University 80
Diamond's department store 94
Disneyland 96, 117
Dugdale, Thomas 43, 164
Duke University 81–2
Durrie, George Henry 166

Eagle Pottery (factory) 155
Earlham College 80
Eastwood Pottery (factory) 155–6
Emerson, Ralph Waldo 54
Emma Bridgewater pottery 155, 158
Empire State Building, New York City 85–7, 148
England and Wales Delineated (1838–60) 43
Erie Canal, New York 61, 68, 70
Ewins, Neil 161, 174

fairs and exhibitions
    1851 London Great Exhibition of the Works of Industry of All Nations 77, 109
    1853 New York Exhibition of the Industry of All Nations 66, 77
    1876 Philadelphia Centennial Exposition 32, 78
    1893 Chicago World's Columbian Exposition 15, 78–9
    1900 Paris World's Fair 17
    1901 Buffalo (NY) Pan American Exposition 78
    1904 Louisiana Purchase Exposition (St. Louis World's Fair) 21, 61, 78
    1925 Paris International Exposition of Modern Decorative and Industrial Arts 35
    1933 Chicago A Century of Progress 78–9
    1939 New York World's Fair 48, 72–3
    1951 London Festival of Britain 109–10
Faneuil Hall, Boston 54–5
Farnham Castle 42
Federal Hall, New York City 73
Fenn, Henry 168
Fennell, Henry (Harry), engraver 42–3, 46, 103, 128

Fennell, "Miss" 41
Field Museum, Chicago 79–80, 84
Finegan, Mary J. 3, 20, 43, 63, 110, 119, 160, 163–6, 169–70, 172–4
Firks, Henry 166
Fisher Bruce Company importer 49
Fiskars company 152–3
Flather, Louise 105–7, 116, 118–21, 123, 130, 171, 173
"flow blue" 3, 19–22, 30
The Flying Cloud (clipper ship) 66, 70, 148
folk life 128–31
Forsyth, Gordon 4, 36–8, 125
Fort Dearborn, Chicago 68, 79
Fort George, New York City 73
Franciscan pottery (Gladding McBean & Co.) 141–2
Franklin, Benjamin 74
Fraunces Tavern, New York City 73
Frederick & Nelson department store 63–4
Frederiksen, Dale 3, 20, 35, 160, 162–5, 169, 171–2, 174
Fred Harvey company 95
Fulton, Robert 66
F. W. G. pottery 13–14

Georgian revival 32
Gibbs, Mark 160, 173
Gimson, Wallis & Co. pottery 80
Gladding McBean & Co. 105
Globe Pottery Co. 11
Godden, Geoffrey 11, 160–2
gold rush 1
Gonzalez, Mark 168, 170–1
Grand Union grocery stores 76
"granite ware" 9, 128
Grant, General (later President) Ulysses S. 54–5
Great War (World War I) 27, 29, 101
Grier, Katherine C. 160
Grimwades pottery 17
Grindley pottery 2, 10–11, 13, 19

Haddon Hall, Derbyshire 43, 103, 128
Hagan, Tere 32, 163
Hamilton, Andrew 67
Hampton Court 103
Hancock House, Boston 67, 70

Hancock, John 67–8
Hanley Pottery (factory) 22, 155–6
Harlech Castle 42
Harrison, Stephen G. 160
Harvard College 54–5, 81
Harvey Hotels 95
Havell, Robert 167
Heere Gracht (Canal Street), New York City 73
Hill, John William 168
Hinton, John Howard 167
Holland, Julie 139
Holmes, Frank Graham 35
Homer Laughlin pottery (US) 29, 74, 92, 104–5
Hotchkin, Rev. S. F. 165
hotel ware 25–6, 39–40
Hudson River, New York 63–4, 66, 70
Hudson's Bay Company 97–9
Hughes, E. pottery 11
Hunsberger, David L. 92–3
Hyde Park, New York 48

Imperial Pottery (factory) 22, 155
Independence Hall, Philadelphia 54–5, 67
ironstone 10, 128
Ives, James Merritt 60

Jefferson, Thomas 54, 65, 67–8, 78, 94, 96
Jenkins, Alan C. 172
Jenkins, Steven 125, 173
Johnson Brothers
  company history 4, 11, 18–19, 22, 29, 31, 49, 131–2, 141–4, 149–51, 155–8
  family 4, 9, 11, 18–19, 22–3, 31, 37–8, 45–6, 59, 110, 113, 131–2, 155, 157–8, 161–2, 173
Jones McDuffee & Stratton Company, pottery and china retailer 53, 55–7, 72, 91

Kansas City, Missouri 68
Keller, Joe 160, 173
Kenilworth Castle 42
Kerr, Miranda 152
King Edward VIII (later Duke of Windsor) 50
King George V 50

King George VI 48
King Henry VIII 103
King's Chapel, Boston 55
Kolich Castle 46
Köllner, Augustus 166-7
Kovel, Ralph M. and Terry H. 162
KPS Capital Partners 152-3

Lafayette, Marquis de 58
Laidacker, Sam 161
Larsen, Ellouise Baker 61, 161, 166
Latchford, Harry, engraver 59
Laura Ashley company 135-6
Lee, General Robert E. 54
Leinster House, Dublin 67, 69
L'Enfant, Pierre 67
Lenox company (US) 34, 163
Lewis, Griselda 161
Lewis, Henry 60
Lexington, Battle of 55
Libbey Glass Company 74
Liberty Bell 67
Lincoln, President Abraham 54-5, 70, 79, 96
Little Falls, New York 63
Liverpool cream ware 8
Longfellow, Henry Wadsworth 54-6
Lowell, James Russell 53-4
Lowenthal, David 172

McKay, Donald 65
McKellar, Elizabeth 163
McKinley, President William 54
McLaren, Graham M. 125, 172
Macy's department store 22, 70-2, 105-8, 110, 118-19, 123
Maddock's pottery 2
Madison, President James 67
Maguire, Patrick J. 101, 170
Major, Charles 171
Manhattan, New York City 66, 74
Marshall Field & Co. department store 79, 84
Marshall Point, Maine 148
Mascheroni, Sarina 137-8
Mason's pottery 11, 114, 131-2, 141, 173
material culture 2, 5, 41
The Mayflower (ship) 54, 74
Meakin pottery 2, 11, 16, 25, 131-2, 141-2

Meier & Frank department store 93-4
Metropolitan Museum of Art, New York City 64, 71-2
Meyer, Herrmann J. 167-8
Michigan Avenue, Chicago 71
Midwinter, Roy 126
Midwinter, W. R. pottery 125-7, 131-3, 141-2
Minton pottery 13, 162
Mississippi River 63-4, 66, 74
Mitchell, Silas Weir 57-8, 165
Moen, Jon R. 163
Moenster, Kathleen 169
Mohawk Valley, New York 63, 65, 69-70
Monarch China Company 74
Montgomery Ward 20
Monticello 32, 54, 67, 70
Mount Rushmore, South Dakota 96-7
Mount Shasta, California 60, 67, 70
Mount Vernon 48, 53, 55, 58, 67, 104
Museum of the City of New York 71-2
Myott & Son pottery 114

Natural Bridge, Virginia 70, 148
New Orleans 68, 70
New York Botanical Garden 107
New York Crystal Palace 66, 69, 78, 148
New York Public Library 71-2
Niagara Falls, New York 67, 69
Niblett, Kathy 173
Nieuw Amsterdam (New York City) 73
Norbury, William
    life 4, 36-8, 42, 45-9, 116, 137, 155, 160
    work as an engraver 4, 37-8, 45-7, 59-61, 87, 96-9, 108-13, 116-18, 121, 123, 128, 131-3, 146, 158-9, 165, 171-3

Old North Bridge, Concord 54-5
Old North Church, Boston 54-5
Old South Church, Boston 54-5
Olmstead, Frederic Law 66
Oneida Ltd. 32
Oregon 67
Oxford 42

Page, Bob 3, 20, 35, 160, 162-5, 169, 171-2, 174
Palmer, Frances F. 166-7, 169

panic of 1907, 26
Pankhurst, J. W. 9–10, 155, 157, 161
"Pareek" pottery 33–5
Parian ware 33
Parkyns, George Isham 104, 171
Parson, Charles 167
Paterson, Michael 173
Pennsylvania Dutch 130–1
Pennsylvania German Folklore Society 92–3
Perry, Michael 151, 173–4
Philadelphia 78
Philadelphia Museum of Art 64
Pilgrims 54–5
Pimpernel company 157
Piranesi, Giovanni Battista 90
Pony Express 74
Portmeirion pottery 109, 157
Potomac River, Washington 67
The Pottery Gazette and Glass Review 2–3, 25, 108, 126, 163
pottery workers' wages 26–7
Precision Studios pottery 131
Prince Albert 50
Prince Charles and Lady Diana Spencer 138, 146
Prince Edward (later King Edward VII) 33, 80
Princess Margaret 48
Psaros, Michael 152

Queen Charlotte (wife of King George III) 82
Queen Elizabeth II 48, 82–3, 103, 128, 142, 171
Queen Elizabeth (wife of King George VI) 48, 142
Queen Victoria 33
Queen Victoria Diamond Jubilee 23
Queensware 82
Quinton, Alfred Robert 113–14, 172

Ragland Castle 46
Ramsay, Gordon 152
Redouté, Pierre-Joseph 107
Reilly, Jr., Bernard F. 60, 166
Replacements, Ltd. 3, 152
Reps, John W. 166
Revere, Paul 54–5, 68

Rhead, Frederick Hurten 74, 104
Rhead, G. W. and F. A. 160
Richardson, A. G. & Co. pottery 58
Richmond, Virginia 65, 71
Ridgway pottery 8, 45
Ridgway, William 8–9
Robertson, Alexander 167
Robinson, Jaime 171
Rochester Castle 42
Rockefeller, Jr., John D. 32, 65, 71, 89
Rocky Mountains 1, 63, 66, 69, 74
Rogaška Crystal company 152
Roosevelt, President Franklin Delano 48, 69
Roosevelt, President Theodore 54–6, 96
Ross, Betsy 74
Rowland & Marsellus Company importers 78
Royal Albert pottery 152
Royal China Company 74–5
Royal Copenhagen china 152
Royal Doulton pottery 132, 151–2
"Royal Ironstone" 10, 18
"Royal Semi-Porcelain" 15–16, 18–19, 23–5
Royal Staffordshire pottery 114
Royal Tuscan pottery 131
Royal Worcester pottery 109, 140, 157
Runnymede, England 42

Sacramento, California 68
St. Gaudens, Augustus 79
St. John the Divine Cathedral, New York City 91
St. Louis, Missouri 1, 60–1, 78, 148
St. Paul's Church, New York City 66
St. Woolstons Kildare 42
San Francisco, California 1, 65
Scudder's Museum, New York City 69
Sears Roebuck & Co. department store 131, 136
Second Trinity Church, New York City 73
Second World War 49–50, 77, 101, 125, 131
"Semi-Porcelain" 11–12, 16
Shearer, Natalie 35, 163
Shepherd, Thomas Hosmer 43
Sheridan, Frank J. 163

Six, Dean 171
South Street, New York City 73
Spode pottery 2, 58, 109, 114, 140, 157, 161
The Stadhuys (The Battery), New York City 73
Stafford Castle 43-4
Staffordshire and Staffordshire potteries 1-2, 7, 29-30, 35, 72, 76, 102, 104, 107, 158
"Staffordshire blue" ware 8, 19, 22, 53, 61, 63-5, 72, 81-2
stage and mail coach 60, 67, 70, 127-8
Stars and Stripes 148
State House, Boston 54-5
Statue of Liberty, New York City 148
Steelite International 132
Stefano, Jr., Frank 78, 161, 165, 169-70
Stein, Aaron 60, 166
Stevenson, Ralph 8, 69, 75
Stevenson & Williams pottery 8, 61, 161
Stoke-on-Trent 2-4, 7, 27, 156-7
Stoke School (College) of Art 4, 36, 38
The Stoke *Sentinel* 29, 141-4, 145, 156, 163, 174
Straus, L. & Sons department store 22
Stulz, Leonora Vance 168-9, 171, 173
Stuyvesant, Peter 66
Sulgrave Manor, Banbury 58
Summers, Dorothy 164
Susie Cooper pottery 36, 131
Syracuse company (US) 30

Tait, Jessie, designer 125-6
Tallis, John 164
Tallman, Ellis W. 163
Tenniel, John 133
Texas oil boom 148
Thames River 65
Thanksgiving 65, 70-1, 74, 113-14, 146
Theobald, Mary Miley 31-2, 163
transfer printing process 7-10, 16, 19, 30, 45-6, 49
Trent Sanitary Works (factory) 22, 155
Trenton, New Jersey 58
Turner, G. W. & Sons 13

Unicorn pottery 132, 141-2
University of Iowa 80
University of Michigan 80
University of Pennsylvania 80
University of Toronto 80
Upper Hanley Pottery Co. 11

Valley Forge, Pennsylvania 58
VanBuskirk, William 19-20, 160, 162-3
Vancouver, Canada 97-9
Vaux, Calvert 66
Venable, Charles 160
Vernon, Dorothy 103
Villeroy & Boch 105

Wakefield, Virginia 58
Walker, John 42-3, 164
Wall Street, New York City 66, 69, 73, 148
Wang, Vera, designer 152
Ward, Jacob C. 168
Warre, Henry James 94, 170
Washington crossing the Delaware (River) 58
Washington DC 70
Washington Elm, Cambridge 53, 55
Washington, George 53-6, 58, 66-8, 72-3, 96, 104, 165
Washington, Martha 54-5
Washington's Headquarters, Cambridge 54-5, 58
Waterford Crystal company 140
Waterford Wedgwood 152
Webster, Daniel 53, 55
Wedgwood, Enoch company 76, 114, 132, 151
Wedgwood, Josiah company
    acquisitions and mergers 105, 131-3, 140-5, 151-3
    museum 4, 164, 171, 174
    pottery 2, 30, 40, 54-8, 75-6, 78, 80-2, 88-92, 114, 145-7, 173
Weehawk, New York 64
Wells Fargo express 67
Westcott, Thompson 165
West Pecos, Texas 148-9
West Point, New York 68-70
West, William 164
White House, Washington 54-6, 67, 69
Whittier, John Greenleaf 55-6
Whittingham, Claude, engraver 59, 123

Williamsburg, Virginia 32, 65, 88–90, 88–91, 170
Williams College 80
Williams-Ellis, Susan 109, 157
Williams-Sonoma 145–7, 151
Willis, Nathaniel P. 60, 161, 167
Windsor Castle 50
Wood & Sons pottery 125
Woodham, Jonathan M. 170

World Wide Art Studios 92
Worthington, Gordon, engraver 118, 123
WWRD (Waterford Wedgwood Royal Doulton) Holding Ltd. 152

Yale College 54
Yale University 80

Zarucchi, Jeanne Morgan 161–2